Facts and Fictions

Books by Ann Bridge

Ann Bridge

Facts and Fictions

some literary recollections

McGraw-Hill Book Company · New York

Library of Congress Catalog Card Number: 68-8659
FIRST EDITION   07732

Contents

Foreword

This is not an autobiography. I may write one some day, but this is not it. It is an endeavour to describe the interplay, in an author's mind, between actual, lived experience, and the situations and events in that author's novels; and how the real impressions and experiences had to be adapted to meet the demands of the fictional characters in the books. I have not held too strictly to my original intention: where a personal experience seemed to me fun, or interesting historically, I have put it in, even if I have never written about it—I do not see why a writer should be tied to too rigid a formula. There is surely room for an occasional book which does not fit neatly into one of the preconceived categories so dear to booksellers.

There is a second interplay which I have, very lightly, interwoven with the main one; the effect of my own kind of life on my writing, and the effect—very marked—of my writing on my life, and that of my family. But this does not amount to an autobiography. And there are two big omissions even in my chosen and limited intention. In each of my novels the main character is a region or a country, and the two countries which have loomed largest in my life I have left out—Ireland, and the West Highlands; though I have written about both, to treat either properly would have swamped this little book. They, like my autobiography, must wait.

Facts and Fictions

I

The First Post I

Our first post abroad was Peking, in many ways the most rewarding of them all. When Owen joined the Foreign Office in 1911 it was still necessary to choose at the outset either the Foreign Office, working in London, or the Diplomatic Service, working abroad; and it was a rule that those who chose the former would not be sent out of England. The choice was usually made on financial grounds; "local allowances", which now make the diplomat, as a rule, far better off in a foreign post than in London, were not then on such a liberal scale. Owen was poor, and chose the Foreign Office, hoping to spend his career in decent obscurity in England. However after the end of the 1914–18 war the Secretary of State was given certain discretionary powers to shift men from one part of the Service to the other; but it remained an understood thing that these powers should not be used at all ruthlessly, and that the views of individuals should be fully taken into account.

Now when the idea of sending Owen to Peking as Counsellor was first mooted, both he and I were far from sure that we wanted to go. Of course it was promotion, and a splendid opening, and all that; but it would be very expensive: it would mean a lot of entertaining, about which I knew nothing, and grand clothes for me and much better clothes, at least, for the children than what they ran about in at home, and a lady's-maid and all sorts of complications—much more china and glass than we possessed or could afford to buy.

But what above all caused us to hesitate was Bridge End. Six years before, in 1919, we had managed to secure an absolutely darling house, in an absolutely darling village, Bridge End, at Ockham, which we had taken for an absurdly low rent from old Lady Lovelace for a term of years. The house, on any showing, was beautiful—the old part fifteenth-century, with beams in its walls and low ceilings; what the villagers still delightfully referred to as "the new end" had the date 1770 on it in blue-ended bricks, and charming half-panelling in the rooms. An aged wistaria climbed up the front, and we had planted pears and plums on the other walls; there was a cedar out at the back, a lawn and a pleasant garden; across the road yet more garden, in which stood the gardener's cottage—two rooms of this were let off to Ursula Nettleship.

Altogether, in those six years, we had established ourselves in the way of life we liked best, a way that we could handle and afford. There was a paddock and an orchard as well as the garden, and we kept pigs and geese and chickens, and made them pay; twice a week the carrier took boxes of our new-laid eggs up to London, and in due season cockerels, plucked, drawn and trussed by me—it was nothing out of the way for me to kill twenty cockerels on a Sunday evening, pluck them on the Monday, and get up at 5 A.M. on Tuesday morning to draw and truss them in the kitchen before the maids came down, because they disliked the smell. Owen was a first-rate joiner, and built the chicken-houses and made the hen-coops himself, as well as the hoppers for the hens' dry mash. We were very scientific about it, and trap-nested our pedigree pullets; Jane's lessons had to be arranged in thirty-five-minute periods, with gaps for preparation in between, so that I could run out to release the squawking creatures, and log up the numbers of their leg-rings on a chart which hung on the hen-house wall. Great was the triumph when Number Twenty-Six laid 230 eggs in her pullet year; birds of that class we mated to a ten-guinea cockerel, and sold settings of their eggs at two guineas a dozen. And people were quite willing to pay the top London price, and part of the carrier's charge as well, because I never let an egg leave the place that was more than forty-eight hours old.

Also, at certain times, we sold eggs by weight. So many amateur poultry-keepers used to lose money when pullets were coming into lay because the eggs were small, below the minimum standard of two ounces; but I routed round small restaurants near Victoria, and found plenty which were not only willing, but eager to take my small eggs and get sixteen for the price of a dozen—they looked quite all right poached, on a piece of toast. In those days, if one took enough trouble, you could make money hand over fist with poultry.

The pigs were profitable too. Through the winter we used to kill one or two about every month—a flight of postcards went out to people in London saying that pork would be available next week, and did they want loin or shoulder or breast, and how many pounds? When the answers came in I would make out a list, and then send for Mr. Miller from May's Green, an outlying hamlet, to settle about the killing. Mr. Miller was a beautiful old man with clear blue eyes, a white beard, and a wise, benevolent face; he looked exactly like Victorian pictures of God the Father. He was also a marvellous butcher. He would stand leaning on the gate of the pigsty, and as I read out my list of joints of loin, he would tap the animals on the back with his walking-stick, and do sums in his head. At last—"Those two, M'm" he would say; "they'll give you about thirty-eight pounds of loin"—and he was never more than a pound or two out. Any surplus we could always sell in the village; country people used to love pork.

The hams I cured. One of the good things about living in a fifteenth-century house, however small, was that there was so much space. At Bridge End, besides the stable and coach-house and harness-room, with a loft over them outside, there was a fair-sized room adjoining the kitchen where I did the washing and ironing, and off that again a sort of pantry with a sink, and a big cellar with a brick floor, a slate slab under the window, and a range of shelves running down one side, on which one could store vast quantities of bottled fruit—it was always my aim to bottle enough in the summer to be able to open six bottles a week through the winter months, and to put down sufficient eggs to be able to use six dozen weekly. The eggs were kept in the vast larder, also brick-floored, but the hams while in pickle lived in the cellar, in large earthenware crocks, two to a crock.

I took great pride in my hams. When Mr. Miller had killed one or more pigs, and cleaned and shaved them, slung from hooks in the coach-house roof, he would first cut off the legs and bring them in to that ample room behind the kitchen where I had ready my bags of

3

bay-salt (coarse sea-salt), alum, and brown sugar. But first I had to set aside the joints for our customers. Then the head, cut in half, went into the house to steep in salted water for subsequent use as brawn; Mrs. Burge, our nearest neighbour, came round with two enamel slop-pails to carry off the intestines and the blood, which she made into "black puddings" and "white puddings"; Mr. Miller himself loved to have the trotters, and some joint of his choice as well; of course the gardener had his piece too. Only when all this distribution was over, the meat covered up, and the coach-house doors shut, could I go in and tackle the hams.

There is something splendid about a ham. One treats it, automatically, with respect, even when carving; how much more when one is engaged in turning the raw material into the noble finished product. When Mr. Miller had completed operations in the coach-house I brought the scales back into the big ironing-room, and began operations, rubbing into the meat the proper quantity of all the dry ingredients; so many pounds of bay-salt and brown sugar, so many ounces of alum, dried juniper-berries and coriander seed; these last two had to be pounded in a mortar. The various processes went on for a month, and then the hams were ready for smoking.

The smoking of a ham is all-important, and at Ockham we were lucky in having a blacksmith, Gammon, who knew all about it, and cared for food with the knowledgeable passion of the old English countryside. He was a huge cheerful man with an enormous hairy chest, who prefaced most of his remarks with the words "Cor', what I mean ter say"; and he would go to any trouble to produce good food. He introduced me to that most delicious form of fish, kippered mackerel, unobtainable in the shops, and taught me how to make it: split them, strew with salt, and leave on dishes for thirty-six hours; then hang up to dry, and after a few hours put in the furnace to be smoked.

Gammon lent himself enthusiastically to smoking our hams. We concerted our times together carefully, so that the end of my wet-pickling should coincide roughly with his "throwing a fellow"—i.e., heating the metal tyre of a cartwheel in his small brick-built furnace. While the furnace was still full of hot embers, Gammon would go up with a wheelbarrow to "the yard", the builders' yard which Lady Lovelace ran on the estate; there he would fill two sacks with oak sawdust. He knew that any kind of pine dust would give "a nasty

4

tang o' turps" to the smoke, and make the hams less than perfect—as it was, he would pick up several handfuls and sniff them suspiciously before he filled his sacks. Back at the smithy he pitched the true, pure oak sawdust onto the embers, and hung up my hams on hooks; then the furnace was closed for thirty-six or forty-eight hours, according to the weight of the hams—after which I would go up with a rucksack and carry them home.

Even that was not the end of the process of producing a good ham. Oh no—they were tied up in loose muslin bags and hung from the ancient black beams in the kitchen to mature; if I could help it I never ate a ham till it was eleven months old.

Owen, what with building all the chicken-houses, setting up the runs for the breeding poultry, and making the hoppers, hen-coops and bee-hives, was immensely active about the place—winter and summer, he was always up and out by 6 A.M., and had put in two hours' work before breakfast, after which he set off for Horseley Station en route for London and the Foreign Office. The most picturesque of his activities was dealing with the daily feeding and watering of the broody hens. We could not afford an incubator at first, so all our chicks had to be hatched under broodies, which we rented from the farmers' wives for 1/- a week.

Owen brought his dealings with those silly creatures to a fine art. On the cement floor of the brooding-shed were set out five bowls of water, five heaps of maize, and five piles of cabbage or lettuce leaves—because a broody is too nervous and fussy to share her meal with another bird. Owen opened five coops, and then, perched on a wooden box, a long willow-rod in his hand, like a ring-master at a circus he somehow coaxed his idiotic charges out, kept them apart while they ate and drank, and finally with the rod guided each hen back into her own coop. There was no fuss, no chasing or grabbing; he never moved till all five were back on their eggs again, fluffing their feathers out to cover every one—then he shut those coops and let out the next five birds.

Well, that was our life, that we loved, and did not much want to leave; but it was not at all like the diplomatic service, or indeed like the lives led by most of Owen's colleagues. Even our friends thought our manner of living rather peculiar. One of my best customers for eggs, pork, poultry and honey was old Sir Edward Thesiger, or rather his daugher Sybil, who kept house for him. On one occasion, to please his son Ernest, the actor, he gave a big cocktail-party at his house in Sloane Street for a member of the Royal Family, an elderly princess, to whom Ernest was devoted; I happened to be in London, and was present. In fact it was all disastrous—Ernest was late, Sybil failed to recognise the Princess, and therefore to curtsey; the Princess was displeased, Ernest distressed. Next morning the old gentleman said at breakfast—"Well, my dear, what are our engagements for today? No more royalty, I do hope."

"No, Father," said Sybil briskly, "only one of the tradespeople coming to lunch." She told me this, gleefully, when I arrived for luncheon a few hours later.

While we havered over Peking, Don Gregory, Owen's head in the Northern Department, decided to apply pressure himself, and on me; he drove down one Sunday and firmly took me for a stroll up Watery Lane, the wet rutted track, shadowed by Lombardy poplars, which ran past the paddock and up to the Portsmouth Road. There Don rubbed it in that it would be downright wicked not to take this chance. I remember some of his very words: "Owen will be the youngest Counsellor in the Service; it will make him a marked man"—he even suggested that it might lead to his becoming, in time, head of the Office. Under this pressure, in the end Owen agreed to go. Bridge End was let—by a great stroke of luck almost at once, and for three years, then the normal duration of a post abroad, and we set about making our preparations.

Goodness, what a lot there was to do!—and only a couple of months to do it in, for we had to sail before Christmas. Everyone impressed on me that I should no longer have time to give Jane all her lessons; and Patrick, now seven, would have to be taught regularly too—so a nursery governess had to be sought, at short notice, and one who was willing to go to the far side of the world for three whole years—moreover someone whom we felt we could bear for so long. How we found Bumpy, as she came to be called, I have forgotten; but after she had been down to see me and the children I had no hesitations, and nor had she. I remember Grania's comment, after the interview; Grania was then four, and had a keen if rather eccentric feeling for words and their associations. "Why's she called Bumpstead?—did she fall off the bedstead?" she enquired.

Then a lady's-maid had to be found. We at once thought of Cissy Welford, who lived just up the road; her father was the head painter at the Yard, and she often made clothes for the children. Naturally this proposition had to be discussed with Mr. Welford—and in the end the answer was No.

"You see, M'm," Mrs. Welford said apologetically when she came to bring me these gloomy tidings, "it isn't as though it were anywhere handy." And I had to agree that Peking, on the opposite side of the world, could not possibly be described as "handy". As so often I turned for help to my Godmother, Nor Wood—and she, also as so often, promptly produced exactly what was required, like a rabbit out of a hat. A young friend of hers was getting married, and inheriting a lady's-maid from her recently deceased mother-in-law. So her own excellent maid, Baker, was going begging; she was at least forty, thoroughly experienced, a splendid needle-woman, and liked foreign travel, to which she was well accustomed—moreover she was a very good hairdresser. I arranged to meet her for an interview in the ladies' sitting-room at the old Haymarket Stores.

This meeting began with a most useful disaster. When leaving to go to the station the old Triumph at first wouldn't start; the gardener was nearly as stupid about motor-cycles as I was, and as I roared up the slope at Horseley Station I saw my train moving out. The next was three-quarters of an hour later—so when, worried and fretful, I walked into the large comfortable ladies' room nearly an hour late, I fully expected my prospective maid to have left in a huff. Not at all—when we had identified each other I found Baker completely untroubled, reading a woman's magazine; she said cheerfully that anyone could miss a train, and then settled down to enquire about the post in the most practical possible manner—in fact it was really she who interviewed me. After settling with her for a monthly wage far lower than I had expected, I engaged her on the spot. I felt that I should be perfectly safe with a person who showed no signs of annoyance at being kept waiting for nearly an hour—and I was not wrong. There is no need to describe Baker—"The Bread-maker", as Jane and Patrick soon called her, in derisive hostility. She is Hubbard, Laura Leroy's maid in *Peking Picnic*.

Even seasoned diplomats, when appointed to some remote and exotic post, are at pains to glean all the information they can about it in advance. Anything less seasoned than the O'Malleys it would be difficult to imagine, and Owen made many enquiries. The wonderful thing was that with ponies at £10 apiece, we should be able to keep horses, and ride—but only astride; and some knowledgeable person told us that we need only get our winter riding-kit in London; once in China the local tailors would copy these for us in drill for summer. So these were duly made, including jodhpurs for Jane; and I got one or two really good dresses for both her and Grania, again to be copied locally in the cheap Chinese cottons when we got there. Then there was the matter of wine, about which we knew nothing, since we were too poor ever to have it in the house. I wish I could remember who the knowing person was who advised us about wine, for his hints and tips were invaluable. Anyhow his advice was that for big dinner-parties by far the most economical thing to do was to pass straight to champagne after sherry with the soup, and to have it in magnums. He also urged Owen to get plenty of half-bottles of champagne; when Owen enquired for what occasions these would be used, this worthy explained that half-a-bottle of champagne was the ideal drink when one came in from riding! We ordered the magnums but not the halves.

All this outlay was a considerable strain on our resources; to raise money for the children's clothes I had a brain-wave. When my (minute) marriage-settlement was being drawn up twelve years before, I had harried and bullied my poor father's lawyer into putting into it a clause to the effect that I might draw up to "one-half of each child's share" for that child's "education or other advancement". In London I went to see the Trustee Department of the Westminster Bank and persuaded the manager, a very kind cosy person, that nothing could be more to the children's advancement, and indeed education, than for us all to go to China—but that to reap the full advantage we must be properly dressed! He actually agreed, and let me have £45 out for each of the children, and £100 for myself.

One of our last activities before leaving was to go over and spend a week-end at Denton, to say goodbye to Owen's parents. The existence of Denton, a house deep in the country some seven miles out of Oxford, was one of the things which had made our life, conducted as it was on a shoe-string, so easy and so pleasant. For summer holidays, for instance, there was never any question of trying to afford cramped lodgings at the seaside—we simply took the children to Denton; if Owen wanted a breather at Easter or Whitsun, we had only to send a line to say we were coming, and went to

Denton—to float in the ease of a big house full of servants, with an abundance of excellent food, and to idle in one of the most beautiful gardens in England. What matter that there was no bathroom, and that the only lavatory higher than ground-floor level functioned precariously with the aid of a garden watering can?—that there was no heating except open fires, and no light but the soft glow of oil lamps? There was every possible comfort, and endless pleasure and entertainment to be derived from the idiosyncrasies of Uncle Edward and Aunt Winnie—as I, like their nephews and nieces, was invited to call my father- and mother-in-law.

A more oddly assorted couple it would be hard to imagine. Uncle Edward had spent a long and happy life in various legal capacities under the Colonial Office, mostly in countries usually referred to as White Man's Graves; these had not affected his health one whit, and had left his mind stored with lively and amusing memories, and his cupboards with delightful scraps and relics—he had always had the wise habit of buying the *common* things in every country where he was posted, and bringing them home. He was full of charm, and had perfect and severe taste; the room which on his retirement he built for himself at the back of the house, lined with bookshelves and cupboards for his relics, with a huge deal table to write at, two armchairs, and a few rugs, was on any showing beautiful. Aunt Winnie on the other hand had no charm at all, either of appearance or manner; her normal dress was some form of stiff and rather dusty black, topped when going out to the garden or the stables by a man's grey felt hat with a hole in the crown. Her taste in household decoration was lamentable. Nothing could really destroy the beauty of the two panelled rooms, the drawing-room and the morning-room, just inside the front door, but what could be done to spoil it she did, with hideous curtains and cretonnes, and dreadful ornaments bought at church bazaars—she was very pious, and rejoiced in the presence of the Bishop of Oxford up on the hill at Cuddesdon, and the College there, full of theological students. Uncle Edward, though good friends with a succession of Bishops of Oxford, despised the students; he liked what he called "good sort of people", that is to say well-bred, intelligent persons of respectable life and habits—immoral peers or divorcing dukes he could not tolerate. Fortunately South Oxfordshire was full of "good sort of people", whom he enjoyed, and as Chairman of Quarter Sessions he had

9

plenty of opportunities of meeting them; but Aunt Winnie did not get on with the county very well, and did not really wish to—the people she liked and felt at home with were the farmers' and villagers' wives, whom she coaxed and scourged into the Mothers' Union.

I think it was really a sort of shyness, coupled with a built-in awkwardness of manner, that made Aunt Winnie so incompetent socially, for she had plenty of intelligence. But her social failings were a sore trial to Uncle Edward.

I remember little of that farewell visit; I suppose my mind was too full of more urgent preoccupations. Uncle Edward was in great spirits, delighted with this rapid step upwards in his younger son's career; Aunt Winnie told me that it was a great mistake to go to the expense of taking a lady's-maid all the way to China—an amah would have done perfectly well; she had had an excellent amah when she was in Hong Kong. They kissed us goodbye on the broad steps, among the two Aberdeen terriers and the Siamese cats, descendants of a gift to Uncle Edward from the King of Siam; then we got into the Wheatley taxi and drove away. From Aunt Winnie it was a final farewell; she died while we were in Peking. (My own parents were both dead years before.)

In the 1920s passengers to the Far East by P. & O. had the choice between joining their ship at Tilbury or at Southampton; for us, living only twenty miles from London, Tilbury was our obvious choice. How deep an impression the gloom and ugliness first of Fenchurch Street Station, and then Tilbury Docks, made on me may be gathered from Chapter Two of *The Ginger Griffin;* years later it made a perfect background to the distress of my little heroine, Amber Harrison. The O'Malleys, however, setting out for their first foreign post, were not in the least distressed; parents and children alike were full of enthusiasm, curiosity and interest. We sailed on December 18th, 1925, in the S.S. *Karmala,* 7,000 tons; not one of the newest or largest boats, but to us she seemed huge. Miss Bumstead and I had adjoining cabins; Jane and Grania slept with her, Patrick with me, in the upper bunk; Baker had a cabin a short distance away, while Owen and his tin Foreign Office boxes, full of "China print", were housed in a stateroom on the boat deck. Before we were out of the Thames Estuary Bumpy and I realised how impossible it was going to be to keep an eye permanently on three

10

lively children on board ship, and we devised a simple rule which might, we hoped, prevent them from falling overboard. If any child was seen so much as to put a foot on one of the boat rails, that child would go to bed in the bunk for a whole day, on bread and water. "It must be something they *will* mind", the little governess said. We summoned them all to the cabin, and with Baker as a witness issued this proclamation; I made them all repeat it, to show that they understood. We guessed that Patrick, at least, would try a dare, but he had no chance next day, for we put into Southampton at 8:30 A.M. and did not sail again till after dark. Sure enough, the following morning, glancing over his shoulder to make sure that he was observed, he put one small fat foot up on the bottom rung; Bumpy was on to him in a flash, and marched him round to me.

"Yes, put him in his bunk and lock him in; you can bring me the key. And only bread and water, mind." Howls and bellows of protest, but Bumpy inexorably bore him off, and in the cabin he stayed all day, and dry bread and water was all he had to eat or drink. Jane thought I was very cruel, and said so, loudly; but both she and Grania took note of the fact that for once a rule meant what it said: the result was a carefree voyage, as far as that particular hazard was concerned.

II

The First Post II

We loved the voyage—for all of us except Baker our first experience of a long sea trip; for Owen and myself the first startling taste of official importance. It had not occurred to us that we must, inevitably, sit at the Captain's table, still less that Owen, as the Number One Passenger, would have to make a speech on the first evening when, safely past Gibraltar and into calm waters, everyone was well enough to assemble in the saloon; I had never heard him speak in public before, but he was very witty, and much applauded.

One or two things still stand out from that journey—especially the Christmas at sea. We had a fair complement of the Navy on board, reliefs for the China Squadron, mostly lieutenant-commanders; they joined in the general demand for carols—but how to get words and music? Fortunately Ursula Nettleship had refused to let us leave for the ends of the earth without an ample supply of those cheap paper sheets, with four-part settings, of the songs we used to sing in the cottage at Bridge End at the week-ends—mostly folk-songs, but she had included several of the more essential Christmas carols; we dug these out of our luggage, and for forty-eight hours the saloon re-sounded with choir-practice. Jane and I, and the one or two other sopranos, had a job to make the air heard above the boom of the basses and tenors, with their main-top nautical voices. But when we sang the familiar words on Christmas Eve it was obvious that it had been absolutely the right thing.

The Navy then said that something ought to be done for the children—there were four or five in the Second Class, as well as our three in the First. Couldn't I produce a rig-out for Father Christ-mas?—Mack was dying to be Father Christmas. Philip John Mack was a huge man, but I did possess a very ample coral flannel dressing-gown with white facings; Baker sewed him up a hood out of a red woollen scarf and trimmed it with cotton-wool, and made him a fine cotton-wool beard tacked onto a piece of gunny-sacking. As for presents, I had a whole suitcaseful for our flock from all their aunts; we took off the labels and renamed enough for there to be a parcel for every child, which Mack stowed, along with crackers from the purser, in a large sack.

Captain Griffen entered fully into the spirit of the thing, and with Mack stage-managed it marvellously. That Christmas Day in the Mediterranean was calm and mild, and after nightfall everyone was mustered on the starboard deck, the children in the centre, but kept well away from the side by the Captain. Suddenly out of the dark-ness, there came a loud hail through a megaphone—"Ship ahoy!" The Captain stepped to the rail and shouted to ask who was there. "Father Christmas. Can I come aboard?" Permission was given, two sailors lowered a rope ladder, and up out of the darkness and onto the lighted deck climbed Mack's huge figure, in his red and white disguise. The whole thing was really breath-taking—as for the smaller children, they were fairly gibbering with excitement as Mack slung his sack off his shoulder, called out their names, and bestowed presents all round. Thanks to that blessed calm Mack had been able to climb out through an opened coal-port; Captain Griffen, tactfully remarking that even Father Christmas must have a drink, presently removed him to the bridge.

Those Christmas revels led to one of the most fascinating parts of the whole journey, a pause of nearly three weeks in Hong-Kong. Soon after leaving Singapore the children in the Second Class de-veloped a rash, and the ship's doctor, a very young man, going East for the first time in his life, diagnosed measles. Our children had only been in contact with them on Christmas night, but contact there had been. The ship's doctor immured the unhappy spotted children in the quarantine quarters, aft the well-deck and adjoining the Second Class; he then directed that our three must be moved there too. With the Captain's support we succeeded in resisting this; they were kept isolated in their cabins, and had their meals there.

13

But obviously they could not be kept in quarantine all the way to Shanghai; the sensible thing would be for them to go ashore at Hong-Kong and wait till it was known whether they would develop measles or not. Owen sent a wireless telegram—we still called them Marconi-grams then—to the Governor, Sir Cecil Clementi, asking if something could be arranged for us all, and received a cheerful reply "Accommodation arranged". But on what scale that accommodation would be we never dreamed.

When we anchored in the harbour at Hong-Kong, and stood on deck gazing up at the Peak, set with houses to its summit, and the bare blue mountains of the mainland, two launches came out to the *Karmala;* one contained the Consuls-General from Canton and Shanghai, who had both come down to greet the new Counsellor, the other the Hong-Kong Medical Officer of Health, come to look at the ship's cases of infectious illness. The M.O.H. was a middle-aged Scotsman, with a long experience of the Far East; he first examined the poor little souls in the isolation quarters, and then came across, shaking with laughter, to us. The rash was not measles at all, it was only dengué fever, a common complaint in those parts—mild, and not infectious. We could perfectly well have gone straight on. However it was now too late to alter all the arrangements, so ashore we went in the two launches—I began to feel that there was something to be said for having a maid when I found that Baker determinedly did all my packing for me, and most of the children's too.

On the quay three large cars were waiting. Through the bright sunny morning air we were swept up the Peak road to a spot where a whole crowd of rickshas awaited us—Tanderagee, the Colonial Secretary's residence where we were to stay, was only accessible by tarmac-ed footpaths so narrow that two rickshas could not go abreast. Along these, in single file, we bowled swiftly; the general dream-like sense of unreality of the whole proceeding accentuated by gardens on both sides of the path full of roses and sweet-peas in bloom, in January! At the house six white-clad servants were drawn up, who greeted us with polite bows; there was also an amah, in blue tunic and trousers, who had been provided for Grania's benefit by the ever-thoughtful Clementis. To add to the fairy-tale quality of the whole performance, the table in the dining-room was laid for lunch; cans of hot water stood under folded towels in the bedroom basins; there were flowers in all the rooms—I could not resist the feeling that if one of us rubbed a coin the wrong way, or used a forbidden word, everything might vanish in smoke. But in fact it was all solid enough—the house was permanently furnished by the Government, and linen, silver, and the admirable servants had all been hired from one of the big emporiums in the town.

There followed a fortnight of almost pure bliss for everyone. After a couple of days Owen went off to Canton with the Consul-General, with the laudable intention of seeing something of South China while he was within easy reach of it. Bumpy started taking the children for long walks; as they were incapable of asking their way in Chinese, she soon came and asked me to procure a map. I telephoned to the Colonial Secretary's office and asked for one. After a good deal of humming and hawing a map was sent up, with a note to say that it must on no account be lost, as it was the only copy. This tiny episode was the first inkling we got of the curious fact that Europeans in China practically never walk; they seem to lose the use of their legs. The map itself was curious: it was on a large scale, and very detailed, but Bumpy was greatly puzzled by heavy blue lines inked in round what, on their walks, she and the children presently identified as the water-sheds between the various valleys, and smaller, irregular splotches outlined in red ink—in these, she reported, they could only find curious earthenware jars and vases, and occasionally small circular walls with a door in each, which would not open. Subsequent enquiry produced the explanation—rather reluctantly given, we noticed. Hong-Kong is chronically short of water, and largely depended for its supply on surface water collected in reservoirs: the red splotches were Chinese cemeteries, out on the open hillsides, so water from those catchment areas was banned as being unhygienic.

While Bumpy and the children patrolled the Colony, and Owen pursued his researches into South China by chasing pirates and shooting duck on H.M.S. *Cicala* in the many-channelled delta of the Pearl River, everyone loaded me with the kindest hospitality. I was taken to the races, I was driven about to see the floating city of sampans at Aberdeen, and the big reservoir with what was then the highest dam in the world. Kindest of all was darling old General Luard, in charge of the troops in Hong-Kong. He, alone, asked me if there was anything I particularly wanted to see or do. I replied instantly that I wanted to go up Tai-mo-Shan, the beautiful pointed mountain in the New Territories, on the mainland, whose blue peak, though only about 4,000 feet high, completely dominates Hong-Kong. He was obviously startled by such a bizarre request, but at once undertook to arrange it, and a few days later, accompanied by some officers and A.D.C.s, up Tai-mo-Shan we went. We drove to the foot, where I was astonished to find waiting for us not only a whole team of mules to carry the food and drink, but saddled animals for everyone to ride. This was not at all my idea of going up a mountain, and I tactlessly said that I would rather walk. This greatly disconcerted the young officers, who had never dreamed of walking uphill for two or three hours; however, one or two took it in turns to keep me company in my foot-slogging, while the General, laughing consumedly, rode up with the others. Tai-mo-Shan is grassy almost to the summit, and till the last hundred feet or so the gradient is quite gentle; it was a lovely, easy walk for anyone fresh from Europe, and the view from the top was infinitely rewarding. It is the highest peak in the coastal range which rises almost directly from the sea; it was only when we reached the summit that we could see what lay behind. From a flat pale-brown floor of paddy-fields rose ranges of dark mountains, bare as bronze and the same colour, as ribbed and spiny as bronze dragons, which indeed was exactly what they looked like; it occurred to me to wonder if this was one reason why the Chinese had chosen the dragon as their symbol of royal power.

This, then, as far as Hong-Kong, was the reality that lay behind the Grant-Howards' voyage out to China at the beginning of *The Ginger Griffin*. But though there are omissions in the book, nothing is invented. The thing that I wished to bring out was the impact of the journey on Amber Harrison, and all that she saw, I saw myself. Illusion about the coast of Arabia, when for a moment she mistook sand and shadows for mist and forests, was mine also; so was the resemblance of Sumatra to the West Highlands, and the breathtaking sight of the fleet of junks at sunrise. It was easy to put myself in her place, to transfer my own feelings to her; but colouring all her impressions with her own so different emotions—her sorrow for her lost young man, her slight timidity towards the sophisticated Grant-Howards, her growing curiosity about what lay ahead of her in Peking. And after Hong-Kong, it was fun to pass the succession of Consuls who came on board to meet Owen in review, as seen through her shy but observant eyes.

16

On our journey North the head of the Hong-Kong and Shanghai Bank presented us, in Shanghai, with a lovely spaniel called Sai-jé, Chinese for snipe; we modified the name slightly to Chargé, short for Chargé d'Affaires, a more suitable name for a Counsellor's dog, we felt. On the way up to Tientsin Chargé lived in a kennel on deck; the kennel, as well as two feeding-bowls and seven pounds of dog-biscuits, was presented to us along with the dog, in the royal style of Far Eastern presents. It soon became very rough and very cold; the ship's rails were hung with icicles, the mountains on the mainland were flecked with snow. We kept fairly close in-shore, to get some shelter from the gale which presently set in to blow. The Captain on this small boat had none of the social expertise of Captain Griffen; he was a cross old man, and more foul-mouthed than anyone I had yet encountered in my countrified life; to sit on his right was no privilege, but I had to. Moreover, he was edgy, and not without reason: only a few weeks before the sister-ship to his had been captured and ransacked by pirates on this very run; he had several four-letter words for the gale which forced him to hug the coast. One day at lunch the note of the engines altered; Owen's ear caught it.

"Captain, you've got a puncture," he said.

"God damn and blast you, sir, what the something something do you think you're talking about?" the old man stormed; but the note altered still more, and as way came off the ship and she swung round into the trough of the waves, she began to roll steeply; within seconds every piece of glass and china shot off the tables and smashed on the floor—she had not been pitching enough before to have the "fiddles" put on. With more and worse oaths the Captain got up and stamped out.

That was an uncomfortable night. We were off a shore known to be infested with pirates, and until the engines were repaired, which took some hours, the ship was completely helpless, and rolled piti-lessly. She was a tiny little thing, and our quarters were so cramped that Grania had no bunk at all, but was bedded down on a sort of settee in my cabin; when I went along to see if she and Jane were all right I found that she had rolled off onto the floor, and lay, still asleep, but half uncovered. There was nothing for it but to tuck her up in my own bunk, out of which she could not roll; in the next cabin Bumpy was being sick, but Patrick, mercifully, was asleep; Baker was being sick too; Owen had gone to bed. I then began to

17

wonder where I should sleep, and remembered the rather sordid little smoking-room aft of the dining-saloon, which had two or three big black horsehair sofas; clutching the icy rails I went along and found it empty—most of the passengers had succumbed by this time. I went and collected some pillows and a couple of blankets, put on an overcoat, and staggered back to the smoking-room—but then I remembered Chargé, the spaniel, so I lurched along to where his kennel was lashed to the rail. He was in a pitiable state—he had been sick, too, poor love, and was shivering with cold, and whimpering miserably. I put on his collar and lead, and dragged him to the smoking-room, where I parked him in an armchair; his whimpering soon stopped, and I bedded myself down snugly on one of the sofas, which wasn't half bad, and in no time was fast asleep.

About two in the morning I was roughly awakened. A torch was flashed in my eyes, and an angry voice shouted—"Who the bloody hell is that?"

I sat up—there was the Captain.

"It's Mrs. O'Malley, Captain."

"What the devil are you doing here?"

"I haven't got a bunk, and I wanted to lie down, so I came in here."

"Why the devil haven't you got a bunk?"

I explained. "Oh, and could you shut the door, Captain? I was getting up a nice fug."

He shut the door and switched on the light, saying "Well, you're a cool one!"—then he caught sight of the spaniel.

"What the bloody hell is that dog doing in here?"

"He's frozen outside—I can't leave him there."

He sat down and began to laugh.

"Mind if I smoke?" When I said no he offered me a gasper; then he pulled a flask out of the pocket of his oilskin and offered me a swig of whisky. For the space of a cigarette he chatted quite amiably; then—

"Mind if I stay?" he asked. "I'd been going to doss down for a bit in here myself." Again I said no, so he switched off the light and settled himself in an armchair; surprisingly, he didn't snore. When I woke in the morning he was gone.

We had heard alarming accounts of the Minister's wife, Lady Macleay, before we left England—in particular that she hated children, and was liable to keep anyone on whom she had any sort of official hold glued to the bridge-table from luncheon till dinner-time. The Counsellor's wife would have been a helpless victim; but I felt I could use my time better in China than by playing bridge, at which I wasn't much good anyhow, so I never touched a card on the boat, and gave out, firmly, that I couldn't play, and was too stupid to learn. Instead, I started learning Chinese, which was much more rewarding; also I wanted Jane to go on with her French and Latin, which Bumpy could not teach her. That largely filled up the mornings, and for the afternoons there was sight-seeing, and the lovely, lovely riding on the enchanting little China ponies—the acquiring of these, and the rides and paper-hunts, are faithfully dealt with in *The Ginger Griffin*. In fact Amber's win in the Ladies' Hunt was achieved by Jane, who turned into a beautiful little horsewoman—again, it was easy to translate this into terms of Amber.

One's degree of enjoyment in any post is to some extent determined by the character of the local diplomatic corps; less so in the Peking of the 1920s than in most places, because with so many new and wonderful things to do and to see, one was less dependent on people outside one's own Legation. Within it we were exceedingly lucky, poor Lady Macleay apart. Eric Teichman, the Chinese Secretary, knew more about China than almost any Englishman then living; he also knew everything about China ponies and their mafoos, or grooms, since he kept a racing-stable as well as playing polo and riding regularly in the Sunday paper-hunts (cross-country steeple-chases). He put all this knowledge, liberally, at our disposal; Nellie, his wife, helped me in every way in her power, and became a life-long friend. The First Secretary, Gordon Vereker, also became a firm friend; he doted on Jane from the start, gave her a beautiful pony, Vanity—on which she won the Ladies' Hunt—and spent hours teaching us to jump, and generally being kind and helpful.

We were fairly lucky with the Corps, too. The Belgian Minister had an English wife, who was very knowledgeable about local customs and personalities, and passed her information on very helpfully; like everyone else she looked on me as a poor helpless Vicarage rose, who needed all the assistance she could get—as indeed I was, and did. The American Counsellor and his wife, Ferdy and Katie Mayer, also became firm friends. Perhaps the most valuable to us of all was the Dane, Henrik de Kauffmann; he had a lovely temple in the Western Hills, to which we often went; he knew Peking really well, and put us in the way of seeing beautiful things quite outside the ken of most people—also he got me my Chinese teacher. The Germans were old, kind, and to us negligible; the French middle-aged and waspish—we were negligible to them. Of the Italians I only remember Theodoli, who was, I think, First Secretary, because he was the most beautiful horseman I have ever seen in my life; he gave me a memorable phrase about "hands" in riding—"the horse should always be searching for the hand, and never find it." And he gave me all three volumes of Daniele Varé's *Novelle di Yen-ching*, afterwards rewritten in English as *The Maker of Heavenly Trousers* and *The Gate of the Happy Sparrows*.

Diplomatic life in fact turned out to be not nearly as intimidating as we had expected. Lady Macleay made no secret of her vexation that I would not learn to play either bridge or mah-jongg, nor of the fact that she regarded me as a poor mutt, but that did not affect me very much—anyhow no one could regard Owen as a poor mutt. She made use of me when she wanted to, of course. Only a few weeks after our arrival the Boxer Indemnity Commission turned up in Peking. This was a commission set up by the British Government to decide how the large indemnity extracted from China for all the damage to British lives and property during the Boxer Rising could best be expended for the benefit of the Chinese themselves—that being the new charitable mood at home; it had been accumulating for years, and now amounted to an enormous sum. It was headed by Lord Willingdon; the financial expert was Colonel the Hon. Sidney Peel, and for the Welfare aspect came Dame Adelaide Anderson. The Willingdons and the Peels stayed in the Legation itself; we offered to put up Dame Adelaide, whom I had known from my childhood, and always called Cissie—she was a dear little old thing, and she and her amah were no trouble. At the end of about a week the chit-coolie brought me a note from Lady Macleay summoning me to see her—I popped across at once.

She told me, rather abruptly, that I must give a dinner-party for the Willingdons as soon as possible. "If Ronald has to sit next to that woman any more nights on end I think he will go mad!"

I promised to ask them forthwith. When I got back Niu, the Number One Boy, informed me that a T'ai-T'ai was in the drawing-room—"She say she wait." Useless of course to expect any recog-

nisable name from a Chinese servant—I hurried in; there sat Lady Willingdon.

She was a good deal more polite than Lady Macleay, but the burden of her message was the same. She wanted me to do her a real kindness, and to ask them to dine with us as soon as possible. "If Willingdon has to talk to that woman much longer without a let-up he will go crazy."

Stifling mirth, I said that nothing could be more delightful, and provisionally fixed a night four days hence. We had to scrape up some people to meet them, but they were such very big fish that this was not difficult. Fraser, the elderly, delightful and learned *Times* correspondent, known familiarly as Father Time, would do for Cissie Anderson, and we already owed the Belgians a dinner; they were free, luckily. (When we had dined with them, Owen, who has never been much good at names, asked me in the car as we pulled up—"Tell me their name again."

"Le Maire de Warzée D'Hermalle."

"Good God!" said poor Owen.)

This was our first real dinner-party, and I was a little nervous—M. de Warzée sat on my right, Lord Willingdon on my other side. We had decided to follow the hint about starting champagne with the fish, and the Belgian Minister's reaction was reassuring—"Ah, comme cela m'est sympathique, de voir le champagne dans un magnum!" he exclaimed. Anyhow no one could fail to enjoy themselves sitting next to Lord Willingdon. He was not only one of the most beautiful human beings ever to walk the earth; he was also courtly, gay, and kind. At the end of dinner, which for me had passed not only easily but delightfully, he noticed that I was becoming a little abstracted, in my frenzied but unsuccessful efforts to catch Lady Willingdon's eye; at the far end of the table she was talking to Owen with something of the remorseless rapidity of a machine-gun. He looked at me with an amused eye.

"You can do nothing with the woman, can you?" he said. "Shall I knock on my glass?"

To us the great value of the Boxer Indemnity Commission proved to be the presence of the Peels. We liked them, they liked us; when Lady Delia had to go home because of the death of a relation, she more or less bequeathed Sidney to us—I promised faithfully to take him for walks regularly, and happily kept my promise, and the

friendship that began then has lasted till now. Peking provided me with another most enriching friend in the person of Lady Gosford. Her son, Lord Acheson, was in China on behalf of the British-American Tobacco Company—he was known locally as the Baccy Baron—and she came out for some months to entertain for him; though she was at least my mother's age we made close friends.

She is Lady Harriet Downham in *Four-Part Setting*, a portrait that was made at the request of Archie Rose, also of the B.A.T. She had been a lady-in-waiting to both Queen Alexandra and Queen Mary, and when in December, 1936, *The Atlantic Monthly* printed an article of mine called "Recollections of Jubilee", a rather gay and informal account of how that great day had been celebrated in Oxford and Abingdon, I sent her a copy. She passed it on to the current Lady-in-Waiting, thinking that it might amuse the King and Queen; but before King George had seen it they went down to Sandringham, the magazine was left behind at Buckingham Palace, and when Queen Mary sent for it, it couldn't be found. Lady G. rang me up and asked me if I had another copy, to post it to Lady So-and-So at Sandringham, which I did. By this time the King was very ill indeed; however the Queen read it aloud to him, and to quote the Lady-in-Waiting, "he guffawed over it", and said he had no idea that simple people, out in the country, had felt like that. I was inexpressibly glad to have been allowed to give that gruff but dedicated old monarch this small pleasure on his death-bed.

Four-Part Setting is a sad book; I wrote it partly because Owen had reproached me with never writing a novel about "people who are being really *pinched* by life." Rose and Antony, both pure inventions, are definitely pinched, not to say wrung. The original of Anastasia—who had never been East of the Reading Room in the British Museum, cared nothing for botany, and had certainly never walked two miles on end in her life—did in fact spot herself, in spite of these disguises, when the party is confronted with the Trappist Monastery, out behind the Western Hills. Of course the expedition over Por Hua Shan, the magical Hill of a Hundred Flowers, was based on a real trip, which I did with the Teichmans and Vereker; it was perfectly simple, in the book, to send five quite different characters on it, using all the actual detail, but adapted to their requirements.

On our way back to Peking, after climbing Mt. Conolly and spend-

ing two nights in the Temple of the Jade Emperor, we stopped for lunch at Tan Chüeh Ssu; we entered this famous temple from behind, and ate our lunch in that delicious little corner courtyard with the island pavilion where half the party in *Peking Picnic* are cornered by bandits, and spend such an uncomfortable time till they are rescued, thanks to Hubbard's Napoleonic machinations. That is how I knew that it was possible to get out, unseen, over the temple wall by the back and foot method, as Lilah did to raise the alarm; and that is how I also came to know of the existence of the back entrance to Tan Chüeh Ssu, where the foreign party are so dramatically rescued by soldiers of the British Legation Guard when they are being marched off into captivity by the T'ao-pings.

That one trip produced material that could be used in two books, *Peking Picnic* and *Four-Part Setting*, as did my sojourn with the children at the seaside in the Counsellor's bungalow in the Legation Compound at Pei-t'ai-ho; for the early part of *Four-Part Setting*, and also for the origin of Amber Harrison's racing-stable in *The Ginger Griffin*. Bumpy and I took that lovely walk along the seashore from Pei-t'ai-ho to Shanhaikwan, and on the way we met a Swedish-American sergeant, who let me ride his pony; he offered to bring me down two griffins from Manchuria, and I accepted eagerly. He brought them all right, but Owen was appalled at the idea of my keeping race-ponies, and I had to sell them at once—without loss. One did quite well on the race-course, though it didn't win the Maiden's Plate; but I learned enough from watching the training of Eric Teichman's race-ponies, and riding some of them myself to exercise them, to be able to give quite a convincing account of them in a novel.

One of the more satisfactory features of life in an Embassy or Legation is that if any interesting or distinguished person visits that particular capital, one almost certainly meets them—anyhow one always can if one wants to. So I was delighted to learn in Peking that Sven Hédin, the famous Swedish explorer, was coming there for some weeks, to assemble and launch one of his expeditions across Central Asia. I had taken a passionate interest in that part of the world for years, ever since reading *The Pulse of Asia* by the American geographer Ellesworth Huntingdon; I had studied Sir Aurel Stein's books, as well as Hédin's own, and was fascinated by the civilisation of almost half a continent now, owing to climatic changes, lying buried under sand. In Peking I had directed Jane's geography lessons to this region; she was as interested in it as I was—and now the man who had done so much to lay bare all that buried past, and the access routes to it, was actually coming to stay in the same town. I was determined to meet him, and if possible I meant that Jane should meet him too.

But to my great vexation I soon learned that this was not going to be perfectly easy. Hédin was believed to have been very anti-British in the First World War, and the Macleays had decided not to invite him to anything; in fact it was hoped that all the Legation staff would cold-shoulder him.

Well, I did not—I arranged to be asked to meet him by Henrik de Kauffmann, and promptly asked him to lunch, where he only met amiable foreigners. He was great fun, and immensely interesting; I asked him again, and this time allowed Jane to be present. In the course of a conversation about Central Asia he suddenly rounded on her with—"*You* don't know where the Yarkandaria is!"

"Yes I do!" Jane replied, rather scornfully. "It rises in the Karakorams, flows North till it joins the Tarim, and then turns East till they both sink away into the sand near Lop Nor."

This unexpected display of knowledge delighted Hédin; for the rest of that luncheon he gave most of his attention to the child, and thereafter always referred to her as "Yane, the little yeographer." This led to a curious incident.

A week later one of our Consuls came to see me; after observing that he understood that I was seeing a good deal of Sven Hédin, he asked if I knew what the object of his expedition was, just where it was going, and how it was financed. It was, he said, to be a huge affair, probably beyond Sweden's power to launch alone, and including some Chinese elements—so—er—well, it would be useful to know more about it, if I followed him. I suggested, rather unkindly, that he might try asking Hédin himself—after more humming and hawing he at last admitted that British Intelligence had exhausted every means of trying to find out the answers to these questions, with no success at all; but it really was important to the British Government to know them.

I saw his point. The expedition was certainly going to cross Central Asia, which in 1926 meant going right along behind the back garden wall of British India, then still a part of the Empire, and constantly under a muted threat from Russia. I could only, in decency, promise to see what I could do. Owen laughed a great deal when I told him of this conversation, but he agreed that I ought to try.

At first it was plain sailing. Chinese incompetence or Chinese stalling, or both, was delaying the expedition's departure; Hédin, fretted by the delay, bored and at a loose end, did not seem to mind how often he came to the Counsellor's House—questions from a family so well-informed about the Tarim Basin were readily answered. The object of the expedition was mainly meteorological; to ascertain the direction of the wind-currents which had laid down so much of the soil of Asia itself—loess is not a sedimentary deposit, but a wind-borne one. For this purpose meteorologists, in twos and threes, were to be dumped all along the route, with a huge supply of small air-balloons, to each of which would be attached a numbered label in three languages, Chinese, Turki, and another, telling the finder to deliver the label to an address in Peking, stating where and when the balloon had been recovered; a good sum would be paid for each label. These balloons would be launched over a period of several months; a careful record would be kept of the dates of launching and so on. Finance?—oh, the Swedish Government was putting up some, the Russians more, and U.F.A., the big German film concern, more still; they were sending a large camera-team and hoped to make a unique documentary, under Hédin's expert leadership. And where exactly were they going? The little man ignored that question —he wanted to tell me more about the supposed past climate changes, and went on pouring out theories.

When I passed this information to my Consul he pulled rather a long face over it. A chain of groups of so-called meteorologists, established all across Central Asia, could form an ideal network of cells, either for spying or for subversion; and a team of German cameramen sounded pretty ominous to him. Of course U.F.A. was a natural source of finance—but Russia putting up money too!—that wasn't so good. Anyhow, where *were* they going?

"He didn't tell me."

"Did you ask him?"

"Yes, but he sort of brushed it aside and went on talking about something else."

This troubled the Consul a lot. He was grateful for what I had found out, and would report it; but what we had already learned made it more important than ever to know the expedition's exact route. He was very urgent about this, and once again I promised to do my best.

But my best wasn't any good. I realised, after one or two more attempts, that Sven Hédin, for whatever reason, was just *not* going to tell me his route—when I reported this the little Consul became almost frantic. I *must* find out; London urgently wanted this information.

This was an amusing situation. While the Macleays and most of the rest of the Legation were frowning on me for my unpatriotic behaviour in making friends with Hédin, British Intelligence was imploring me to use that same friendship to find out for them what they could not learn for themselves. And in the end I did think of something—rather reluctantly I decided to let Yane, the little Yeographer, see what she could do.

I sent a chit to the Swede asking him if he would mind coming to luncheon with no other guests, only ourselves and Jane?—I wanted the child to have the chance of talking to him herself, and hearing his incomparable first-hand accounts of the Pamirs and so on; the good-natured creature agreed at once. Then I coached Jane. I wished her to ask Dr. Hédin where he was going—I should leave them alone together, and if she wanted the big atlas, it would be in the schoolroom; after twenty minutes I should come back and send her off to rest, when she was to go straight to her room and write down any names he had mentioned. Never mind about the spelling, just write down the *sounds;* but she *must* remember the sounds, and put them down at once. And she was not to talk about it to Pat, Bumpy or anyone, because it was a secret, and rather important.

Jane—she was only eleven then—accepted this assignment with fewer questions, and less argument than I had feared; she liked Hédin enormously, and the idea of having him all to herself pleased her, I think. All went according to plan—after lunch Owen returned to the Chancery, and presently I made some excuse and left Jane and the explorer alone in the drawing-room. I fretted and fidgeted for twenty minutes, or a little longer, and then went back and told Jane she must go to rest at once—I apologised for having had to leave my guest, and sat on talking with him till at last, after four o'clock, he left. One could never be bored in Hédin's company, but I heard little of what he told me that afternoon—I was in a fever of

26

anxiety to know if our stratagem had succeeded; as soon as he had gone I flew upstairs to the nursery wing.

Jane was sitting on her bed, the atlas open on her knees; across the double spread which covered Central Asia ran a heavy black line, along which Jane, her tongue out in her concentration, was writing down names unless, recognisably, they were there already—then she had underlined them, also in heavy black. The atlas was ruined; but when she had finished I took it downstairs, got a piece of tracing-paper, and copied the whole thing. When I summoned the little Consul and showed it to him he was astonished—and delighted. But how on earth had I got it?—and was I sure that it was correct?

Dead sure, I told him; it was completely correct. But when Hédin came to say goodbye I felt rather like Jael with Sisera.

III

The Return

In the spring of 1927 the children and I went home. Patrick and Grania had both had scarlet fever, combined with diphtheria, the previous summer, quite badly; Dickie's illness in *The Ginger Griffin* accurately pictures both its origin, and that anxiety. Soon after we all had dysentery bar Jane, and spent four lovely weeks at a borrowed temple in the old Imperial Hunting Park, out in the Western Hills, to recover from it—going for walks in the cool of the morning, and having long chats with the peasant-women over their tasks of hoeing and apricot-picking; I learned quite a bit about Chinese life and Chinese husbandry during that calm, unsocial spell. In the following March Patrick somehow contracted septic pneumonia—he had it in both lungs, and very nearly died. That, we felt, was enough; and indeed Dr. Dipper (the original of Dr. Hertz, in both Picnic and Griffin) said flatly that he would never live through another hot weather in the Far East. By the same token it was thought too risky to return home as we had come, through the tropics; instead it was decided that we should go on round the world—across the Pacific, across Canada, and finally across the Atlantic. Owen stayed on alone.

Now Bumpy had always been promised that when we left Peking she should be given her fare home, and on the way visit some relations in Australia; but I had assumed that Owen would be with us, to deal with the mechanics of the actual traveling, like pursers

28

and luggage, while I coped with the children. As it was, Baker and I had to manage as best we could by ourselves, handling a party which included, besides the lively three, a pet squirrel given to Patrick by an admirer, and a short-tailed mouse similarly presented to Jane. These gave me a lot of trouble: nuts and apples had constantly to be produced for the squirrel, fresh beans and unmilled grain for the mouse—moreover they were looked on very sourly by all immigration authorities, who muttered ominously about quarantine, and had to be talked out of it. We left Peking, inauspiciously, on Friday the thirteenth of May; went up, by train, to Mukden, and down through Korea to Fusan, where we crossed to Shimonoseki in Japan; we spent a couple of nights in Osaka, where I left the children with Baker for a day, and made a solitary dash to see Kyoto and the Temples there—then on to Tokyo. The Tilleys were endlessly good to us; though the Embassy proper had been shaken down by the great earthquake, and they and their staff were living in temporary quarters, we were all fitted in somehow while we waited for our boat—Grania stayed with Charles and Catherine Peake, and they formed a lifelong friendship with the child. There was another, small earthquake while we were in Tokyo; by great good luck it took place by daylight, and I happened to be looking out of the window, and saw the water in the pool on the lawn sloshing to and fro and slopping out onto the grass banks—a singular spectacle which I would not have missed for anything.

The trip, by a C.P.R. boat, across the north Pacific was dull and chilly. The only feature of interest was crossing the 180th meridian, when we had an extra day, Meridian Day, which had no date in the calendar—yet on it, so the wireless informed us, Call-boy won the Derby! It was great fun explaining this to Jane, who, being a little yeographer, easily took it in.

We landed at Vancouver early in the day, and I was rather aghast to find that the transcontinental express only left at midnight; while I was dismally enquiring about hotels an angelic lady came on board, said that I had been kind to a cousin of hers in Peking, and swept us all off to her house, where her solitary Japanese manservant produced a delicious lunch—then the children were put to lie down, and she drove me out to see those marvellous gardens, where all flowers seem larger, and more abundant, than anywhere else in the world.

At the station, to which our luggage had been sent direct from the ship, a major difficulty arose. The Foreign Office had of course agreed, in the circumstances, to my returning with the children, and all our reservations had been made for us before we started, I presume by the Chancery in Peking. Whoever made them, though, was ignorant of the peculiarities of railway travel in the New Hemisphere; we had three and a half first-class tickets, but no berths had been booked in addition—and as on Canadian and American trains a berth by night is a seat by day, our tickets only entitled us to stand in the corridor all the way from Vancouver to Quebec, some four days and nights. The rather unhelpful Canadian Pacific Railways official who explained this to me suggested that I should take two "drawing-rooms", small private compartments like European sleepers, only much larger; I inspected these, and agreed that they would do very well—but he wanted me to pay for them on the spot, and I had nothing like the hundreds of dollars necessary. I had only been provided with a modest sum as petty cash, for food and tips, since it was assumed that proper accommodation had been paid for in advance for our whole journey. Becoming desperate, I also became rather tough. I said the children must go and at least *sit* in the drawing-rooms while we got something settled. This done, and Patrick and Grania lying down, I rounded on the man. Mercifully Lord Willingdon had recently arrived in Canada as Governor-General, and I told the C.P.R. person to go and ring him up at Ottawa, and ask him, personally, if he wished his friend Mrs. O'Malley and her children to stand in the corridor the whole way across the continent, or whether he would guarantee that the British Government would later pay for our drawing-rooms? Somewhat shaken, the official went off; what actually transpired I don't know, but he presently returned and told me, a good deal more politely than before, that it was "all right". And as our kind hostess's Japanese manservant had produced an ample supply of beans for the mouse and nuts for the squirrel, I was at last able to bid her goodbye, and settle down for the night.

The Rockies were something of a disappointment. Compared with the Alps, their geological structure seems rather ugly; instead of rising from the valleys in clear sweeping lines from base to summit, more than half their height consists of huge squarish masses, on which the actual peaks are perched, looking like small pointed spires on a square church tower. But the Fraser River, foaming and tumbling below us next morning, was lovely, and so were the wild strawberries and fresh trout brought for our approval by a steward.

The children were highly amused by the names of the places we went through, such as Moose Jaw and Medicine Hat; and once we were out on the prairies there was the endless entertainment afforded by the gophers, little marmot-like creatures whose method of concealment was to stand bolt upright, so rigid and motionless that they looked exactly like small wooden stakes—till they suddenly decided to bolt like lightning into their burrows. And we had one great piece of luck. Right out in the middle of the prairie our engine broke down, and the great train came to a halt; someone climbed a telegraph pole and I suppose tapped the wires, anyhow a fresh engine was summoned. I got hold of a sort of super-steward, and persuaded him to let me and the children get out and go for a walk; the new engine was unlikely to arrive for an hour and a half, he said. Steps were produced, we climbed down, and set off to walk over the actual prairie, here mostly shortish pasture, not very green, full of small bright wild-flowers. We walked directly away from the train; when we had gone a mile or rather more it looked quite small, a thin black line in an expanse that stretched away on all sides as featureless as an ocean, and to a horizon as remote as an ocean horizon—a most remarkable sight; not a house, not a tree to be seen. Presently we noticed smoke rising in front of us in this apparently empty waste, and pressed on to the lip of a hollow, which opened quite suddenly before our feet; in the bottom of it lay a farm, with buildings, and chickens and people moving about. We longed to go down and see more, but I was afraid to let the train, now looking smaller than ever, out of my sight; we turned back, the children loudly lamenting, and reached the line of coaches just in time to see the new engine, a plumed speck in the distance, humming towards us. I find it impossible to explain why that prairie walk was such a wonderful experience.

At Montreal, where there was a long halt, we got out to stretch our legs; on the platform was an A.D.C. from Government House, who greeted us with deferential politeness and handed me a note from Lady Willingdon, inviting me warmly to go back to Ottawa and stay with them till our boat for Europe left in a week's time—there was however no mention of the children. This seemed to me impossible. So I found my despatch-case, and scribbled a regretful note explaining that I could not come, and gave it to the A.D.C. It was only when we got to Quebec, and I told Owen's cousin Angus about this, that he made me realise that in my innocence I had perpetrated a most frightful gaffe—an invitation from the Governor-General, or his wife, amounted to a royal command, and could not possibly be refused. So I wrote Lady W. a second letter, deeply apologetic, stressing Patrick's fragile state of health; and then settled down to enjoy myself in the humbler milieu afforded by Angus and his friends.

Quebec is a strangely beautiful city; very grey and very French, with its pointed slate-tiled roofs, seated high above the St. Lawrence. The rooms which Angus had taken for us were not in any hotel, but in one of a row of eighteenth-century houses opposite the Citadel: we looked across at its grey battlements from the window of our big, lofty, rather sparsely furnished room. Angus, who thinks of everything, at once provided us with the two volumes of Francis Parkman's *History of Canada;* I read these at night, and every morning assembled the children on my huge double bed and read them suitable portions aloud before breakfast and the day's excursions. These, also organised by Angus, were many and amusing. We went down by steamer to the Ile d'Orléans, and drove about it; I remember especially a strange sort of hawthorn, whose heads of very large flowers were set as flat as plates and almost as large, growing in flowery meadows; and how, as we came to the crest of a gentle slope, the thunderous sound of the Montmorency Falls suddenly came to us across the water from the further bank of the St. Lawrence. Another day, without the children, Angus and a friend drove me out into the "bush", the virgin forest which Price Brothers, so profitably, were diligently cutting down; there I saw for the first time the striking white or reddish three-petalled flowers of the wild Trilliums, and encountered the terrible stinging gnats and flies so vividly described in Nevil Shute's *No Highway,* and the fallen boughs and trunks which make walking a nightmare.

Of course we were duly shown the Plains of Abraham, but in a rather pleasing and unusual way: Pat and Jane, after these early morning lections from Parkman, were wild to climb up the very glen by which Wolfe's troops made their surprise attack from the river. This emerges in Wolfe's Field, a private estate which then belonged to a very old Miss Price; of course Angus knew her, and was able to arrange it—Patrick, hawk-eyed, examined the ground minutely, and actually found a contemporary musket-ball in the loose soil at the mouth of some wild creature's burrow. The Citadel itself was naturally a thrill; Georges Vanier was then the Commandant, and showed us everything; both lots of children played together.

It was mid-summer by the time we reached England; Bridge End was still let, so we went first to Denton. Owen's mother had died in the spring, but Uncle Edward and Eva O'Malley still kept the house hospitably open. However we couldn't all stay there indefinitely, so I engaged another governess for Patrick, and the children's old Nannie returned to take care of Grania—thus attended they could be sent off as small units on visits to friends and relations. This was just as well, as I was suddenly told that I must have my appendix out; Geoffrey Keynes did it for me, very cheaply—but what neither he nor I realised was that in those pre-antibiotic days an abdominal operation on anyone who had had dysentery within the previous three years meant a septic wound. This I duly got, so instead of the normal ten days I was laid up for a month.

Owen came home in the autumn, but still we could not get Bridge End back. Patrick's health was very precarious, and on a specialist's advice it was arranged that I should take him out to Château d'Oex for some months; we stayed in a pension, the Villa Prima-Flora, and he went as a day-boy to the English School. Another governess was engaged for Jane, and they stayed at Pendell Court with May Bell, her godmother; Grania and Nannie Comley continued to pay long visits, Owen lived at the Club. It was an uncomfortable, disjointed sort of spell in our family life.

It was at this time that I began writing for money. I had lectured for years, long before we went to China, but only in an unprofessional sort of way. On my return from China the requests for talks increased; I was even asked to give one or two at Château d'Oex, which I did, rather nervously, in French. And I wrote little pieces about China for various small Church-y magazines, and articles on bringing up children for *The Nursery World:* "The Invalid Child", "The Child at Sea", "The Child Abroad"—which paid surprisingly well. But serious writing began in a rather curious way.

In May 1928 Owen and I were on a motoring holiday in Scotland, and spent a fortnight at the hotel at Roy Bridge. While there I got

colitis and had to stay in bed, sipping arrowroot; in this dismal
situation I read one day in the paper that Chang T'so-lin, the Manchurian war-lord, formerly a bandit, was reported to have been
murdered by the Japanese. Now I had met Chang when he came
down to Peking; Eric Teichman had taught me the most flattering
Chinese titles and phrases that he could think of, and I had used
them on the old boy when he came, more than once, to parties at
the Legation, with considerable success; he nattered away to me
about magic as a cure for this and that, and also about his wish for
modern Western armaments. I got quite fond of him; and lying in
that dismal hotel bed, in that dismal state, on reading the report of
his death I snatched up a pen and amused myself by writing the
following poem.

They say that Chang T'so-lin is dead.
I shall be sorry if that is true,
Seeing again his round black head
Which nodded above his robe of blue
When, gravely polite, he spoke to you.

He looked like a little Oxford don
With his gentle voice, and his secret smile,
A don in a gentian dressing-gown
Full of humor and quiet guile—
Where was the bandit, all the while?

I remember him last at a foreign dance
In a gown of black brocade, that night,
Sliding his slow mysterious glance
Over the guests, from left to right,
As they filed before him, faintly polite.

To each as they passed him, face to face,
He gave his little cautious bow;
But when he saw me he left his place,
Smiled, stepped forward down the row
And clasped his hands, and said "Nin hao?"
                                    [Are you well?]

I clasped mine, and said "Ta Hsuai hao?"
    (How may the Great Commander be?)
Chang beamed at that, and bowed very low
He liked the ancient flattery
Of the Viceroy's title that used to be.

We went together and drank champagne,
Touched glasses, each with a courtly bend;
Chang spoke of the latest hydroplane,
And magic, and said to me at the end—
"Nin wo-ti peng-yo" (You're my friend.)

Very soon after we came away—
I've not seen Chang T'so-lin since then,
If he's really dead, as the papers say
I shan't drink wine with him again—
Oddest of friends among all men!

I had my typewriter with me, to finish another article for *The Nursery World;* I typed this effusion out, signed it "G. Allenby", and sent it to the *Spectator.* Almost by return of post came a cheque for four guineas, and a letter saying that the editor would be glad to consider any articles about China that I cared to submit.

That opened the door to a steady output of articles. Looking back, I can see why. It wasn't a particularly good poem, but it could only have been written by someone who knew China—and Chang—at first hand; China at that time was "news", and editors couldn't have too much of lively, first-hand accounts of it. More articles went off, all over the ridiculous signature of "G. Allenby", which was a recondite joke at Vereker's expense—he was always talking about Lord Allenby, and what they had done together in Palestine. But my first short story about China, "The Buick Saloon", I signed "Mary O'Malley" when it appeared in *The Cornhill;* dear old Dr. Huxley who was then the editor gave me fourteen guineas for it, and within a twelve-month it was taken by Lady Cynthia Asquith for inclusion in her first collection of ghost stories, *When Churchyards Yawn*—for another fiver. In fact by 1929 I was making between £150 and £200 a year by writing, which in the then state of our finances meant a great deal.

At that stage I had the idea of translating Daniele Varé's Chinese short stories into English—I wrote to him, sending a sample, and received permission. Armed with this I asked Harold Raymond, of Chatto & Windus, whether he would care to publish these if I did enough to fill a book? The Raymonds were neighbours and friends, and I occasionally read French and Italian novels for Harold, to report on whether they were worth translating. Harold's reply was memorable—"I'd much rather you wrote us a novel about China yourself." And someone else rather well-informed told me that if I did succeed in having a novel published I should get far better prices for my articles and short stories, and find them easier to place.

I hesitated a good deal over this idea. I had no expectation of getting more than perhaps £50 as an advance from some rather dim publisher—for I didn't take Harold's remarks at all seriously—and I was reluctant to forego my small but assured income for a whole year while I wrote a novel on spec. However, in the end I decided to risk it, and settled down to write *Peking Picnic*. By this time we were back at Bridge End, and the pig and poultry industry was going more strongly than ever; Patrick and Jane were both at school, she at reduced fees, but even so we couldn't possibly afford any sort of attendant for Grania, so a job was found for Nannie C. with May Bell, and I became Grania's nannie-cum-governess, as well as doing all my farm jobs. The only possible time for writing was before breakfast: I usually managed to wake about six, and wrote hard for two hours; at eight, however absorbing the situation my characters happened to be in, I had to shut my writing-book, get up and dress, and leave them till the next morning. In fact I believe that this tightly disciplined way of writing, sandwiched in between practical tasks, many of them manual, may have a rather wholesome effect on a writer's work; at least there is no time for fads, or "trends", or thinking about what other authors are doing.

This is not to say that I did not discuss the book with anyone—I did, constantly, and the dedication shows those to whom it owes most. Most valuable of all was Jock Balfour. Being bilingual in French (as indeed in many other languages), he rather enjoyed, I think, helping me with Henri Delache's remarks. I knew what I wanted Henri to say, but I could not put it into idiomatic French as Jock could.

And I continually went over on the old Triumph to see a really *very* plain friend—whose firm character and laconic speech were the foundations for Lilah—and discuss her activities; this precious creature was under no illusions about her looks, and gleefully told all her friends, "Mary Anne is putting me in her book, disguised as a beauty." It was in the house of this friend that, very late in 1931, I met a young man from a well-known firm of publishers who specialised in books about foreign travel; hearing that I had just finished a novel about China, he urged me to send it to him. I had only typed half, but that I sent, excited by what I thought a marvellous stroke of luck. A couple of weeks later there arrived by the early post a printed contract form, offering me £30 advance and royalties of 7½ per cent; but reserving to the publisher all American, film, and translation rights. In my ignorance I was quite ready to accept this, but mercifully Dominick Spring-Rice was staying with us; he insisted that if a publisher of the status of X.Y. was willing to make a contract for a book of which he had only seen half, I must have a literary agent to advise me. He drove up to London that morning with Owen, and worked fast; an appointment was made by telephone, and next day, in his office, I met for the first time A. D. Peters, who has been my literary agent ever since.

A.D.P.'s ultra-detached manner makes him a slightly intimidating person at first, and that morning he nearly frightened me out of my wits. When, with timid pride, I showed him the contract, I have seldom seen a man so angry. "This is a flat-trap!" he said furiously, striking his hand on the printed form; and lifting the telephone he demanded to be put through to X.Y.

"You have the manuscript of half a novel by a Mrs. O'Malley in your office," he said, when he got the publisher. "Peters here; please have it sent round to my office, *now*, by hand. Yes, I am acting for Mrs. O'Malley"—and he slammed the receiver down. Then he explained that the terms were quite monstrous, and asked if I knew any publishers. I said that Harold Raymond was an old friend; he telephoned to him immediately, and asked if he would care to see the first half of a novel about China by Mrs. O'Malley. "X.Y. has seen it, and wants it, but the terms are not satisfactory." And when the parcel of manuscript arrived, a messenger was sent straight up with it to Chatto & Windus in St. Martin's Lane. A few days later a very different contract reached me from Peters: £50 advance, 10 per cent royalties up to 1,000 copies, 15 per cent to 6,000, and 20 per cent thereafter; all American, film, and translation rights reserved to the author. Dominick had done me a very good turn.

But that was not the end of A.D.P.'s good offices. He had an associate firm in New York, and knew that *The Atlantic Monthly* had run into trouble over its new biennial fiction prize of $10,000, only started four years previously. The first one, in 1928, had gone to Mazo de la Roche for *Jalna;* in 1930 no book had come up to Ellery Sedgwick's exacting standards; now, in 1932, 749 manuscripts had already been seen, and none was liked—it would be a fearful flop if the prize had to be withheld a second time. Accordingly Peters cabled to Sedgwick that two London publishers were competing *for the first half only* of a novel by an unknown author; the second half must be typed, and it was very improbable that this could be finished in time for the script to reach Boston by February 1, the closing date for entries for the prize. Sedgwick cabled back—"If your manuscript can be mailed in time to bear the London postmark of January 31, it shall be deemed to have reached Boston on February 1."

I posted the whole manuscript to a typist well known to Peters, who did all J. B. Priestley's work; he made a rush job of it, and the parcel for Boston duly went off on January 30. Then we waited—the result of the competition would only be announced at the end of March. I hardly dared hope that *Picnic* would be successful, but oh, how badly I needed the money. Patrick was now at Radley, Jane at Hawnes; to meet their school fees I had had to fall back on my marriage settlement again, and for the spring term we had scraped the bottom of the barrel—how their summer fees were to be paid we had no idea, unless, impossibly, I won the prize.

Radley is only a few miles from Denton, and at the end of term I drove over to collect Patrick in a very ramshackle old car which had been given me by the same kind friend who had furnished the character of Lilah; we went on to Denton for lunch, and while there the telephone rang. It was Jane.

"Peters has been telephoning like a madman—he says you're to ring him up the moment you get back."

"What does he want?"

"To tell you you've won that prize, I think."

I ran upstairs to tell Eva, who was in bed. She was very damping.

"How can you be so silly, Mary Anne! Have you forgotten what day it is?"

I had, of course—April 1, All Fools Day. But would Jane have played me a trick like that, when she knew how much it meant? Hardly—but the seed of doubt had been sown, and in that uncertainty we drove back to Bridge End. It was nearly five when I hurried into the study and rang up Peters. Then all doubt was at an end. Yes, I had won it all right; he was full of congratulations. He was having the money cabled, so that I should get it in a few days. Completely ignorant about such things as the sterling-dollar rate, I asked what it would come to in English money. About £3,500— perhaps a little more. Then he went on to explain that he had spoken to Harold Raymond about postponing the English edition; the book was to have been published in London in May.

"Oh, why?" I was disappointed; I was longing to see myself in print. Patiently Peters explained that of course the Atlantic Monthly Press in Boston would want their edition to appear first, if only by a matter of twenty-four hours; and they could not get the book out before August. But Raymond had been very nice about it, and had agreed at once to postpone the Chatto version; he too sent his best congratulations. This was the first of the many kindnesses which Harold Raymond showered on me while he was head of Chatto & Windus.

In his autobiography, *The Phantom Caravan*, my husband wrote of this episode: "It enabled us to rebuild Bridge End and to raise our standard of living to a point which has kept the family on the verge of insolvency ever since." But at the time it did not seem quite like that; the relief was too immense. My daughter Grania has reminded me of a curious and illuminating little incident. The post came early at Ockham, and the house-parlourmaid used to bring my letters up to my room; it was Grania's daily duty to present herself to me there for inspection after she had got up, that I might see whether, as was constantly enjoined on her, she was "washed and dressed, and combed and curled, and a delight to the eye of the beholder." One morning of that April she came in, and was terrified to find me in tears; she hugged me, and begged to know what was the matter. For answer I handed her a letter from my bank in London, informing me that the sum of £3,600 had been paid into my account. The child was puzzled as to why this good news should make me cry, a thing she had never seen me do—those who have experienced a sudden relief from desperate anxiety will understand. I soon recovered myself sufficiently to write a cheque. Poor Owen had had to deny himself many of his small pleasures, and even to sell out capital to meet those awful school bills; now, with infinite pleasure, I wrote out a cheque "For one thousand pounds only", and took it down to him at breakfast. (From then till Patrick and Jane had finished at Oxford, he never had to pay another penny for the children's education.)

However, I was puritanically anxious that wealth should not corrupt my family, and to inculcate a taste for simple pleasures I took Jane and Patrick, those Easter holidays, on a walking tour—I had happy memories of similar expeditions with my sister Cora; for me a romantic, "open road" aura still hung about them. We were to walk along the Sussex Downs, sleeping two nights on the way, and do it all on foot, except for the return from Steyning to Midhurst. But from the start the children were resistant to the hardy and romantic aspects. We left the car in a friend's barn at Harting; as we climbed up onto the ridge, to dip down again through the gap at Cocking— "It's topping hiking from Harting to Cocking" rose their mocking chant. They complained of the weight of their rucksacks, and presently took them off and slung them from a stick, of which each carried one end. In the afternoon it came on to rain, which afforded a splendid excuse for leaving the downs, eating a huge tea in a pub, and going on to Fittleworth by bus. Next morning they hurried me down to the cross-roads near Amberley, presided over by an A.A. Scout—"We mustn't miss the bus." I protested that we weren't going by bus. "No, but the rucksacks are"; Patrick had arranged it all with the Scout in the bar the evening before. I was forced to realise that my own offspring were already living in another day and age to mine.

It presently occurred to Owen that something must be done about submitting my novel to the authorities, and he arranged for me to drive over one week-end to see Van—Vansittart, then head of the Foreign Office—at his house at Denham. "You're not asking me to read it?" Van exclaimed, looking horrified, when I unfolded my errand. I said no, we only wanted permission for it to appear—and explained that there would be a certain amount of publicity, at least in America, as it had won a prize over there. "The Pulitzer?" Van asked; he had married an American. "No, the *Atlantic Monthly.*" "Ah yes—that's much richer, I believe. How much *is* it?" He was kindly congratulatory about the $10,000, and said that Owen should give the manuscript to Sir Stephen Gaselee, the librarian, who would blue-pencil it if necessary. But on one point he was very firm. I must use a pseudonym, and *no one* was to know my real name; I must promise that. There had for a century or more been a tradition in the Service that if a diplomat's wife put pen to paper she would either ruin her husband's career, or provoke an international incident, or both.

Back at Bridge End we discussed the question of pseudonyms; Jock Balfour was down again that Sunday, and suggested taking Ann from "Mary Anne" and Bridge from "Bridge End"—and so this new entity was hatched. We were just in time to prevent my real name from becoming known in America; and over here Chatto, Peters, and everyone else who knew were sworn to secrecy. This led to a funny little episode. Later in the year Ellery Sedgwick came to England; he was naturally determined to meet his new author, and through Peters it was arranged that I should meet him for tea at Rumpelmayers—I told A.D.P. to tell him that I was tall, and should be wearing a black satin dress. Alas, as all too often, I was rather late; when I had parked my car in St. James's Street—yes, one could do that in 1932—and went into the tea-shop enquiring for "a Mr. Sedgwick", I was led up to a rather cross and highly embarrassed little old gentleman, who was being practically held captive by a very forbidding manageress. *Poor* Ellery, most correct of Bostonians—as the time passed, in his desperation he had accosted so many tall ladies, in black satin frocks, asking if they were Miss Ann Bridge, that he had more or less been taken into custody. However he soon got over his justifiable vexation, and so began a very happy relationship—from that day forward he always treated me as a sort of cross between a grand-daughter and a gold mine; for my part, I was devoted to him.

Authors, new ones especially, got much more fun out of reviews in the 1930s than they can possibly do today. A reviewer would seldom review more than one, or at most two books at a time, and would use as much space for a single novel as editors today allow for a batch of six; it is not, I think, mere fancy to remember that having this extra elbow-room they reviewed with more interest, and therefore in greater depth. The reviewers were amazingly kind to *Peking Picnic*. I rubbed my eyes in astonishment; could this be my book, that I had been so tentative about? It was a heady experience for a beginner, and the anonymity on which Van had insisted added to the fun. People who knew we had been in China were constantly asking—"Who *is* Ann Bridge? Did you meet her in Peking?" As one cannot very well meet oneself, I could truthfully say that I had not.

Then there was the fan-mail, which flooded in in such quantities as almost to swamp us; to answer this in sufficient anonymity I had paper printed with A. D. Peters' letter-head in Adelphi, London, W.C.2. For a time I let Jane answer some of it: she generally managed to bring in a reference to "my first husband, the late Canon Albert Bridge, who was a missionary in China". But not all the fan-mail was foolish; there were some letters which I treasure still. Laurence Binyon was then at the British Museum, in charge of the department which contained the Chinese pictures; he wrote, via Chatto: "People are pouring into the Museum to look at 'The Earthly Paradise', because of what you wrote about it. It is a lovely thing, but there are others even more beautiful; if you could spare the time it would be a pleasure to show them to you." I went, taking Jane; scrolls in wooden boxes, too fragile to bear the light of day all the time, were taken out of presses, unrolled, and hung up for us. In fact I still preferred "The Earthly Paradise", to which George Mallory had introduced me as a girl, years before.

IV

The Adriatic Novels

In 1930 my friend Frances Wills had invited me to spend a few
weeks with her in North Italy; she was to be for a fortnight with
friends in Florence, and as she knew no Italian she suggested that I
should come out and meet her in Venice, at her expense; show her
that, and then we could wander about "as the spirit moves us". I
knew quite well how the spirit would move me. Arthur Wood had
recently been to Dalmatia, where in those days practically no
English people ever went; he had lent me Sir T. Graham Jackson's
book on the architecture of that coast, and his own descriptions—
particularly of Ragusa: "It is like living in an opal"—had given me a
burning desire to see this strange and novel part of Europe. Out to
Venice I went, and showed Frances the sights there—including Tor-
cello; but I had little difficulty in persuading her that it would be
more amusing to take a boat down to Spalato and Ragusa than to
potter about in such places as Padua and Bologna. Frances, though
not exceedingly pretty, was of a dazzling fairness which Italian men
find irresistible; it had been bad enough in Florence, but Venice was
worse—she was delighted to go anywhere where she would not, as
she said gloomily, "be chased all the time". So we booked rooms,
and set off for Spalato.

The journey was precisely as described in *Illyrian Spring* (includ-
ing nearly getting left behind at Pola) except that there was no Dr.
Halther on board, and that Frances took the place of Nicholas
Humphreys. She was well off, so there was no trouble about hiring

cars for trips to such places as Trogir and Clissa; we spent a very
happy week in Spalato, and then went on to Ragusa. But there we
ran into trouble. Frances had been ill, and was anyhow a highly
nervous creature; she suffered badly from insomnia. The hotel at
Ragusa where we had taken rooms was building a new terrace, and
from dawn to dusk workmen were chipping away at the marble
balustrade; this drove her to a frenzy. I went over by tram to Gruz
and found a small quiet hotel, across the harbour from the ship-
yard, and we moved there next day. But that was no good either;
when urgent repairs were going on the shipwrights worked by flood-
light, and all through the night the sounds of hammering and clang-
ing travelled across the water; Frances came into my room at two in
the morning, white and distraught—"I've taken a third pill, and *still*
I can't sleep. What am I to do?" She was almost in despair.

That was how we came to stay at Komolac. Next day we took a
sailing-boat up the river Ombla, and picnicked on the way among
the wild-flowers which so charmed Lady Kilmichael; we saw the
mysterious source of the river, pouring silently out of the solid
mountainside; we climbed the cliffs above and found the wild irises
in bloom; finally, on the way home, we stopped for coffee at the
Restauratija Tété Jélé. I investigated the bedrooms, and in a torrent of
"Perché no?"s from the Signora Antonio (her real name) I took them
—next day we drove out in a taxi and settled in. Here at last was
silence, except for the nightingales and the low voice of the river;
here was peace; and here we stayed in great contentment, till it was
time to go home. We explored the countryside, we—or at least
I—constantly went in to Ragusa and examined that thoroughly; I
was completely enchanted by the beauty and strangeness of the
whole place, and by the wild-flowers. When we returned to
England, with the help of Dr. Turrill of Kew, who had written a
book on the flora of the Balkans, I managed to identify most of
them.

After *Peking Picnic*'s resounding success I was naturally rather
nervous lest the second book should be a flop—however *The Ginger
Griffin* went all right; none of the critics suggested that Ann Bridge
was a one-book writer. All the same, I thought it would be a good
plan to give China a rest after that, and I was longing to "tell the
world" how lovely Dalmatia was; from a small child I had always
loved writing down descriptions of places, and what could be more

worth describing than that opalescent coast? As to the plot, I had been painfully struck by the fact that so many women in my own age-group were in the habit of going to bed in tears three or four nights a week, because their daughters were so horrid to them—and though I did not quite do that, my own experiences in my family, and with their young friends, had given me a very fair idea of the problem, and an inkling of some possible solutions. So Lady Kilmichael was easy to describe, and by creating Sir Walter and Nicholas—for both of whom models abounded on all sides—adding Mrs. Barum for good measure, and throwing in a psychologist to help clear Grace Kilmichael's mind for her, there was my plot—and lovely Dalmatia still vivid in the mind for it to be played out in.

The fact that no adequate small guide-book to that coast existed in English was an excellent excuse for being rather detailed about the buildings, which I was longing to describe anyhow; and even Sir T. Graham Jackson, in his three bulky tomes, had not spotted the connection with the West Highland carvings. Naturally enough— that is a small and very specialised section of European art; but it so happened that Owen's uncle, Robert Graham of Skipness, had written an authoritative book on the subject, and for years I myself had been engaged in trying to make a *corpus* of the carved tomb-slabs with that characteristic interlaced ornament, sailing and tramping about the West Coast and the Outer Islands, and making rubbings on linen or calico, which were gladly housed by the Museum of Antiquities in Edinburgh. So it was immensely exciting to find specimens of the same thing on the shores of the Adriatic; and that, too, I could not refrain from introducing, for the sheer fun of it—and also in order to make the compartments of knowledge rather less water-tight.

Illyrian Spring (Harold Raymond produced the title) came out in the spring of 1935, and accidentally created a new fashion. Miliça Banač, the wife of the Yugoslav shipowner, was a friend of Princess Marina, and gave her a copy; she liked it, and in turn gave a copy to the Prince of Wales—which was why he took the yacht *Nahlin* down the Adriatic on that much-publicised trip with Mrs. Simpson and a party of friends. The public followed suit: within the space of twelve months the number of American tourists to Dalmatia had doubled, the English influx was multiplied four-fold. By this time the secret of my identity had leaked out; I met Madame Banač, and when she heard that I was going down to Albania to stay with the Hodgsons, our Minister at Durazzo and his wife, she invited me to stay in her villa at Çavtat for as long as I liked, on the way. This was a delightful plan; there was still a lot to be seen in Ragusa, for which Çavtat was quite handy, and I wanted to visit the Meštrović mausoleum in Çavtat itself, and to revisit all manner of places and pictures that I had enjoyed six years before. But I was quite unprepared for what happened on that second journey.

The first surprise was on the steamer. I had booked in London through the Yugoslav Express Agency, and had reserved an ordinary cabin on one of their boats; but when I went aboard at Venice I was shown to a stateroom. I protested that I only wanted a single cabin; a stateroom was too expensive. With bows and smiles the purser explained that the stateroom was free—everything was free for the Gospodja!—and what would I like in the way of drinks?—brandy, or slivovitz, or Cinzano? Nothing to pay! In this very agreeable fashion I came to Spalato, where on leaving the hotel I was presented with a bill, receipted!—and it was the same in Ragusa, where I spent a night before going on to the Banaçs' villa.

From there I drove over one day to Komolac, and again had a surprise. I went first to the source of the Ombla, and fell into conversation with an old man on the bridge over the river, who spoke German—"I suppose", he said presently, "you have come to visit our village because of the Book [Das Buch]. Everyone who comes to Komolac has read Das Buch." Startled, I asked how he had heard of it, and learned that an English lady who had stayed at the Tété Jélé the year before had given the Signora Antonio a copy; the Signora's schoolmistress niece (who had been ejected from the house to make room for Frances) knew English, and during the winter evenings the good people of Komolac had gathered in the priest's house while she read the relevant chapters aloud, translating into Serbo-Croat as she went along. "Ah, what she has done for us, this English authoress!" the old man said. "So many visitors!—such wealth!—to us who were poor."

I simply couldn't resist it—"I wrote the book," I said.

I thought for a moment he was going to hug me—he came to me with arms outstretched, saying "Sie? Sie? *You* have done this?" But he just took my hands and wrung them up and down, saying "Sie!" over and over again; at last—"How can you ever be thanked?" he said. It was one of the most moving things I have ever known.

All the same I was rather taken aback when I walked round to the village, and into the garden at the Tété Jélé. On the gravel between the trellises, where Frances and I used to drag out the heavy old wooden table from the tiny dining-room when we wanted to eat out-of-doors, stood several small metal tables, neatly laid; two young waiters in smart white jackets hovered among them. I asked for the Signora—when she came out she *did* hug me, warmly; we sat, and she told me how wonderful everything was. Presently she said—"But why have you not brought the Signorina, who wrote The Book?" Rather indignantly, this time, I repeated "But *I* wrote the book—why should you suppose the Signorina wrote it?" Signora Antonio got up and hugged me again with more "Sie's"; then she explained how she had come to make her mistake. When the English lady (it was D. K. Broster, in fact) had sent her the book, and the niece had read it aloud, she realised that either Frances or I must have written it, since no other foreigners had ever stayed in the house before. But, she said, the Excellenza (me) was always so active and cheerful, going for walks, talking and laughing—not at all like an author; whereas the Signorina had often sat silent, her head on her hand, looking sad and thoughtful, as authors should do —so naturally they assumed that she had written the book. Suddenly the Signora looked amused, and rather smug—"So all the visitors have been paying to see the wrong room!" she said.

I went into this. Oh yes, they all wanted to see the room of the author, and it was quite a labour, taking them upstairs all day; so she and Signor Antonio decided to charge them three dinars (then about 3d.) a head.

She gave me a marvellous lunch, and a bottle of Grk to take with me when I drove back to Çavtat. I could not help being very happy about the whole thing—it was nice to have brought so much prosperity to such kind, warm-hearted people.

But it was only in Albania that I realised properly how general that prosperity was, and how greatly envied. Owen was now in the Southern Department of the Foreign Office, and Albania was part of his diocese, so to speak; since I was staying at our Legation it seemed natural enough that the Foreign Minister should invite me to a luncheon, and the Prime Minister to a dinner—both given in what was then Tirana's one and only large hotel. But these two gentlemen had something in mind beyond doing a courtesy to the wife of an official. In turn they took me aside and asked, urgently, if

I would not write a book about Albania. They had seen, they said, what had happened just over the frontier in Yugoslavia—the tourist industry booming, splendid foreign currency flowing in. Could I not do the same for them?—they needed it even more, they were still poorer than their Yugoslav neighbours. When I said that I didn't know their country nearly well enough to write a proper book about it, they brushed that aside—I could stay as long as I liked, in this very hotel, as the guest of the Government; they would provide guides and pony-teams and an interpreter to take me anywhere I wanted to go. It was all rather tempting and very flattering, and the real obstacle was one I could not mention, namely that Albania was simply not ready then for a sudden increase of its *turismo*. Yugoslavia had already had plenty of perfectly adequate hotels, hitherto mostly used by Czechs and Germans, it had roads and transport facilities—whereas Albania had hardly any hotels, and to get about —it was its great charm—one had to take ponies along mountain tracks, and camp in tents.

These embarrassing interviews, however, took place towards the end of my stay, after the lovely expedition through High Albania, described in *Singing Waters*. The journey down from Ragusa was of course exactly like Gloire Thurston's. There was one rather odd feature about that book, though. When I at last decided, seven or eight years later, to write it, Owen had been suggesting for some time that I should make mild fun of myself by introducing a woman writer into one of the novels, and this Albania book seemed a suitable place for her to appear. All novels of course reflect one's own experience to some extent, inevitably; but I have never so definitely and deliberately introduced myself into a book before or since, let alone as *two* characters—Susan Glanfield and Gloire Thurston.

I decided to write it in the end, inadequate as I still felt my knowledge to be, to satisfy King Zog. Not quite three years after my visit, in Holy Week, 1939, the Italians invaded Albania, and their airpower really swamped the local resistance; the King and his delightful Hungarian wife, with her new-born baby, had to flee, and in the end came to England. He asked me, urgently, to write about his country, so that "it should not be forgotten." I was greatly touched by this request; but as before I pointed out that I did not know nearly enough to do Albania justice. For answer the King used words I have never forgotten—"You know enough to create a climate of sympathy." So I agreed to do it. I spent some time mugging up Albanian history, ancient and modern, and pestering with questions those who really knew the place and the people inside out.

By this time, too, I had been to the United States for the first time; and since Albania furnished such an admirable example of the European way of life and its origins, as opposed to the American, I decided to put out at least one more flag for Europe's ideas and ideals. The result, when the book was finished in 1944, was more of a "novel of ideas" than I had ever attempted before, and A. D. Peters was aghast.

"This is a letter I never thought I should have to send to you," he wrote, in his own hand—and went on to complain that the book was a sociological tract, not a novel at all; he begged me to withdraw it, and write a treatise if I must, but not to ruin my reputation as a writer with something so certain of failure.

He was right up to a point. When the manuscript was sent to Boston the late Alfred MacIntyre, then head of the Atlantic Monthly Press, wrote sadly that he could not publish it as it was; there were too many "British anti-American cracks" in it, and they would have to be cut before it could possibly sell in the States. In reply I wrote to Alfred, saying that the criticisms I had voiced were not simply "British", I had heard them in France, in Germany, in Italy and Hungary, Switzerland and Spain—it was a European point of view that I was expressing, and it had got to stand. If he could not publish it, he must break his contract.

He did so. Peters, nobly refraining from saying "What did I tell you?", set his New York office to try again. There followed, for me, a very uncomfortable three months of suspense; then came a cable to say that the Macmillan Company of New York had accepted the book, without asking for any cuts—and two or three months later came another, with the quite astonishing news that *Singing Waters* was the choice of the Literary Guild of America. In those days to be a Guild "choice" meant a lot: a guaranteed edition of over half a million copies, and $90,000 to be split fifty-fifty between the author and the publisher—to say nothing of all the enhanced sales of the ordinary edition.

But to go back to 1936. That trip with a pony-train through High Albania was one of the most wonderful things in my whole life— which has been full of wonderful things. The originals of the Robinsons were Colonel Hill, the English Gendarmerie officer from Scutari, and his wife; like Gloire I had stayed with them on my way down, while Sir Robert, in the hotel, really had that ridiculous interview with a well-wishing Albanian contact, who told him that an English lady, a cousin of Mr. Anthony Eden's, had arrived that very day for important political consultations with the Bishop! The fourth, in our real-life party, was Lady Hodgson; she was Russianborn, and not much accustomed either to walking or to roughing it; the fatigue attributed to Mrs. Robinson was really hers—Mrs. Hill was perfectly tough. We did visit the Abbot of Ourosh (the real Torosh) after Whitsun High Mass, and stayed, though only for a night or two, with Prince Marc-a-Gioni and his massive wife, and saw that marvellous Old Testament life in its fullness of vigour and calm activity; we did all sleep on the floor of the one and only guestroom, wolves really did howl outside at night; the local gendarmes accompanied us all the way, with their charming ritual of saluting and reciting an oath of loyalty.

And from beginning to end there was the ceaseless enchantment of the woods full of nightingales, the clear rivers, the mountains—and the flowers! After all the difficulties over identifying my Dalmatian flowers from descriptions only, I was determined to make a proper collection this time, and borrowed a wire press with sheets of lint and blotting-paper; like Miss Glanfield, at the end of each day I faithfully pressed the latest finds. Back in England I set them on sheets of foolscap, numbered them, and wrote out a list on which, next to each number, was recorded where the plant had been found, the approximate altitude, the aspect—south, west, or north—and the names of any identifiable plants growing near it, and sent the whole thing off to Kew. The Royal Botanic Gardens did identify them all right, but asked if they might keep the lot!—they had not, they said, had any such complete and detailed collection from precisely that area.

Writing that book was an enormous pleasure, partly because the subject-matter was so unusual—it was a keen enjoyment to recall, for example, the peculiarities of the Legation at Durazzo, built half in, half on, the massive mediaeval Venetian fortifications, and the curious habit of the pelicans on the lagoon of *sailing* up it before the wind. It was also a very taxing exercise to work in so much past history and so many current political and economic problems with

say—it was fascinating to spend half a morning in the "Etche Ona", watching the proprietor and his family making *pâté de foie gras*, packing the raw goose-livers and the sliced truffles—which last smell quite horrible raw—into tins, sealing them with a soldering iron, and then putting them into a vast shining copper to boil for hours and hours; from these friendly people we learned that local experts prefer not to eat *pâté* till it is at least three years old. The Embassy work was not so strenuous as to prevent Owen from constantly driving us out on charming expeditions: to eat the famous stew of *palombes*—wood-pigeons trapped on migration—in a black sauce, at the inn at Ascain; to be led through the Grotte de Sare; to admire the old fortress at St. Jean Pied-de-Port. For a celebration of our silver wedding Owen drove to the foot of La Rhune, the isolated peak rising nearly 7,000 feet from the coastal plain, and we walked up it; geographically the frontier runs right over the summit, but we saw for ourselves how nearly impossible it was to define it, out there on the empty hills, and how hopeless was the border-watching task of the Non-Intervention Commission, many of whom lived in our hotel. By road, however, no one could approach the frontier without a *permis de circulation;* blue-clad Gardes Mobiles patrolled even the by-roads in pairs.

Down at Irun there was no possible doubt about the frontier and its whereabouts. Red and white wire barriers, manned by police and Customs officials, closed both ends of the bridge over the Bidassoa; all passengers on the Sud Express, the great international train between Paris and Madrid and Lisbon, had to get out and cross the bridge on foot; their luggage, after a detailed examination, pushed after them on wheelbarrows, to rejoin the train on the further side. Even diplomats could only leave or enter Spain if, over and above their passports and *laissez-passers,* they could show a *salvo-conducto,* a special document issued, very restrictedly, by the Franco régime; the names of the holders of these coveted objects were all entered in long-hand in a huge ledger, and had to be verified, usually very slowly, each time one crossed, by a rather illiterate Spanish official. We frequently went through this elaborate performance, for we were constantly dodging over to Burgos when Owen had to see Bob Hodgson about something—while he was at the Agencia, as the Spaniards called it, Grania and I used to explore the town—the glorious Cathedral, and the lovely buildings at the Cartuja, the

Carthusian monastery. We always stayed at the Condestable, a large charmless hotel; Burgos was crowded, but room was always made at the Condestable for official visitors or diplomats, on Government orders. Food was adequate but dull; Nationalist Spain was enduring shortages of every sort—a girl with whom I fell into conversation one day outside the Cathedral, in the bitter cold of a Spanish winter, had shoes on, but neither stockings nor gloves. She told me she had been praying for her brother, who was at the front; her hands were raw with chilblains, and I took off my gloves and begged her to accept them. She fingered them almost tenderly; then, thanking me with grave courtesy, she shook her head. Her brother had no gloves, and since he was fighting for Spain with cold hands, she would not keep hers warm, she said.

Some of the foreign diplomats lived permanently in the Hotel Condestable; so did the few journalists allowed in Franco Spain, among them Kim Philby, whom we took to greatly—so intelligent, and likeable, he seemed to us then. How he ever came to defect to Russia remains a sinister mystery, to friends who knew him well. Outside, in St. Jean, journalists of all nations of course swarmed, particularly at the Bar Basque, which was also frequented by some of the other diplomats from Madrid, as well as the refugees and the spies; among them rumour flew ceaselessly, as it does among reporters at loose ends. We got to know a good few of them—whenever we returned from a trip into Spain, even if it was only to San Sebastian for lunch with the German Ambassador, or a joy-ride to La Loyola or Zarauz, they always came hovering round Grania and me, hoping to pick up some morsel of news interest. This familiarity with journalists and their curious mode of existence was invaluable when I came to write *Frontier Passage*, because they formed what books on French cookery call "a base"—not quite a foundation, something at the bottom, but some element, like a sauce, in which all the other ingredients are combined and held together. From motives of prudence I gave most of the newspaper-men in the book place-names from the County Mayo as surnames: "Milcom" is a country house, "Crumpaun" a river, as is "Hever"; "Newport" a small town, "Carrow" a bridge—even my English family, the Oldheads, derived their name from a promontory on Clew Bay.

From the point of view of diplomatic entertaining St. Jean de Luz was a most care-free post. For one thing there were very few diplomats besides the stout cheerful Frenchman from Madrid—whose name was Bonjean, but who, from his figure, was commonly known as Jambon—and a Spanish diplomat *de carrière*, who held a sort of watching brief for France, and lived in great poverty in Biarritz; when we asked him to lunch he came over by bus. He was great fun; we called him Pepe, and he told us the life-histories of most of the refugees. There were of course some permanent British residents, and through a godmother with French connections I met some of the French gentry round about: but we had no obligations to either of these sections of the community, as one has to the local society in a foreign post; we could see as much or as little of them as we chose. Even if we did give a luncheon all I had to do was to inform the manager and the *maître d'hôtel*, and then forgot all about it till the time came—most painless. I only remember giving one cocktail-party, to which I invited everyone I could think of; it was held in a sort of ballroom, and was a most frightful flop. The Napiers had sent us out a huge Stilton for Christmas, and I thought it would be an amusing change from the ordinary cocktail eats to give everyone Stilton and brown bread; I had masses of small wholemeal loaves specially baked, broke them into crusty pieces, buttered them, and set them on the buffet, with plates of cheese ready scooped out, and the noble Stilton standing as a centerpiece. But to most of the foreign guests this seemed not only strange and rather nasty, but mean too—they had hoped for tinned caviar and stale smoked salmon. That taught me a useful lesson: never be original in diplomatic entertaining—stick to the beaten track.

Thus blessedly free from social obligations we explored the countryside, we explored the neighbouring parts of Spain, we familiarised ourselves with the highly individual life of St. Jean itself—the refuse-collection was done by a man with a barrel on a bullock-cart, who emptied the trash-cans; he was called *le bouvier*. We went to Bayonne and watched the ships going in and coming out of the port on the tide, ate the delicious local oysters, at 3d. a dozen, and had powder made up to suit our skins, while we watched, for an equally derisory price. And all this, like the journalists and their goings-on, and what Pepe told us about the lives and characters of the refugees, was to give, later on, a certain quality of intimacy and immediacy to the book I came to write about the Spanish Civil War.

This was the first of several novels which I call my "modern historicals"—novels dealing with historical events that have taken place in our life-time, of which I have come to have first-hand knowledge; fiction, but made as factual as possible, consistently with concealing the identities of real people; and giving close and intimate details of what it was really like on the spot, at the time, to individuals. If any of my work comes to have permanent value, I feel it will be these books: *Frontier Passage, The Dark Moment, A Place to Stand,* and *The Tightening String.* It was my great good fortune to be an eye-witness of such happenings, and also to meet people who could tell me, directly and at the time, of episodes which I did not see with my own eyes. And one such person was the white Spaniard whose experiences in a Republican prison form an essential part of *Frontier Passage.*

Some time before Christmas, 1938, Owen had to go down to Gibraltar; he went by car, driving himself. I went with him as far as Burgos and stayed for a day or two, as usual in the Condestable. While I was in the hotel a man, not from the Agency, asked me if I would mind giving a lift to a Spanish officer who had just been exchanged for a prominent Republican prisoner; his family was in France, and he wanted to get out to them. Public transport being practically non-existent, I more or less had to say yes, but there was a slight hitch about this worthy's clothes; he had come out in rags, and a suit was being made for him in a hurry, at his friends' expense —once one of the richest men in Spain, he now could not afford the price of a pair of ready-made shoes, let alone a suit, as all his property was in enemy hands. I was worried about the clothes, as I could not very well delay Sir Robert's car, which was to take me back; however, late on the evening of the day before we were due to start, he was brought up and presented to me, as the Marques de ———. (I have truly forgotten his name, but I should not have used it in any case.)

The drive from Burgos to St. Jean takes between five and six hours; one usually allowed seven because of the delay at the Bridge at Irun. (The Non-Intervention couriers did it in less, but they drove much too fast, and were so well-known that the frontier formalities hardly delayed them at all.) Sir Robert's chauffeur drove the Rolls very sedately, and for most of a winter's day the Marques and I, muffled in rugs, sat talking as the big car purred almost noiselessly along. He spoke French with a deplorable accent, but quite fluently, and during those long hours of conversation he told me all about the conditions of his imprisonment in Republican hands, in a room with ten other men; of the air-raids, and how they used to bribe the gaoler with sugar or cigarettes to bring them up teak from ships wrecked in the harbour, and broken glass from ruined houses to carve it with—at one point he showed me, proudly, a belt-buckle made of four interlocking rings of teak which he had carved from a single piece for his wife. More, he told me the story of the young girl whose execution he had been marched out to witness in the prison yard, and how she put a red carnation from the bouquet which a friend had brought her into the button-holes of each of the firing-squad. His wife I never met, and I know nothing of the circumstances of their life—after I dropped him at Hendaye I never saw him again. But there was the core of my book. There were quite enough rich rakish counts who were unfaithful to their wives in Spain to make the plot, as I eventually evolved it, not in the least implausible, nor the "Conde de Verdura" particularly recognisable; and my passenger had given me what I could never have got otherwise, that first-hand account of life in a Spanish prison—straw palliasses, soap-boxes for seats, high windows and all.

The final Franco offensive broke round about the New Year, during one of the hardest winters that South-east France had ever known. Patrick and Jane had come out to us for Christmas, driving my little Talbot coupé—and a hard drive they had of it. Owen, suddenly recalled from Gibraltar to deal with the "bag episode" —when the Spaniards planted some bogus maps in the Consular bag coming from San Sebastian to St. Jean, and opened it at Irun— took ship, car and all, to Marseilles, and piled up the Humber Snipe against a tree on the icy road near St. Gaudens; however it was repaired in time for his next summons. Towards the end of January, 1939, when it became clear that the Republican resistance was crumbling, Ralph Stevenson was instructed to close the Embassy at Barcelona, H.M.S. *Devonshire* was sent to take off him and his staff, and Owen was ordered to go at once to meet him at Port Vendres and arrange temporary accommodation in France for the whole outfit. The cat had jumped unmistakeably, and the British Government was forced off the fence at last.

I went along—little realising how much that journey would mean. We spent the first night at Pau, and started at seven next morning; on the long straight road running due east the low sun, reflected off the glossy bonnet of the Snipe, was completely blinding—we pulled up, I broke the ice on a ditch and smeared the bonnet with mud and water; after that Owen could see to drive. We paused in Perpignan to book a room in the hotel, and then drove on to Port Vendres. Our first sight of Mare Nostrum, as the Italians liked to call the Mediterranean, showed us very reassuringly the huge grey shape of *Devonshire,* lying offshore, rolling, so the harbour-master told us, through eighteen degrees; he thought there was no chance of a boat coming off. But we had to find out—and applied to the Captain of a French destroyer, who had just brought his own Minister away from Barcelona. With the utmost kindness he allowed his wireless operator to make a signal to Stevenson, and gave us whisky in his cabin while we waited for the reply. The French "Sparks" was not very strong on English; the message he presently brought in, written in purple pencil, confirmed that the cruiser was rolling too much for a landing to be possible, and went on "Proceeding torngth Marseilles." We rightly interpreted TORNGTH as "tonight", and presently returned to Perpignan, but not before we had seen that ghastly confusion of refugees and crates of rotting oranges, littered all over the quays and streets of the pretty little town.

That whole business of the flight of the Spanish civilian population across the frontier into France, and the shilly-shallying of the French Government about whether to allow the Republican troops in as well—one day "Yes", the next "No", the day after "Yes" again—was I think on any showing one of the most horrifying episodes in any modern war; and for the French, one of the most discreditable. Of course the local authorities had their problems: next day we called on the Préfèt, and heard his woes. Then we went on to Le Boulou and saw the internment camp there, and the awful train, crammed with foodless women and children, standing hour after hour in the station, since no one had given orders as to where it was to go. On up to the frontier at Le Perthus, where we saw the crowd of *miliciens,* as the French called the Republican troops, crammed in thousands against the chains hurriedly set up to keep them out, howling like wolves; everywhere the civilian refugees, dragging or carrying children and piteous luggage—and the ceaseless beating rain; it never stopped for seventy-two hours. The only hopeful sight was three lorries manned by young Englishmen, doling out soup and coffee from their field kitchens.

Next day, like the three journalists in the novel, we drove up to the other frontier post at Cerbère, and on the way had that unbearably moving encounter with the five *miliciens* who had trickled in over the frontier: Owen told them that at Cerbère they would be given food, and sent to an internment camp, and in gratitude for these good tidings they threw that packet of cheap cigarettes into the car—I have it still, with the picture of a ship in full sail over the name "Homeward Bound". They had had no food for thirty-six hours, and yet they insisted on giving us their one form of comfort. Up on the pass at Cerbère we saw the line of cars, their roofs shining in the rain, jammed nose to tail for eight or nine miles; they had been standing there for forty-eight hours, and a chauffeur really did offer to sell Owen a brand-new seven-seater Packard car for 2,000 francs, then about £25, or $100; while women put their heads out of the car windows to offer me typewriters, or even jewels, for prices equally derisory—anything to get some francs.

That night we went to Amélie-les-Bains to stay. We disliked the noise and overcrowding at the hotel in Perpignan, which in any case was so choked with journalists and the wealthier refugees that it was hopeless to try to get rooms there for Ralph and his staff, so we had telephoned to the Hotel des Thermes Pujades for rooms in the morning. We arrived at that extraordinary establishment after dark, to find the bureau locked and no one about—the whole thing was like a very strange bad dream till we found our way, in the rain and darkness, along a drive to the restaurant in another building. But it was a nice place when one had learned one's way through its peculiarities; we settled in there very happily, booked rooms for Ralph and his party, and sent a message to that effect to the Consulate-General at Marseilles. Then we resumed our explorations. From the charming Sous-Préfêt at Arles-sur-Tech, a little way up the valley— he was an importation from Paris, sent to help in coping with this alarming situation—Owen procured a special pass which enabled us to go anywhere, even up to the frontier itself; and we drove up and down the Vallespir, as the valley in which the river Tech flows is called, observing the ingenious wigwams of box or turf, built round chestnut poles, which the *miliciens* were constructing for themselves in the hastily improvised camps along the valley, watched over by small contingents of the French Army. We went over to Bourg Madame and Vernet-les-Bains and saw the horribly inadequate camps there.

But Argelès was the worst—a major scandal, which the O'Malleys between them managed to expose and put an end to. When at last it was decided to let the *miliciens* in and intern them, the French authorities massed 90,000 men behind barbed wire, on a stretch of sandy seashore, with no vegetation and no shelter of any sort; when the wretched prisoners tried to dig trenches to shelter in, in three feet at the most they came on brackish water. Naturally pneumonia, dysentery, and gangrene were rife, but the French refused to allow any foreign observers in lest these ghastly conditions should become known, and extended this ban to the Quaker Hospital Unit, the International Red Cross, and the Swedish Red Cross; I saw with my own eyes four motor hospital-vans of the last-named, fully equipped for operations, standing outside the gate and being refused entry, and heard the despairing pleas of the Quakers to be allowed in with their supplies of bedding and medicines.

At this point we heard that Grania, who had been sent to stay with friends in Paris when we made our dash to the Mediterranean, had been taken ill; I caught the night train from Perpignan and went up to look after her, while Owen followed by car. The poor child had got jaundice, and was quite bad; but when she had been installed in the American Hospital at Neuilly, and Professor Chiray (the Nobel prize-winner) had been laid on to look after her, I promptly busied myself about Argelès. I got hold of Gordon Water-field, then with Reuters, and told him the whole appalling story. He in his turn got hold of one of the Rodds, and made me repeat it to him over a meal; this gentleman got in touch with London, a special correspondent was sent out, and within a week a blistering article appeared in *The Sunday Times*—an article so blistering that the French Government, cringing, had to allow medical relief to be given. Owen meanwhile had been to see Sir Eric Phipps, the Ambassador, who was greatly shocked, and promised to do what he could; what that amounted to we never knew, but as I say, between them the O'Malleys put an end to the worst horrors of Argelès.

When Grania began to recover, Professor Chiray recommended us strongly not to take her back to London, but to keep her in a mild part of France for some time. We had such nice memories of Amélie-les-Bains that I suggested that, and he jumped at the idea—it was he who described Amélie as possessing "un climat plutôt Africain". The poor little Embassy at St. Jean was by now in process of being wound up; we went back there, and then Owen drove the convalescent child down in his more comfortable car, while I followed in my own. In a few days, Jane joined us at Amélie and Owen went home.

There followed several fascinating weeks, during which we saw, at close quarters, the aftermath of the Spanish Civil War in France. The nice Sous-Préfêt at Arles-sur-Tech gave us another of those all-powerful permits, and armed with this we—Jane and Grania especially—did what Rosemary and James Milcom are described as doing in the book: driving up onto the frontier throughout its length, making friends with Gardes Mobiles and Franco frontier-guards alike, witnessing those extraordinary spectacles on the summit—abandoned cars and typewriters lying about like boulders and stones on a beach whose shingle consisted of rifle bullets, presided over by the two flags, the tricolor of France and the "mustard and blood" of Spain, leaning tipsily out of the same cairn of rocks. It was an astonishing experience—and most astonishing of all was the Col d'Ares.

I was with the two girls that day, and saw that awful sight. From our earlier journeys we had already become familiar with the curious French habit, in that part of the Pyrenees, of not completing their roads right to the crest of the frontier, to connect with the Spanish ones, but of stopping them anything from a half to two kilometres short of the summit, leaving a gap of stones, scree, and boulders which could be crossed on foot or by mule, but was too rough for wheeled vehicles—hence the abandoned cars and typewriters which stretched at intervals all along the ridge. And this was the case at the Col d'Ares. On the Spanish side a fine military road led right to the top, and up this a whole Republican division had driven, hoping to escape into France; when they found that the road ended in an impossible wilderness of rocky slopes, they simply drove everything—guns, lorries, ambulances, cars, motorcycles, off the road into the ravine below, where they set fire to them. This wreckage stretched for *four miles*—we saw it. Like Milcom and Rosemary in the novel, we sat with the Franquista guards in their funny little shelter, built out of car wreckage, and over cigarettes—

ours—heard the whole story; we too were joined by Gardes Mobiles, in the usual cheerful fraternisation of those remote spots, and heard how they had carried 2,000 Spanish wounded down to the head of the French road, through three feet of snow. (The walking wounded accounted for the blood-stained bandages on the roadsides, which had startled and horrified us on the way up.) And one of the Spaniards truly asked us if we had read *Don Quixote,* which he was perusing in a splendid tome bound armorially in leather, and admired; and they lit our cigarettes with spills made from the pages of a *History of Social Progress.* Even the irony did not have to be invented on that occasion!

In fact, as must be obvious, a great deal of the latter part of *Frontier Passage* is almost pure *reportage,* with our own actual experiences transferred, complete and whole, to the journalists, but especially to Milcom—a character invented with some care to be the mouthpiece for my own strong feelings on the Spanish Civil War as a whole, on the various aspects of foreign intervention in it, and above all on the behaviour of the French.

British officialdom impinged on the book twice, in ways which caused us a certain amusement. Of course it had to be submitted to the Foreign Office, and Sir Stephen Gaselee, who read it, very kindly sent my husband a note of warning. There was, he said, nothing objectionable in the book from the Office point of view; but Spaniards were touchy people, and "your wife has made all her Spanish characters so uniformly unpleasant that if, at any future time, you were to be appointed to Madrid, the Spanish Government might very conceivably refuse their *agrément,* or at least make it a condition that she did not accompany you." We wondered what on earth he could be thinking of, since Raquel was my main heroine, and as delightful as I could make her; however Owen was willing to risk it. The laugh came when the French and Spanish translations appeared, almost simultaneously, in Madrid, some time in 1946. According to Walter Starkie, then a sort of uncrowned king of all literary milieux in Spain, Spaniards of any political views devoured it rapturously. They had been justifiably irritated by the fact that most foreign novelists had presented the Civil War purely from the Republican point of view, and inaccurately at that: Arturo Barea flayed *For Whom the Bell Tolls* for the psychological ineptitude of placing an Andalusian at the head of a band of *Aragonese* partisans —something which could not happen. But here at last, as reviews and fan-mail alike testified, was a book by a foreign writer who held the balance justly and evenly between Red and Whites, Republicans and Nationalists, and they greeted it with enthusiasm.

The other episode reflected more creditably on at least one public department. When the book appeared, late in 1942, I was in a nursing-home in Edinburgh after a major operation. Within a week there arrived a letter, forwarded by my publishers, to the effect that it was evident from the novel that I had an extremely detailed knowledge of the Basque coast of France, and the writer would be much obliged if I would answer, as promptly as possible, certain questions. The stretch of shore, for instance, between the Chambre d'Amour near Biarritz, and the river-mouth at Bayonne, where "the girl Rosemary" had met the spy—would it be possible for vehicles to drive up from the beach into the pine woods behind, or would the unfinished sea-wall and the blocks of cement prevent this? Were there gaps in the wall or did it run the whole way? And the pine woods themselves—how dense were they? Would they afford cover from the air—and how firm was the going in them? Then some very precise questions about particular roads and bridges: how deep was the river at Y?—how firm the banks? If the road between C. and D. were blown up or rendered impassable, would the ground on either side permit of a diversion for *heavy* vehicles? And of course, I realised that all this must be kept completely confidential? If I could come in person and talk about it, that would be much the most satisfactory.

I was charmed by this. Plans for a second front, of course!—and all possible preliminary facts being assembled in advance. But *how* smart of them to have got hold of the book practically on the day of publication—and to have read it so carefully. Of course I couldn't go, being flat on my back, but Jane had come to Edinburgh to look after me, and I got her to write to this mystery department and explain, and also to suggest that they should see Grania, who was in London with her father. Then, through the Matron, we got hold of a shorthand-typist, to whom I made an elaborate spiel about preparing a geographical and botanical paper, as a cover-story. The typist was a middle-aged Edinburgh body, not very quick at the uptake; but I must have overdone the botanical aspect in my desire for secrecy, as I discovered when the typescript came back—where I had dictated "firm going on both sides of the road", the worthy woman had put "ferns growing on both sides of the road".

VI

Being a Chef-ess—Hungary I

While we were still at St. Jean de Luz, driving about the green country below the Pyrenees, we fell in one day with a group of gypsies, and stopped to talk to them—Owen has a passion for gypsies. Of course they wanted to tell our fortunes, and the youngish woman who told Owen's informed him that he would soon be leaving the place where he was, and going Eastwards. (This was long before Christmas, when there was still no firm indication of when the Civil War would end.) Pressed for more details, she said that he would be going to the country from which many of her people came. Now Owen had always longed to go to Hungary, and had in fact let this be known to the Private Secretaries; Hungary of course is full of gypsies, and he was highly pleased when, in the following spring, some time after our return from France, he was appointed Minister in Budapest; and on May 4, 1939, his fifty-second birthday, he set off by car from our flat on Chelsea Embankment for this new and most rewarding post.

In his autobiography, *The Phantom Caravan*, my husband has written an excellent assessment of exactly *why* it is so agreeable to be a British Minister or Ambassador abroad, and why it was so particularly agreeable for an Englishman to be *en poste* in Hungary before the destruction of its way of life by the Communists—the similarities of outlook of the two nations making one feel at home and at ease there.

As in the case of Mexico, Jane soon joined him, but I remained to look after Grania. We thought a spell in the Alps would be a good tonic to clear off any after-effects of jaundice, and in August she and I went out to Rosenlaui, in the Bernese Oberland; she already had a strong taste for climbing, which I was eager to encourage, and the small rocky peaks of the Engelhörner afforded a succession of short days and exciting rock-work, just the right thing. For these expeditions we engaged one of the local guides, and I was amused by the contrast between him and the Grindelwald guides of my youth— magnificent climbers, but still complete peasants, wearing thick cloth suits and in some cases speaking even *Hoch-deutsch* with a certain difficulty. Grania's guide Arni Glatthard and his colleagues wore Harris tweeds, talked Oxford English, and took it as a matter of course that they should eat with us in the hotel after a climb, or at least have a drink in the bar; they were delightful creatures. "Sie geht wie eine Kleine Katze!" ("She goes like a little cat!"), Glatthard said to me enthusiastically one evening when they came down after a successful ascent of a particularly difficult peaklet, the Kleine Simmelistock. (Much later he was chosen to go out to Katmandu to direct a rock-climbing school for Sherpas.)

The Wetterhorn was the only one of the main peaks round Grindelwald that I had never been up, and as there was an easy route from a hut just above Rosenlaui, only a snow plug, I was keen to do it. The guide had to go over to Grindelwald for three or four days to do a long-planned climb with two elderly members of the Alpine Club; it was settled that we should do the Wetterhorn as soon as he returned. But when he came back and met Grania in the hotel bar to settle the details, he told her, laughing, that we most certainly should *not* go by the easy route, but by a tolerably exciting rock ridge. Grania protested a little; she knew I no longer wanted a stiff day—I had done no climbing since my marriage. But, still laughing, he was firm. "Miss Sanders does not take snow walks up mountains!" he told her. His elderly English clients had told him what "Mrs. O'Malley's" maiden name had been.

But I never did get up the Wetterhorn. The very next evening, in the bar, we heard over the wireless that Russia, as the Swiss wags said at the time, had joined the Anti-Comintern Pact; not wanting to panic, I rang up the Consul-General in Geneva next day to ask if he thought we ought to go home. "Mrs. O' Malley? Good God, are you still here?" he exclaimed, and told us to get back to England at once; we packed in a hurry, raced down to Meiringen, and set off.

The journey was rather a nightmare. It would have been much more of one but for what I had seen in Spain only a few months before; as it was, I filled our rucksacks with food—ham, cheese, buttered rolls, fruit and biscuits and chocolate, plus two bottles of Vermouth—and all the cigarettes I could get in the hotel. This was fortunate, for such a mass exodus of the British from Switzerland was suddenly taking place that all restaurant-cars were cancelled. At Thun we saw Laurence Collier, from the Foreign Office, and his wife boarding the train, humping their own luggage; we hailed them into our carriage, and learned that Switzerland had begun a partial mobilisation, so no porters—we were in a through coach to Paris, mercifully. But once in France it began to seem more and more uncertain whether our train would ever reach Paris. Grania and I still speak of "The Hell of Belfort", to describe the three hours or more that our train stood in that station, under the dimmed blue lights, while across the platform the French mobilisation was trying to take place. Shouts; orders and counter-orders; soldiers scrambling onto a train, and then being hustled off again; sobbing families, parcels bursting open; the train moving out a few yards, and then being shunted back again. We and the Colliers supped from those useful rucksacks; when at last our train moved out we all got some sleep.

As we drew into the Gare de l'Est next morning I put my head out of the window to appraise the situation. As we had expected, no porters—but right at the far end of the platform, as we passed, I saw that there were several flat luggage-trolleys, all empty. Shoving my way along the corridor I opened the train door, and stood on the step; as it slowed down I jumped off, raced back along the platform, and secured a trolley. Laurence and his wife, and Grania, had got most of the luggage out by the time I had wheeled it back, to cries of "Where did you get that?" from fellow-passengers—"Plenty more up there," I told them. People constantly tried to put their own luggage onto our trolley, but we only allowed this to a few elderly ladies, who were apparently alone—when I had time to notice them I realised that they were all Jewish. One of the horrifying features of that confused *sauve qui peut* from Europe in September, 1939, was the preponderance of Jews among the crowds struggling to get to England.

At the station entrance there were no taxis, of course, and we saw little hope of being allowed to wheel our trolley all the way to the Gare du Nord. Laurence suggested ringing up the Embassy; we found a telephone and I tried for Charles Mendl. He was away, but his maître d'hôtel knew me well, and rather reluctantly agreed to bring his master's car for us; he sensibly came himself, so that he would recognise me, and he and the chauffeur between them fended off the desperate people who tried, by bribes or main force, to get hold of the big saloon. The station forecourt was now a seething mass of stranded humanity, wondering how on earth to get across Paris; the car just took us four and our luggage—unhappily there was room for only one of the elderly Jewish ladies. No trolley at the Nord, but Laurence and Charles's servant got the big stuff to the train, and Grania, Mrs. Collier, and I managed the rest.

At Boulogne the boat was already crammed; it had waited for our train. Here English sailors—blessed sight!—gave a hand with the heavy luggage; there was no chance of a seat, but Grania and I scrambled up onto a large square erection containing life-belts and covered with tarpaulin, and hauled Mrs. Collier up after us—here we could sit and dangle our legs, and survey the crowd below. In this we soon spied Ursula Nettleship, and shouted; she climbed up and joined us, dragging a small child after her—she had, we knew, been staying with Owen in Budapest, and she gave us a lively account of how he was sending all the British women and children home as fast as he could; the mother of the child she was escorting was ill, and could not leave.

Ursula and her charge were starving too—the queue for the steamer restaurant stretched all round the deck. We fed them, and drank Cinzano. Presently there came a hail from the mob below. "Mary O'Malley, where did you get that Vermouth?" It was Arnold Lunn, also on his way home; we told him to come up and have some, and he was glad of food too—the two rucksacks were pretty light by the time we got to London.

The flat on the Embankment was of course empty, but we routed out one of our old chars and scratched along while we settled what to do next. Grania soon got a job in the Censorship, and was despatched to Liverpool, rather to my relief; even before the heavy raids began, the threat of them in London was constant, and unpleasant. I was soon attached to the Ministry of Information in a rather vague capacity—I was to use such contacts as I had in the States to place articles on England's war effort over there, to ascertain the right type and length of article, and then to coax English writers to produce them. This was the sort of job for which no office or fixed hours were required, and I rented a furnished cottage out in the country at Cobham, not far from our beloved Bridge End; the children's Nannie Comley had written to say that she would like to make me her war work, and she and I settled down there in great contentment. In the mornings I wrote, letters or sketches for articles; in the afternoons Nan and I drove out into the woods below Telegraph Hill, and collected wood for our fire, which I chopped up on the verandah—once a week we went up to the flat for a couple of nights, when I talked to writers, and reported to my department. On one of these trips petrol-rationing was suddenly announced as imminent. Eager to lay in at least a small supply I hastened to our regular garage. They had plenty of petrol, but not a single jerrycan left to put it in!

On such occasions I always sit down, light a cigarette, and tell myself—"There is something sensible to be done about this, if you will only keep quite calm and think what it is." It usually works, and it did then. I drove across the Bridge to Battersea and went to a large oil-shop, where I first purchased a gallon of paraffin; then I asked if they had any empty cans with air-tight stoppers. They had, of course, of every shape and sort: cans that had held turpentine, linseed oil, or furniture polish—these we carefully rinsed out in their yard with the paraffin. I went on to one or two more oil-shops, and drove back across the Bridge with containers for nearly one hundred gallons—the garage proprietor filled them. Next day I left Nan in the flat and took this dangerous cargo down to Surrey, where I parked it with various friends.

How thankful I was for this flagrant piece of hoarding when only two or three weeks later Patrick rang up, from Aldershot, to say that he had got forty-eight hours' leave, and would like to spend it at the cottage, but could we fetch him? Aldershot certainly meant embarcation leave. Before he came, while in London, I went to the French bookshop near Leicester Square and got two copies of the

Guide Gastronomique; he took one, so that he could always give me an idea of where he was by writing on a card—"Dined last night at the Coq d'Or (or whatever) and had a splendid"—and mention some "plât régionnal" peculiar to that inn; a tip used by Lucilla Eynsham and her fiancé in *The Tightening String.*

Petrol was not the only thing it was important to secure in good time. Owen and I had been to Ireland in 1938 and bought Rockfleet in the County Mayo, then really only a Regency ruin; Owen had planned out the alterations and additions, and the cottage and garage were already built, but the house had not gone very far. A quarter of a century earlier we had learned that a war means shortages of everything, and a steep rise in prices; it occurred to me that it would be a good plan to make sure of an adequate quantity of baths and fitted basins, and Hal Goodhart-Rendel put me onto a small firm which supplied these very reasonably. I hadn't even got the plans of the house, but I had a rough idea of what would be needed, and ordered, and paid cash down for, twelve basins and six baths, and had these despatched to the plumbers in Dublin who were to do the work—plus, on Hal's advice, 400 feet of copper piping for the hot water; they arrived even before the insurance rates for freight by sea had gone up because of submarines. I got one bath too many and two basins too few; but by the time they were installed the price had more than doubled, so it was better than leaving it to chance.

When the phoney war had lasted for nearly six months Owen decided that it would be reasonable for Grania and me to come out and join him. We travelled quite normally through France, Italy, and Yugoslavia, and then into Hungary across the frontier that was later to become such a main escape-route for the interned Poles—a very different journey from that disorderly and uncomfortable return home the previous autumn. And life in Budapest was totally unlike life at St. Jean de Luz, my only previous experience as wife of the head of a Mission. The Legation in Buda had been a palace during the Turkish occupation; a *porte-cochère,* locked at night, led from the street into a paved courtyard, another at the opposite end out into the garden, right on the lip of the mediaeval Bastion which surrounded the Old City; the harem-lik, the women's quarters, had been in these apartments, and the archway still had its massive wrought-iron gates, but now that end of the house contained guest-rooms. The Office of Works had built on an extra storey right round the courtyard, to house the kitchens, offices, and servants' quarters; the Chancery occupied the ground floor on the right of the entrance —from the glazed passage on the first floor Grania and I could see, on our way to the drawing-room, whether the First Secretary, seated at his desk, was really writing minutes, or—as sometimes happened —tying flies for his next fishing trip. From our bedrooms we had a superb view across the Danube to the lower city of Pest and, close at hand, we could look into the tops of the trees which clothed the slope below, and watch the blackbirds building their nests, and catch sight of that explosion of daffodil-yellow which indicated the sudden movement of a golden oriole.

My husband has noted, in his book, how a place among the domestic staff of the British Embassy or Legation was much sought after in most foreign capitals, and certainly the servants at the Legation at Budapest approached perfection. He has mentioned Erich, our faultless and devoted butler; I for my part owed much to the thoughtful administrations of Margit, who maided me and the two girls. But my favorite was the chef, a huge man, completely bald, who looked exactly like my most admired film star, Erich von Stroheim—ordering the meals was a daily delight. People who have never actually lived through the quite arduous routine of official life abroad—the constant entertaining, the ceaseless round of lunches and dinners, cocktail-parties and calls, for which one must always be perfectly dressed—find it hard to realise how important a good domestic staff is to the proper performance of those official duties (none the less official for sometimes being very pleasant) for which in fact the British tax-payer foots the bill; they even tend to be contemptuous about the need for such appendages as ladies'-maids and chefs, and all the behind-the-scenes apparatus of diplomatic life. This however is merely ignorance—the job is a job, like any other, and has to be well done; as it only can be with good and well-trained servants. There are only so many hours in the day, and so much physical strength; if a Minister's or Ambassador's wife had to wash her own stockings, press her own dresses, and clean her gloves and shoes, she could only get through that much smaller a proportion of the work for which her husband is paid. Diplomacy may be an indifferent way of conducting international relations, but while it remains the way in which they *are* conducted, it is foolish to think—

let alone say—that it is unimportant to do the job as well as it can be done, and to condemn the necessary means to that end.

My first official task was of course to call on the wife of the Head of State, Madame Horthy. The Regent lived in what had been the Hapsburg royal palace, up on the hill in Buda, and thither, when an appointment had been made by the Chancery, I betook myself one afternoon. It was an imposing place. From the entrance-hall a long flight of stairs led up to the official apartments, and on both sides of this staircase, on every alternate step, stood halberdiers in white breeches, high yellow boots, and long red cloaks lined with yellow, with herons'-plumes in their casques, each holding a gilded halberd; they stood, motionless as statues, while some official led me up between them.

But if the entrance was impressively formal, Madame Horthy was simplicity itself—after passing through several huge saloons I was shown into a small comfortable sitting-room, with an open wood fire, and a low table set for a thoroughly English tea; my hostess made the tea herself from a spirit-kettle. Though past middle age she still had great beauty, and immense charm; like most Hungarians she spoke perfect English, and nothing could have been pleasanter than her complete naturalness and lively interest in everything English—I began to regret that my instructions were to make a move to leave after twenty minutes at the outside. But that proved to be impossible. Presently the Regent himself walked in, in his admiral's uniform; shook hands, threw a log on the fire, sat down and began to tuck into crumpets, talking and laughing like the jolly sailor he was before he was forced to take the tiller of the ship of his small, menaced state. The Horthys were not *Magnaten*, great landed noble families like the Zichys or the Esterhazys or the Karolys; they were small country squires, with a long ancestry, but always modest folk, often serving in the Army, and, under Austria, in the Navy—the choice of a ruler from this class could provoke no dangerous rivalries, and was wise in itself: the Regent was shrewd, intelligent, and extremely sensible.

Presently he said that he wished to ask "a great favour" of me; of course I answered that if it was in my power, it should be done.

"I want you to write a novel about Hungary," he said bluntly, and went on to emphasize that it should be about "the *real* Hungary; not only night-clubs and paprika-chicken!"—English novelists, he complained, were apt to concentrate on the night-life of the capital, and ignore everything else. Greatly astonished, I promised to do as he asked—it seemed incredible that he should actually have read any of my books. He had, though—*Peking Picnic* and *Illyrian Spring*—and talked very knowledgeably about them both. Alas, by the time I was able to keep my promise and sent him *A Place to Stand* he was in exile in Portugal, living in a small villa in Monte Estoril; when I went to tea with them there he opened the door to me himself—no ranks of plumed halberdiers now! But he was still as merry and cheerful as ever.

In fact the books had become almost a political weapon. Two had just been translated into Hungarian, but with typical graceful gallantry the publishers held them up till I arrived in Budapest; then they appeared, and were given big window-displays, with a photograph, in the main bookshops. This exasperated the Germans, and a week or two later the shops were forced to fill their windows with *Mein Kampf*, surrounding a portrait of the Führer, as a come-back. I am sure this nonsense was nothing to do with von Erdmannsdorf, the German Minister, who was a delightful and most civilised person; he and Owen were good friends till the outbreak of war—after that they had perforce to ignore each other's existence officially. But if they met in the course of their afternoon walks on the Bastion, they would grin cheerfully and furtively at each other if no one was about.

Though the Regent and Madame Horthy now occupied the great Hapsburg palace, there were still some actual Hapsburgs living in Budapest—two Archdukes and their wives. For some curious reason the men bore the same Christian name, and as they were anyhow rather colourless creatures, the two families were differentiated by the names of the wives—everyone called them "the Annas" and "the Augustas". I knew both pairs; the Augustas were rather intimidating and not very amusing, but I got very fond of the Annas. She in particular was a charmer, and a very good botanist; she drove herself about in a little red sports-car, and used to take me to see special rarities in the hills and woods round Budapest. Archduchess Anna was not a Hungarian, she belonged to the royal house of Saxony; this made it the more complicated when her husband said to me one day—"Why do you not ask us to your house? We should like to come." There is a certain protocol—which I have never fully understood—about H. M. representatives abroad *not* entertaining ex-royalties; we had plenty of bother about that in Lisbon later on. At the time I felt I had a good excuse; the phoney war was over by then, England stood alone, and in dire peril—Owen had very properly issued an edict that we should give no white-tie parties for the time being. But when I explained this to the Archduke he merely said—"Let it be a black-tie party." That wouldn't do either, I told him; for him it must be white-tie. Undefeated, he said—"Then have us to lunch, alone; a *parti-carré!*" He was really a most innocent creature.

Fortunately no such official embargo extended to princely families not of royal blood, of whom there used to be several in Central Europe. We could see all we wanted to of Prince Georgy Festetics— the original of Prince Willi Terenyi in *The Tightening String*. He lived at Kesthely, at the far end of Lake Balaton; we made great friends, and I stayed there often, and learned a vast amount about Hungarian, and indeed European, history from him on those visits. Kesthely really *was* half the size of Versailles; I had been warned that the Prince had a mania about punctuality, and when he escorted me to my room on my arrival I took a furtive peep at my watch and timed myself on our way from the drawing-room—on that occasion the walk took four minutes. But along with the troops of servants, the formality, and the almost regal state kept up in that house, Georgy Festetics worked as hard as most tycoons, and was a benefactor to his district, and indeed to his country. His grandfather had started an agricultural college, I believe the first in Europe, at his own expense, and the Prince still maintained it; if he amused himself by breeding race-horses, which he bought from people like Lord Derby in England, he also brought in improved stocks of vines from Germany, and distributed them to the peasants, as well as making wine himself on a big scale; Hungary owes to his initiative the foreign currency which she now earns from her renowned "Hungarian Riesling". There were always three or four men at work in the huge cellars of that enormous house, blending, bottling, and labelling.

The gardens were vast, and beautifully kept, but not only for show; regular consignments of flowers went up from the beds and greenhouses to the florists in Budapest. Georgy's mother had been a daughter of the Duke of Hamilton, and he had a proper Scottish sense of the rightness of putting everything to good use, and the positive sinfulness of mere wasteful display; let money be put to making more money, in some practical manner, not just spent. He had, too, a strong religious sense—Mass was said daily in the private chapel; and before All Souls Day the teams of gardeners were at work making wire frames, clothing them with greenery, and finally covering them with flowers from the greenhouses, not only for the family wreaths, but for all the peasantry round about—on *All-Heiligen* itself, after Mass in the village church, the Prince walked with his people in a long procession to the churchyard, where all together laid wreaths on the graves of their dead. I know it is fashionable now to deride this sort of thing; but it was a reality, and a very happy and valuable reality too. There is neither pleasure nor merit in the class antagonism of what Rebecca West has called "the mindless, traditionless, possessionless urban proletariat", with which so much current writing is concerned—antagonisms which were non-existent in pre-Communist Hungary. Contentment, happiness, and warm traditional relationships are not really so despicable, whatever those who have never encountered them may say.

Georgy Festetics, in spite of these solid qualities, was also a great card, in a very un-Scottish and completely Hungarian way—Hungarian men are tremendous gossips, and he was no exception; he had a vast fund of rather malicious and very funny stories about everyone in Hungarian and Austrian society, in most of which, at an early stage, occurred the words—"I said to him [or to her] 'You will see, it will all turn out very badly'." It always did, of course. A phrase of more auspicious omen was—"I think I had better have a little talk" with So-and-so. "A little talk with the Old Boy" (i.e., the Regent) resulted in our being allowed to use the official labels of the Hungarian Red Cross for all the thousands of parcels which the Legation sent to the British prisoners of war in Germany—an arrangement which meant absolute security, and of course no charge whatever for postage or freight.

Social dealings with the Corps were necessarily a little complicated by the War. We could not meet the Germans, which we regretted, nor the Italians (which we did not), nor, after the fall of France, the French—for the French Minister and his half-Syrian wife stuck to the Vichy régime; we didn't terribly regret them either. With the Americans, Mr. and Mrs. Montgomery, and their staff, all was ease; they showed me no end of helpful kindness—to the point of lending me their own very remarkable addendum to the usual printed Diplomatic List: a small manuscript book in which were written down the names of who was whose lover or mistress, and which pairs it was customary, and polite, to invite together. In fact this was a little too progressive for us—I was thoroughly imbued with the notion that the wife of the head of a British Mission must be a sort of mixture of Britannia, Queen Victoria, and Mrs. Grundy rolled into one; so I was not able to take full advantage of this American thoroughness. I also made great friends with the Turkish Minister, Ruşen Eşref Ünaydin, and his wife Saliha; at one point he had a serious operation, and to distract her a little in her anxiety, as often as I could I used to take her out for drives in the afternoons. This small kindness they repaid a thousandfold by inviting me to stay with them in their villa at Prinkipo, on the Sea of Marmara, when later in the summer he went home to convalesce; I went, with results which shall be told in their place.

There were other Hungarian country-houses, a good deal less like Versailles than Kesthely, where we often stayed—in the winter, for the shooting, at the Mautners, down in the Alföld, where something like 300 beaters turned out to drive the game, and 2,000 cock-pheasants was a normal day's bag; the women rode out in sleighs to meet the men for lunch, which we ate sitting at tables on the snow, in the sun and out of the wind. It was coming back from one of these al fresco meals that I saw a "hares' parliament"—between fifty and sixty of the creatures sitting in a circle, their small upright shapes dark against the snow.

Madame Mautner was one of the many Weiss sisters, members of the family which had given Hungary its main heavy industry; from their factories flowed locomotives and rolling-stock which found a ready market all over South-east Europe. The Weisses were an example of that curious Hungarian phenomenon, the Catholic Jewish families: Jewish by race, by religion devout Catholics for three or four generations. In the summer we went as often as possible to dear Tommy Esterhazy at Devezcer (the original of Terencer in *The Tightening String*) and bathed in the big pool under the oak-trees, or were driven by Etti, his wife, in a dog-cart through the Forest of the Bakony, where one saw wild boar wallowing in their sloughs, and deer darted away down the dim glades. Etti handled

77

her pair of pure white Arabs beautifully—I have never gone so fast in any horse-drawn vehicle before or since.

One of the more tedious duties that came my way was the *jour*, or At Home day at the Legation. Geoffrey Knox, Owen's predecessor, being a bachelor, had abandoned it, but strong pressure was brought on me to revive it, which I dutifully did; it had traditionally been held on a Monday, and—less smart than Mrs. Eynsham in *The Tightening String*—I agreed to this, not realising how it would constrict our week-ends. The *jour* has been fully described in the novel: during 1940 it really did become a sort of barometer of Central European opinion of England's chances of survival; and how we honoured those Hungarians who braved the field-glasses of the Secret Police spotters in the window above the greengrocer's shop across the street, and steadfastly came during the darkest days, as after the fall of France—people like the old Markgraf Gyury Pallavincini, Jeanne and Jenkö Pongracz, and Daisy Karolyi. We didn't hold it against those who always stayed away, for the Hungarians were in a desperately difficult situation; but we did rather despise the more notoriously pro-Nazi people who, when there was some fairly striking Allied success, suddenly showed up.

Owen and I have often wondered why Hungary should have had such a consistently bad press in England, and to a lesser extent in America too. People still use the phrase "the Horthy Régime" as if it was a dirty word. Why? The Hungarians are a brave, intelligent, and deeply religious people; they were, like England, a constitutional monarchy, and were the second country in Europe to have a Parliament—which they did less than one hundred years after Simon de Montfort set up the English model. Their peasantry lived, for the most part, in excellent conditions, with free grazing for their pigs, cattle, and geese, and a decent plot of land for each household in addition; they were hard-working, moral, and contented. The liveliness of the Hungarian character, the unusual food—above all the gypsies in the restaurants and night-clubs—made the night-life of Budapest so uniquely picturesque that novelists and journalists alike described that, to the exclusion of the solid merits in the background, about which they knew and cared nothing. Admittedly there was a good deal of surface frivolity among the upper classes of Hungarian society—but so there was in Poland and Austria and

78

Rumania; yet they were not denigrated, year in year out, as Hungary was.

I think one possible reason for this moralising disapproval—the source of the prejudice, so to speak—was, besides plain ignorance, the lack of an established middle-class intelligentsia, whom foreign journalists normally meet; public opinion is fatally dependent on what it is told by the Press. There was in Budapest the bourgeois world of the *petits fonctionnaires,* the lesser civil servants, bank employees, and so on; but the young writers and artists and musicians (who in London or Paris had for long consciously hived together, formed a vigorous entity, aware of themselves and interested in the stranger) in Hungary were still much more isolated, disconnected from one another. Why this was I do not know; there was not time to find out. But a few people in the upper strata of Hungarian society were aware of this lack, and were actively working to remedy it. Princess Odescalchi, for instance, sought these young people out, and brought them together at her house; she drew the exiled Poles in too, and gave them all gay evenings, to which she also firmly dragged young girls of established position—the daughters of her innumerable relations and even of diplomats, to give more breadth and variety to her parties; Grania—Kate—was so drawn in. (It was in Hungary that Grania finally insisted on abandoning her rather unusual Christian name and being called Kate, to which she was also baptismally entitled—the Poles, rather sweetly, turned it into "Ketush".) Kaia Odescalchi was a splendid person, full of energy and originality; she kept a gold brick by her, to have something in hand in case of emergencies; it was with her when she was killed by a stray bomb, fleeing to the Adriatic coast with our Naval Attaché when the Germans came into Hungary in 1941. Her efforts to create a true Hungarian intelligentsia were one of the many good things in Europe which the Nazis blindly extinguished.

VII

Being a Chef-ess—Hungary II

In Budapest, over and above the normal routine of diplomatic life, Owen and I each had a special preoccupation: his, to facilitate the departure of as many as possible of the 40,000-odd Polish troops interned in Hungary, to go down to Egypt and to reform as units of the Allied forces; mine, to get food, clothing, and cigarettes to the British prisoners of war in Germany. The two Hungarian novels reflect these activities.

A Place to Stand deals with the Poles in Hungary. It is really Kate's book; she planned it, and actually wrote 14,000 words; but other activities prevented her from completing it, and she burnt what she had written. Much later, when I was casting about for a new book, she offered the plot to me; together we planned out a detailed synopsis, chapter by chapter, from which I could work alone.

Now I never saw, and could never have seen, some of the places described in the novel—they were not such as Ministers' wives frequented; but Kate, a pretty child in her late teens, slipped in and out of them with the familiarity and ease of a little mouse; she has a great gift for description, and enabled me to record them accurately. For instance I could never have gone to the Söröző, the shabby restaurant with two doors, where the old flower-seller who stood outside used to come in and offer pot-plants to the customers if he saw men from the *Deuxième Bureau,* the Secret Police, approaching; the customers, those who needed the warning, would go down a passage past the lavatory and slip out by a side door, while the woman who ran the place swept their plates and cups into the sink before the agents came in. Kate actually saw this happen, often. I must say that I was rather aghast when years later, safely in Ireland, I learned what she had been up to in Budapest when I thought she was amusing herself with her Hungarian friends.

Though I only learned about the Belgrade bombing at second-hand, much of *A Place to Stand* is not only pure history, but a first-hand account of events as they happened—especially Chapter VIII, which describes the Germans being allowed to come through Hungary to attack Yugoslavia, and Count Teleki's suicide. On that March morning in 1941, Erich, our butler, came himself to my bedroom, a thing he never did normally—he would send any message by Margit—and told me that Count Teleki had committed suicide; Teleki's manservant was a friend of Erich's, and had told him this himself, including the details about the Prime Minister's Scout uniform being laid out ready for him to wear when he took his troop of little boys to early Mass, and his being called for that purpose at 6:30 A.M. Almost as an afterthought Erich mentioned that the German panzer-divisions were pouring through the city, and when he had gone I went along to Jane's and Kate's sitting-room, overlooking the river, threw up the window, and heard the hideous din they made; a little later, like Hope, my heroine, I went down to the Chain Bridge, and saw them close to, and the Szallascists—the small but vocal Hungarian pro-Nazi party—giving the Nazi salute to the splendidly turned-out young soldiers on the tanks and trucked vehicles, and heard what they said. As to the reasons for Teleki's suicide, we guessed at once that he had done it because, after all the assurances that he had given to my husband personally that this would never happen, someone had given orders that the German armour was to be allowed through—without his knowledge, and behind his back. Of all the complicated manoeuvres, the comings and goings, and Teleki's own movements on that night, we only heard piecemeal at the time; afterwards Professor Aylmer Macartney, the historian, fitted all the bits of the puzzle together in his monumental book *A History of Modern Hungary*, and allowed me to read and use the relevant sections in typescript.

In the novel the Kirklands, Hope's parents, leave Budapest the night before the bombing of Belgrade. So they missed Count

Teleki's funeral. We however attended that most moving service, in the high-domed Parliament building down in Pest, and saw, among the magnificent ceremonial vestments of the Prince-Primate and his assisting clergy, and the huge elaborate official wreaths, Teleki Paul's own troop of very small Boy Scouts, in their shirts and shorts, being sent up first to place their little bunches of wild-flowers on the black and silver catafalque. And we realised to the full the intense surge of public relief which filled that most Catholic nation when, earlier, the news broke that the Vatican had telegraphed permission for there to be a religious ceremony and Christian burial, in spite of the certainty that this great and good man had died by his own hand.

The Tightening String treats of my quite different private preoccupation, feeding the British prisoners of war in Germany; and treats too of a different aspect of Hungarian life. I felt that the first book only partly fulfilled my promise to the Regent to write about "the real Hungary", since it contained almost nothing about the life of the countryside, the good conditions under which, for the most part, the peasants lived, and their cheerful relations with the land-owners. The main plot is not the rather slight love-affair between Lucilla Eynsham and Hugo Weissberger, but the efforts of the Prisoners' Relief Committee to get food, clothing, cigarettes, and anything else they wanted to the British prisoners in Germany, and my personal struggles with British officialdom, and especially with the British Red Cross Society, to that end. These efforts and struggles could only have been carried out by the personnel of the Legation, it was no good trying to pretend anything else; nor could the dates be changed, since the capture of the Highland Division at St. Valéry, which began it all, and the entry of the Germans into Hungary, which ended it, were matters of historical fact—yet at the relevant period there had been a real Legation in Budapest, full of real people, occupying specific positions. There was only one thing to do—to sweep all the real characters out, and replace them in the book with fictitious ones, and this I proceeded to do.

Readers familiar with Oxfordshire may have noticed that the names of all the English characters are taken from places in that county; they seem to sound exactly like ordinary surnames, and I think fit the characters quite well. I had rather a worry over Sonia

Marston, the unsatisfactory woman journalist, who intrigues with the Germans and is sent home by the Minister; no such treacherous person ever existed, but there had been an English woman journalist in Budapest before Kate and I arrived, and oh the bother of finding out when she left! However it was established eventually that she had gone elsewhere well before the time at which the novel opens.

As for the behaviour of the British Red Cross, it seems even more incredible in retrospect than it did at the time. While their letters from London enquiring about the numbers of prisoners in each camp were taking six weeks to reach Geneva—telegrams were impossible, for some reason—and the replies another six weeks, I had only to lift the telephone on my desk, ask for the International Red Cross, and be connected with Geneva in a few minutes; while British Red Cross parcels piled up month after month, on the quays at Lisbon (where they had been sent by sea in the idiotic hope that they could be sent on across France to Switzerland), our parcels, with their Hungarian Red Cross labels, were reaching even the remotest camps in three or four weeks, week after week, with absolute regularity. What the old gentlemen in Grosvenor Crescent could not realise was that this was World War II, not World War I. Between 1914 and 1918 Switzerland had been the neutral country adjacent to Germany, with an open frontier to an Allied country—Italy—to the south of it, and access from the sea; parcels had been shipped to Switzerland, and sent on quite fast. But in 1940 Italy came into the war on the German side on June 10, so that Switzerland, though still neutral, was completely encircled by enemy territory; Hungary now occupied that useful position of the neutral with access from the sea, and a common frontier with Germany, and it was through Hungary that parcels should have been routed, for the first eleven months at any rate.

As late as February, 1941, eight months after Italy's entry into the war, it came to our knowledge that the Red Cross had bought 40,000 sets of woollen vests and pants from Middle East Command in Cairo, with instructions that they were to be sent to Switzerland via *Genoa*. This so exasperated my husband that he telegraphed to Miles Lampson in Cairo, and succeeded in having this zany order ignored, and the stuff re-routed via the Piraeus, to come up to Budapest for despatch; we *just* got the whole seven freight-wagon loads unpacked, divided, repacked, and sent off before we had to leave

83

ourselves—even so, our spies reported that the goods train with this vital cargo on board was still sitting in the West Station forty-eight hours before we were due to leave ourselves. Whereupon I did in reality what Rosina Eynsham does in the book—rang up Pista Horthy, the Regent's son, who was Director of the State Railways, and told him flatly that until I heard that the *sieben Wagonen* had crossed the frontier, *I* should not leave Budapest, whatever the rest of the Legation personnel might do. It would have been even more embarrassing to the Hungarian Government to have the Minister's wife stay behind than the Counsellor's wife, and the stuff went across all right—we had a telephone call from the frontier just twenty-four hours before we left.

Mrs. Eynsham's journey down through the Balkans to Turkey, raising money and ordering supplies as she went, is of course directly taken from my own activities in August and September, 1940. I really did meet the charming Bulgarian chocolate-manufacturer in Sofia, and having settled with him for half-a-hundred-weight of chocolate, in quarter-kilogram cakes, to come up every week, at a very reasonable price, he did truly insist on having each half-pound packed as fourteen separate fingers in silver foil, because these would make nicer presents for the prisoners to give one another than pieces broken off a slab; he had been a prisoner of war himself in the First World War, and felt very pro-British.

The refusal, in the novel, of the Red Cross to finance the purchase of more than 10,000 of the absurdly cheap quilts from Turkey was all too true, and made us very angry. We *knew* what conditions were like in the camps: at any time our good friends in the American Legation could ring up their Embassy in Berlin and get the answer to a given problem in a matter of hours; they passed on to us the reports of their investigators, who toured the camps regularly. Like the Committee in the novel, we all wrote angry letters to highly placed people in England, protesting at the failure of the Red Cross to feed and clothe our prisoners themselves, and their refusal to give us funds with which to do so; I wrote, through a friend, to Cosmo Gordon Lang, the Archbishop of Canterbury—I knew she would let him see my letter, and she did. He wrote back rebuking me for my intemperate language!—but one way or another a change came over the people in London. Early in January, 1941, came a telegram via the Foreign Office, asking me to become British Red

Cross Representative in Hungary, agreeing to pay for what I sent, and instructing me to charge expenses "through the Foreign Office".

This rather went to my head. I telephoned for flannelette from Yugoslavia by the thousand metres, and got more and more food and clothing in from outside Hungary—I think I was perhaps a little reckless. I conveniently "forgot" that the Red Cross wished us to confine our efforts to Oflag VII C., and sent stuff to Stalags as well—bed-ticking to cover the straw on which the men slept, and, in particular, 500 mouth-organs to one very large Stalag on the Polish border, which had asked for them. Much later, in America, I got a letter from Field-Marshal Lord Chetwode, an old friend from St. Jean de Luz days, remonstrating with me about all this: I had only been authorised to send supplies to one camp, whereas in fact I had sent food and clothing to camps all over Germany; and the accounts they had now received from our archivist showed that, strictly speaking, I owed the British Red Cross Society something over £7,000. This shook me a little at first, but I soon recovered myself; I was devoted to Lord Chetwode, and wrote him an affectionate letter, to the effect that I couldn't say I was sorry, because our wretched prisoners had got, through my instrumentality, a little of what they so desperately needed; and I didn't think he really meant it anyhow. If, when I got home, they wanted to sue me for that £7,000—"I shall conduct my own defence, and have the time of my life doing it, and the British Red Cross will wish it had never been born." I got a sweet reply, more or less admitting that he had been obliged to write the earlier letter, and saying that I was not to worry.

When I came to write the book I had to be rather careful. I definitely wanted to expose the failures of the British Red Cross, so that nothing of the sort could ever happen again. But if there is one thing all publishers are terrified of it is libel actions, and I knew that Chattos would be frightened out of their wits by the hair-raising facts in the novel. So when it was finished, and typed, I took all the relevant chapters to a renowned libel lawyer in Grays Inn and asked him to vet them for me professionally; I learned some interesting facts as a result. One may not quote another person's letters or telegrams, because the sender has a copyright in them—so some of the most destructively damaging communications from the Red Cross had to come out. When I had altered the text I got the lawyer to write me a letter stating that the book now contained nothing actionable, and sent it to Chattos with the manuscript; which saved all trouble.

David Eynsham, Rosina's husband, is an invented character, and one I like particularly. I gave him heart trouble, because I have always found it a good plan to have an illness in a book, if possible; it adds to the interest and tension. I learned this from the eager fan-mail I got, from doctors especially, about Little Annette's illness in *Peking Picnic*, my first book: they all wanted to know how *I* knew that the symptoms of sunstroke and meningitis are so alike? In fact I got the basic idea from a doctor friend, and the details from Selfridge's Information Bureau—sheets of typescript packed with information, all for free. I didn't need so much help over David Eynsham because I had had two coronaries myself, and his visits to the old heart-specialist and his stay in the Nursing Home fitted in very well with the plot, since in the book the two escaped British prisoners are parked in the Home till they are brought up to the Legation—in real life a Polish priest told Kate where they were down in Pest, only I couldn't very well put that in. But my husband really did let them in by the garden gate after dark, like Sir Hugh Billingshurst, and put them in one of the spare rooms, till he took them down, disguised as a manservant and a clerk, to Belgrade, whence they went on to Cairo.

And it seemed to me that to have David die during that horrible time at the Russian frontier gave a sort of finality to the end of the book. Except for his death, all that episode is completely true—the special diplomatic train, sent by the Russian Government to meet us, drawn up 200 yards away from the one in which we arrived, with no light in it, and only two porters for the luggage of some sixty people; while the menfolk argued in the station with the illiterate Russian colonel who had been sent to facilitate our entry into Russia, but had never heard of a *laissez-passer*, teams of wives and typists themselves humped all the hand-luggage through fifteen inches of snow and hauled it up into the darkness of the empty waiting train—we made that trip *five* times. We had two invalids, Harry Blake-Tyler, our Assistant Military Attaché, who in fact had heart trouble himself, and Kate, who was suffering from acute sinusitis; the beds in the sleepers had not been made up, and the discomfort and worry were immense; it was our first encounter with the Russian combination of ignorance and obstructiveness, both *total*—and it made one feel strangely helpless. It is plain fact that the station staff had never seen a gramophone, and insisted on playing all the Passport Control Officer's scores of records before they would let this official special train leave at 7 A.M.—we having reached the station at ten the night before.

"Gradually gathering speed, the train glided slowly down into Russia." So the book ends, but our actual story went on, and so did the Russian unpleasantness. After twenty-four hours there was no water left in the tanks which supplied the basins and W.C.s on the train; all representations from our two Russian-speakers were unavailing, till at Tarnopol (I think it was) we were joined by a woman Intourist guide, who spoke a little English. She didn't pay much attention to requests for the tanks to be filled at first, till I had the happy idea of telling her that I was an authoress, Anni Bridgeova, and should be giving lectures in America; of course the Americans would most wish to hear about Russia, and I wished to be able to say how wonderful conditions were there—but why people read my books all over the world was because they knew that I always told the exact truth about the countries I described, and I should have to go on doing so. The Americans were fanatically clean people, and would take a poor view of Russia if I told them, as I certainly should, that the Russians cared so little for cleanliness that there was no water in the basins on long-distance trains. I made this oration to encouraging murmurs of "Keep at it, Bridge" from Owen, and before we left that station the train tanks were re-filled.

I forget who the well-informed person in Budapest was who told me that if by any chance we stopped at Kiev we must at all costs see the Lavra Monastery, with its chain of underground cells and chapels running down to the river, and their paintings and treasures, but we were all grateful to him or her. At Kiev Miss Intourist, who wore an imitation leopard-skin coat, announced that we should pause there for several hours; we were to lunch at an hotel in the town, but before that, cars had been provided to drive us to a collective farm. I took a hurried census of the party's views: most agreed that they would just as soon see the Lavra Monastery, and the rest by this time didn't care what they did, so long as it was contrary to poor Miss Intourist's ideas. So I explained that *first,* anyhow, we wished to visit the world-famous shrine, and rather crossly she took us there. It was in fact a most remarkable place— the little narrow tunnels leading from chapel to chapel and from cell to cell, all carefully lit by electricity, and full of treasures and wall-paintings; but the most illuminating thing of all was the big church at the top, which had been turned into an "anti-God Museum". The altars, and the big icons in their silver frames, had been left in position, though all the jewels had been picked out of the frames, leaving jagged gaping holes in the silver; groups of young soldiers and workers were being led round by guides, who jeeringly derided religion as the "opiate of the masses" to their flocks—while at the chancel rails a few old women, and still fewer old men, knelt in prayer while the tide of godlessness washed round their feet. It was rather moving.

The town of Kiev itself startled us in one respect: the almost total absence of "consumer goods" in the shops; these were numerous and well-built, though now shabby and badly needing a coat of paint; they had big windows, but these were either empty, or full of balalaikas! Every other shop had a huge display of balalaikas. Some of the party, as an Intourist-tease, asked to be taken to a shop where they could buy something to remind them of Kiev; they returned with one faded and utterly withered half-pound box of Fullers' chocolates, which had cost 14/-, or two dollars. Lunch in the hotel, for which we waited an hour, was very poor when it came; but top marks went to the Station, which had a beautiful modern façade in the shape of a Russian crown, lavatories that actually flushed when one pulled the chain, and hot water in the basins—not surprisingly, the Ladies' Room was full of Russian women having a wash. These poor souls were highly entertained to see Kate and Rosemary Blake-Tyler using their lipsticks; they held out their hands for them with eager cries, and then, shrieking with laughter, scrawled their bare legs with red.

The three days' journey to Moscow seemed long: the countryside, at winter's end, was bare and dreary, and at intervals we were confronted with the sight of labour-camps where political prisoners, their unshod feet bound in rags, were being marched out to work over the frozen ground by guards armed with rifles; at intervals along the barbed wire perimeters more guards manned tall towers with search-lights and machine-guns on top of them.

At Moscow we were met, and most kindly welcomed, by Sir Stafford and Lady Cripps; they put Kate and Owen and myself up in the Embassy for the first three days. Then, when it became obvious that the Russians were going to take some time over arranging our further transport on across Siberia, Lady Cripps, with her usual tactful kindness, thought that we should be happier in a ménage of our own, and contrived for us to be lent a Consul's flat. We were startled to hear the building in which this flat was situated was referred to as "the Starry Dome"; but later learned that this poetic title merely meant "Stary Dom", the "Old House", in Russian. The flat was a splendid arrangement, if only because of the two Russian maids: one had had a mother from Yorkshire, and so spoke some English, the other was a "Volga German", i.e., a descendant of the German colonists planted down that river by Peter the Great—in either case we could communicate perfectly easily with them, and a present of a pair of silk stockings each made them our slaves.

From these two nice women, and from doing my own housekeeping, I learned a little about the complications of daily life in Russia. As diplomatic visitors we of course had special ration-cards, but for rationed foods the coupons were only valid for one day, so if we wanted a duck or a chicken we could not use two days' coupons and buy a whole bird—oh no, it was cut neatly in half down the middle; next day we could purchase the other half. Unrationed foods one could buy without limit—these included butter and fresh caviare, and my mouth still waters at the thought of our breakfasts in Moscow: a rack of freshly made toast, heaps of glorious golden butter, and a dish with half-a-pound of grey-green caviare, for each person.

We also learned a bit more about the shortage of consumer-goods, partly from the maids. In the rush of departure from Budapest, difficulties over getting off the last of the prisoners' supplies, and the endless farewells, I had had to leave most of my packing to Margit; now, in an empty room in the Consul's flat, I went through all our cases, selecting and repacking, to cut down the luggage as much as possible. I had told Margit, hurriedly, to be sure to pack plenty of dress-hangers; I meant the pretty padded ones, but she had filled one whole suitcase with the common wooden things, costing perhaps a penny each, on which the Budapest cleaners were wont to send one's frocks home, fluttering from a small pole—impatiently I threw them out onto the floor. One after the other the two maids came sidling up to me and asked, timidly, if I could spare one of these objects. I asked some questions. Oh no, you couldn't buy them in Moscow; they had never seen one before—but they were *so* practical. I gave them four dozen each, and it was plain that they had become millionairesses, and would be able to bribe the whole quarter with this sudden wealth.

The well-informed person who had sent us to the Lavra Monastery had also advised me to take any old clothes we didn't want to Moscow, where they would fetch fantastic prices; so when I had presented Margit and Minnie, Erich's fat wife, with a suitable amount of cast-offs as perquisites, I brought the rest along. In Moscow Kate and I sorted out whatever we could spare, and then, escorted by a Russian-speaker from the Embassy, we took the stuff, a little at a time, to the old-clothes shops and sold it. This was highly illuminating. In Moscow in 1941 there were four hundred and three of these shops, all run by Jewesses; we visited about twenty of them, and the prices were in truth fantastic. An ounce of fact is worth a pound of generalisation, so I will give one concrete example. Seven years before I had bought, at a sale in London, a green open-work hand-knitted jumper for 25/-, or three and a half dollars; it was worn and washed and worn and washed till it became too small for me, and I passed it on to Jane, who wore it out riding for a couple of years; when it got too small for her she passed it on to Kate, who wore it under the jacket of her ski-suit. The thing was by now really a small, shapeless, shrunken piece of greenish felt; but a red-haired Jewess in one of those Russian shops gave me seventy-five roubles for it—these I exchanged at a cocktail-party with an American journalist for dollars, at fifteen roubles to the dollar; he wanted roubles, we, en route for the States, wanted dollars. Seven years old, practically ruined, and in Moscow it fetched nearly double what I had given for it in the first place.

It was no good taking things like tea-gowns or evening frocks to the shops; these—quite a lot of them—I sold privately through the *Daily Telegraph* correspondent, to the only people who could either use or afford them, the singers and ballerinas. He also helped us with the rouble-dollar exchanges; but Kate and I soon got into the habit of always carrying several hundred roubles in our handbags wherever we went, on the chance of effecting a swap.

Lady Cripps continued her kindnesses, sending us in a car to see one or two of the Orthodox basilicas, which had not been quite as roughly treated as the Lavra Church at Kiev, and taking us out into the country to see such wild-flowers as were out, mostly dandelions and coltsfoot. She and her two daughters belonged to the Wild-flower Association, as we did, and we compared our printed wild-flower diaries: the Crippses were miles ahead of us, and had found all but about one hundred and fifty of the thirteen-hundred-odd English species. We were constantly asked to lunch or dine at the Embassy, where it usually fell to my lot to sit by Sir Stafford Cripps; I found him rather a sad creature, with a gloomy outlook on life generally, and pretty thoroughly disillusioned about the Russians. He had gone to Moscow after being in India, full of Labourish enthusiasm—"They *asked* for me" he told me bitterly, more than once; "I was sent here at their special request. Now I've been here nine months, and I have only seen Molotov once! When I ask to see him, I am put off with some junior minister."

The Crippses entertained in rather an unusual fashion. Unless it was a big party, with a lot of diplomats, everyone wore day dress for dinner, and after it we sat in his study; moreover the whole family were vegetarians, and they had a very indifferent chef, who certainly swindled them: while they consumed a delicious carrot souflée, their guests chewed away at leathery steaks or chops. At one of these quiet dinners I was introduced to a banker, a Dr. Nüssbaumer, who was the Swiss member of the Bank for International Settlements; after dinner, sitting in the Ambassador's study, we had a long conversation. I began by talking to him in Berner-Deutsch, his native tongue, which surprised and amused him; then I asked him what he was doing in Russia. He made no bones about telling me—he had come to buy a kilogram of platinum, which certain firms in Switzerland wanted for some special purpose; but on his way through Berlin the German Government had asked him to get a kilogram for them too—in spite of the Ribbentrop-Molotov pact they had had difficulty about getting it for themselves, it seemed. He agreed that the Russians were difficult to deal with. He had been in Moscow a whole week, and had seen Molotov four times already, he said, and still he had not got his platinum. Always ready to make a little honest mischief, I called to our host—"Sir Stafford, Sir Stafford! Dr. Nüssbaumer has only been here a week, and he has seen Molotov four times!" Cripps looked more vinegarish than ever, but only vouchsafed a scowl in reply, which indeed was all this teasing deserved.

Then the fascinating thing happened. Out of pure idle curiosity I asked the Swiss how much longer he expected to stay in Moscow. Not more than another week or ten days, he hoped—and then he said the significant thing. "Anyhow, the Oberkommando Wehrmacht in Berlin told me that it will be all right provided I am back across the Russo-Polish frontier by May 10, or at latest the eleventh." This was April 22. I made no comment then, but when I repeated these words to Owen we agreed that this could only mean one thing—that the Germans intended to invade Russia, Pact or no Pact, in the middle of May. It is well known, now, that this was Hitler's original intention, and that the Allied landings in Greece caused a delay of six weeks, since they siphoned off several German divisions to the Balkans; in fact the Germans marched into Russia on June 22. Fatal delay! It gave General Winter his chance to defeat Hitler as he had defeated Napoleon; the icy cold fell like a sword on the German armour when within sight of Moscow; oil and petrol froze, nothing could move—the capital was saved, and Eastern Europe lost. (I heard about all that six years later from a taxi-driver in South Tyrol, and the appalling helplessness, when even tanks and guns were immobilised, within sight of their goal—"We could see the tram-lines!" he told me.) But it was absorbing to hear of this projected invasion before it happened, when Russia and Germany were still supposed to be allied to each other.

The over-riding impression that we all got from Moscow was of a profound drabness and dreariness, pressing down like a sort of miasmic fog, over everything and everyone. The populace trudging and shuffling along the pavements, plain to begin with, with pale eyes, faces often marked with small-pox, and snub noses, were dressed with dismal uniformity: the men mostly in dungarees, the women wearing identically cut coats, all dark blue or dark brown, with rabbit-fur collars, and rather dirty white woollen berets—and all wearing galoshes. Of course I went into this with the two maids. Oh no, they did not *buy* their overcoats; these were issued to them by the *Dom-Kom*, the House Commissar for their block—one had to show one's old coat when applying, and if the *Dom-Kom* thought it had another year's wear in it, no new one was issued. The only colours were blue or brown. I asked about mourning. No, black coats were not made—at least, they had never seen any. (The helpful *Telegraph* correspondent subsequently explained to me that a good black dye is both expensive, and requires a considerable degree of skill in its production; the nearest they had got to it in the Workers' Paradise was a dim pepper-and-salt. The galoshes were the result of a successful bulk purchase of rubber; all the available leather was required for boots for the army.)

Now we noticed that these dense, ugly, trudging crowds moved along with glum faces, seldom speaking. I was so much struck by this that one day, waiting in the car outside the principal chemist's while a prescription was being made up, Kate and I began to count how many people we saw laugh or smile. After ten minutes the chauffeur came back, and we drove off. In that period 400 people had passed us: Kate's score was one smile; mine was nil. Now this is *really* abnormal—in London, or any European capital, a similar count gives dozens of smiles, several laughs, and constant animated conversation. Our general impression of gloom had been a perfectly valid one. We were all glad when the time came to leave Moscow.

VIII

Towards Home

The first six days of the journey eastwards across the Trans-Siberian Railway are pretty dull. The central Asiatic plain is flat, and early in the year, day after day, one sees only greyish rectangles of arable land alternating with dark rectangles of conifers. Our sleepers were reasonably comfortable, but the food in the restaurant-car was both expensive and bad, and the table-cloths nearly as dirty as the blouses and hands of the waitresses. The train-boys objected strongly to our brewing coffee on Owen's Baby Primus, the Intourist person—a man this time—to our giving sweets to the children who swarmed round the train at the three daily stops—morning, midday, and evening; we all got out then, and walked about on the platform to stretch our legs, and to buy milk and eggs from the cheerful but ill-clad peasants who brought their wares to the stations. At these times the train-boys wandered about on the tracks picking up lumps of coal fallen from the tenders, with which to stoke the fire at the end of the coach which provided the heating; sometimes, for lack of anything better to do, I used to help them in this occupation, and gradually they became a little less sour, and turned a blind eye on the Primus—also I learned where they kept their stocks of coal and kindling, which was to come in handy later on. But the general Russian hostility to us as English-people remained marked. We were a diplomatic party, and should all have been together; but the Dutch were put in the next coach, and three Germans were installed in ours—in fact they were quite inoffensive, and I often talked to them; Harry Blake-Tyler objected strongly to that!—he accused me of fraternising with the enemy. They were civil engineers, going to China to a job; they told me they found it hard to get jobs at present—"since we can no longer be employed in the Empire." Puzzled, I asked what Empire?—they were all young-ish men, and Germany had lost all her overseas possessions more times our train drew up in a siding to let them pass; more often, as there?" they said laughing.

On that journey across Siberia we got pretty good confirmation of what Nüssbaumer had told me in Moscow. Day after day, waking early, as I usually did, I saw west-bound trains full of troops; some-times our train drew up in a siding to let them pass, more often, as we steamed slowly eastwards, the troop-train was in a siding, and in the early light we could see the soldiers washing their feet in the half-frozen ditches. How the authorities contrived that these en-counters should always take place at day-break I don't know, but we never saw them at any other time; Owen suggested that we were meant to pass the troop-trains at night, and that the arrangements, like so many Russian arrangements, had gone slightly wrong.

As we approached Lake Baikal the monotonous flatness of the great plain broke up into rolling country, with deep valleys full of white-stemmed poplars just coming into leaf, the young foliage as bright as new pennies in the sun, a lovely sight. And Baikal itself was very splendid—an incredibly vast expanse of inland water, stretching away out of sight. We rejoiced at the new beauty of the scenery, and at the fact that we were about to leave Russia; every hour brought us nearer to the Manchurian frontier, though oddly enough as we got further East it became colder again. It was strange how acutely every member of the party, various as were our ages, sexes, and backgrounds, looked forward to getting out of Rus-sia.

However, we rejoiced too soon. At Otpor, the last station before the actual frontier, we ran into trouble. A sinister-looking police official came onto the train, examined our passports, and then, through the Intourist interpreter, informed the unfortunate Owen that as our passports had no Manchurian visas we could not go any further until he received fresh instructions. In vain Owen pointed out that we had correct Japanese visas (Manchuria was then in Japanese hands), that the Russian Foreign Office had itself arranged

our papers and assured the Embassy that no difficulty could arise—
no, we must stay at Otpor. Could he telephone to Moscow, or to our
Consulate-General at Harbin, in Manchuria? No. Was there an hotel
in Otpor? No. Was there a station restaurant? No—and in any case
we should not be permitted to leave the train. All Owen was allowed to do was to send a telegram—*in Russian*—to Sir Stafford
Cripps telling him of our plight, which cost 3,000 roubles; it was
never delivered. To the question of whether the heating would be
kept on in the coaches the answer was another no—with the grinning remark: "You would be colder in an air-raid shelter in
London!" The restaurant-car was then detached, the train-boys went
round locking all the pillows and blankets into the upper bunks,
leaving the two-berth sleepers as mere seats, the Germans were
taken out and put into the next coach, where the Dutch were; the
doors were locked, and we were left to our own devices for the
night.

Our situation was really very disagreeable indeed. Mercifully we
had had dinner, so we were not hungry yet, but it was obviously
going to get very cold—we could see the frost-crystals glittering on
the snow outside, and hear the icy crunch of the two sentries' boots,
as they marched up and down with fixed bayonets. Poor Owen—a
whole party on his hands, including two invalids, Kate and Blake-
Tyler, and all at the mercy of Russian ill-will. We all put on our
overcoats, and disposed ourselves to sleep in a very gloomy frame of
mind.

I did not lie down—as so often, I lit a cigarette and did some
thinking. After nearly an hour, I peeped cautiously out of the corridor window and saw, as I hoped, that all the lights in the station
buildings were out; only the arc-lamps above the platform showed
the sentries tramping up and down outside. I got a torch and went
and turned off the lights in the corridor; no reaction from the sentries, so I pulled down all the blinds. Unluckily there was no blind
on the window of the train door giving onto the platform, which
was precisely where I wanted to be screened from Russian eyes, for
the stove which heated the coach was just inside it. Never mind—on
all fours I crept to the stove, found the handle and opened the door;
a splendid heap of red embers still glowed inside. I knew where the
boys kept the coal and the kindling-wood, in bunkers on either side
of the passage into the next coach; still on all fours I fetched a heap

of kindling and threw it onto the glowing embers, and then put lumps of coal on top, a little at a time. There was, I knew, a handle up on the wall which controlled a sort of register to increase the draught; cautiously straightening up, I found it with my torch, and pulled it out a little way—a reassuring roar from the stove showed that it was working. I waited, putting on coal at intervals, till the stove was three-parts full and burning splendidly; then I reduced the draught and went back to my sleeper.

But I dared not lie down, for fear I should go to sleep. I got the whisky out of the pigskin bag—there was still a little left—opened a bottle of soda-water, and sat, reading a book and sipping whisky at intervals, all night. Every hour I went along the corridor, now pleasantly warm, stoked the stove and went back to my book.

About four in the morning, when I had just finished another bout of re-fuelling, Owen appeared, and asked what I was up to. "It seems quite warm," he observed in surprise.

"Yes, I know—I've kept the fire going."

"Let me see."

"Well, kneel down," I told him, and opened the stove door. Grunting approval, my husband went back to his sleeper, fetched the despatches he was taking to the Tokyo Embassy, and burnt them— which on the whole I think was a wise precaution. We had no means of knowing to what lengths Russian malevolence might go in this remote spot. Then he asked if I had written any letters during our eight-day journey. Of course I had—heaps; there was little else to do. "Are they indiscreet?" he asked.

"About Russia? What do *you* think?"

"Hand them over," he said inexorably. So all my lively descriptions of Russia were committed to the flames.

Between five and six, when day was beginning to break, I thought morning tea would be a good idea, but the Primus was in Owen's compartment, and I didn't want to disturb him, so I investigated the train-boys' samovar, at the end of the coach opposite the stove. It had gone out. I knew where they kept the charcoal which was its main fuel, but what I could not find were the long thin spills, like straws, which they use as kindling. However we had masses of boxes of chocolates still left over from the farewell gifts in Budapest; some were half-empty, so I quite emptied one, and with my nail-scissors cut it into long narrow strips—these, with tissue-paper underneath, did the job perfectly. I added charcoal, little by little, filled the brass container with several jugfuls of water from my basin, and presently had the satisfaction of hearing it bubbling inside. I found the boys' stock of tea and sugar too; the tea I put into the appropriate hole in the container, and some sugar in a glass—when I turned the tap and filled my tumbler I was quite pleased with the brew. While I was sipping it Johnnie Reed appeared, looking rather haggard—I gave him a glass of tea.

"Mrs. Min" (the staff in B.P. always called me that), "how long do you think it will be before we get out of this jam?" he asked rather anxiously. I told him I had no idea, but that once we *had* got out, it was something we should be very glad to have gone through, for we should be able to dine out on it for the rest of our lives! Then I told him to go along the coach and find out if anyone else was awake and would like tea. While he was doing this I thought that if many of the party wanted tea there would not be enough tumblers, so I went through into the next coach and began taking down clean glasses out of the rack by the samovar there—while so occupied I was accosted by one of my German engineering friends, who like Owen asked what I was doing.

Getting glasses for tea, I told him, and invited him to come over and have some—he refused, because the Russians had forbidden them to leave their coach, he said. "Is it not terribly cold?" was his next question.

Not in our coach, I said; it was lovely and warm—come and try it. He came as far as the middle of the concertina-like passage, and stretched out his hands, which were in fact blue with cold, yearningly towards the warmth. "They keep up the *Heizung* for you?" he asked in surprise.

"No, and they said we weren't to—but we kept it going ourselves, just the same."

He stepped back, alarmed. "They may shoot you for this!" he exclaimed.

"Then we shall die warm!" I told him, laughing. It was at that point, I think, that I decided that Germany was going to lose the war.

Most of our party came and had tea, and biscuits out of the lunchcase, and I took some across to the Dutch. However our trials were nearly over. Between seven and eight the Russian officials came onto the train again, returned our passports, which they had impounded, and said that we should be going on into Manchuria almost at once. Our big luggage, which had been in the van, was piled into the two coaches, higgledy-piggledy—every single piece had had five or six figures 1½ inches high scrawled on it in indelible black paint, a last touch of spite; then an engine was attached, and we steamed on into Manchuria. At Mandchouli, the first station beyond the border, we had to change trains, and all bundled out; Owen and I, with a strong sense of home-coming and pleasure, found ourselves once again among the cheerful, smiling, helpful Northern Chinese—their raucous accents were music in our ears, their wrinkled faces beautiful to us, after what my husband has so rightly described as "the dirty crazy barbarism of Russia". We were met by a young and inexperienced Vice-Consul from Harbin, and greatly relieved he was to see us at last; he had expected us to arrive the evening before, and could learn nothing as to the reason for the delay. In fact no explanation for this very peculiar treatment of a party of inoffensive diplomats was ever forthcoming.

By now we were all pretty hungry; the young Vice-Consul had laid on an open horse-cab, and our two invalids, Kate and Harry Blake-Tyler, were put into it, along with his wife and myself, as an advance party to go to the hotel and organise breakfast. Cheerfully we jogged through the untidy, tumble-down, sunny streets, rejoicing at being out of Russia, and in the free world again. At the hotel, once more all was pleasantness: with millennial politeness, smiling, bowing and kow-towing, the manager, his wife, and his staff made us welcome and—in Chinese—asked our pleasure. Now if you had asked me only twenty-five minutes earlier if I could still speak any Chinese, I should probably have said no; but the sight of those familiar faces, the sound of those nasal voices, in some strange way brought back part, at least, of my always rather moderate stock of "Peking Colloquial"—I told the bowing manager that first we wanted *K'ai Shui* (hot water). When we had been led up to a nice clean bedroom and bathroom, and had had a good wash, we went down to a dining-room where a huge table was set ready for forty people with bread and butter; a strong delicious smell proclaimed coffee in the background, and to the manager's enquiry as to what we wished to eat I was able to ask unhesitatingly "Jee-Zerh yo mayo?" (Eggs got-not-got?) When he replied with a thundering

"Yo!" (got) and asked how many we should want—"Ikö jen san-kö" (one man three piece), I told him. And soon we were all sitting down to a splendid meal of eggs, bread-and-butter, and excellent coffee.

Our train journey onwards formed the greatest possible contrast to our last week of travel. Being Japanese-run, the coaches and dining-car were all spotlessly clean, the food good and neatly served; and the country that we saw from the windows was full of all manner of different enchantments. The north-western part of Manchuria is mountainous, and strewn with lakes; owing to the broken terrain one often met the same lake, so to speak, over and over again—seeing it and losing it, seeing it and losing it. But at that moment of the year the wild geese were coming in, and onto a lake that one saw at first, in the distance, as a curved scimitar of blue brilliant as enamel, the great birds came skeining down like brown rain, more and more at successive glimpses, till at one's last sight something like half the blue scimitar had become greyish brown. Further on, on the bare golden uplands, small China ponies, like those we had ridden in Peking fifteen years before, ran in vast flocks, like parti-coloured sheep, tended by herdsmen on horse-back; the dark conical shapes of their yurts, the felt tents which were their only habitations, stood out in vivid groups, almost black—and all this against a background of blue mountains, flecked with the last snow; painted mountains, almost unreal, like the back-drop on some enormous stage. When the train stopped at a local station, some of the herdsmen would board it and sit down in the dining-car for a meal or glasses of tea; they were a remarkable sight, dressed in magnificent quilted robes of brocaded silk in dull pinks or greens or blues, but in every case *filthy*, with huge clasps and buckles of silver set with corals and turquoises—a strange get-up for horse-masters, to our Western eyes. After two or three stops they would get off again, mount more small ponies, and clatter away into the distance —leaving the O'Malleys thinking how unbelievably lucky they were to be seeing such unimaginable beings with their own eyes, in this unimaginable country.

Harbin, where we spent a couple of nights, seemed a dull, rather featureless modern town; but at least it had such conveniences as hairdressers, and we all badly needed a shampoo, after the protracted filth of the Russian train—Kate and Rosemary also wanted "facials", and insisted on my having one too. These treatments were administered to us by beautiful fair-haired girls with soft voices, fine features, and slim delicate wrists, who attended to us with the utmost gentle courtesy; we were astonished—and aghast—to learn from the Consul-General that they were White Russians, whose parents had fled before the Revolution and had been cast up, like jetsam, on this rather dreary shore, to earn a living as best they might. Another train took us to Dairen, where we boarded a small Japanese steamer for Kobe. On this boat, once again we ran into trouble with insolent or ignorant officialdom, Japanese this time; in fact I think it must have been deliberate insolence, for the ship's company knew quite well who Owen and I, at least, were, and had given us the two main double staterooms on the boat, roomy and charmingly furnished. However, two Customs officials, who came on board, demanded to examine our luggage. Owen—like the recent U.N. Mission to Aden, and with better reason—protested, pointing out that we had not only diplomatic passports but *laissez-passers* as well, stamped by the Japanese Embassy in Moscow. With an outward show of politeness, bowing, grinning, and hissing, the Japanese nevertheless were very insistent—they absolutely must open our luggage. This rather angered me—I was in Owen's stateroom too—and I put my oar in, muttering that he really must not give way, or it would be selling the pass for other diplomats in the future. My poor husband, driven beyond endurance, said coldly and politely— "My dear, would you mind leaving us?" I retired to my cabin, rather ashamed of myself, but still furious with the Japanese; for the short trip to Kobe all my luggage had been put in my stateroom, and I now went round and locked every single piece, including my despatch-case, and put my key-ring down the front of my dress. Presently Owen knocked and ushered in the two Japanese —"Now, these two gentlemen would just like to glance at some of your luggage."

"I see. Would you mind leaving us?" I said in my turn; Owen perforce did so. Then, turning to the two officials I said, with effusive regret, that I had had a most distressing misfortune—leaning out of the window, I had accidentally dropped my keys overboard! It was extremely unfortunate, and all my luggage was locked—but what could I do? And I too bowed and smiled. So did they, and hissed too; but there was nothing *they* could do about it, and presently they retreated, discomfited.

When, later, we reported this episode to our Ambassador in Tokyo, he did not seem particularly surprised. The Japanese hatred of Westerners was a pathological thing, he said, and strongest of the English and the Americans; they would preserve the outward forms of courtesy if it suited their book, but if they thought they could get away with offensive behaviour to either nation, they would lose no chance of displaying it. And for good measure he told us some horrible stories of what had happened to English passengers in taxis, at night, on lonely roads. Eight months later, on a Sunday in December, I was to remember this assessment.

The last part of that short sea-trip was enchanting. We passed through the Inland Sea, among little hilly islands tufted with dark pines; in the distance they were exactly of the deep blue of Japanese colour-prints, indeed we seemed to be steaming through Japanese colour-prints—but close at hand, down almost to the water-line, every island was carpeted with wild azaleas of the soft clear pink of apple-blossom, in full bloom.

At Tokyo we were most kindly put up and entertained by Sir Robert and Lady Craigie. The Embassy was very different now from what it had been in 1927; built up, large and splendiferous. The Craigies did everything they could for us, and caused us to do quite a bit ourselves; Owen had to lunch with the Chamber of Commerce, and tell them as much as he thought fit about Russia; I was caused to lecture on Hungary and Spain to various gatherings of women. We enjoyed more being taken to that austere, immense, and noble monument, the Buddha at Kamakura; I think Kipling must have seen it himself, or he could not have written the poem— one almost felt impelled oneself, like his heathen, to pray "to Buddha at Kamakura".

One night they took us to a display of Japanese wrestling, a most peculiar and comical performance. Two huge men, enormously stout, hairless, and naked except for dark trunks, moved ponderously onto a stage, empty except for a small table on which stood a bowl of salt. Very deliberately—all their movements were immensely slow—they first bowed deeply to one another, and then, in turns, took salt from the bowl, and with further bowing sprinkled it towards the four points of the compass. More ceremonious bowings; we began to wonder when something would happen. At last they moved towards one another, and got into a sort of clinch; but after a few moments they parted again, only, with careful steps, to approach once more, and twine their massive golden limbs about one another, making deep grunting sounds. To a Japanese I suppose there were some fine points to be appreciated in this solemn performance, for they were both noted champions, but to us it seemed very dull and highly absurd; but the Craigies had warned us in advance that we must on no account laugh. The following night, however, we were able to laugh our fill, for the Ambassador and his counsellor, Houston-Boswell, repeated the performance themselves in the drawing-room after dinner—it was one of their favourite parlour tricks, and made a very good turn. Houston-Boswell I suppose weighed fourteen stone, while Sir Robert was a small neat man; in their dinner-jackets they went through all the slow elaborate posturings, bowing, sprinkling imaginary salt, grunting, advancing and retreating—it was much funnier than most ambassadorial entertainments.

While we were in Tokyo we heard that Rudolf Hess, in his Messerschmidt, had landed in Scotland and been captured by a Home Guard armed with a hayfork. Everyone was puzzled by this peculiar démarche.

We went on to San Francisco on a Japanese boat, the *Tatsuta Maru*. This crossing of the Pacific, though at about the same time of year, was much more pleasant than the northern route to Vancouver which we had taken in 1927; the air was balmy, the sun shone, we wore summer frocks. We spent nearly forty-eight hours in Honolulu, and were startled by the contrast between the sky-scrapers in the town and the tropical vegetation when we drove up a sort of mountain behind it. We surf-bathed, helped by the beautiful brown-skinned Hawaiian youths and girls, who were as much at home in the water as seals, and as delightful to watch; we skimmed about the approaches to Pearl Harbor in a boat with a glass bottom, through which one was supposed to see the tropical fish; in this we were not very successful. We noticed the neat market-gardens on both sides of the road leading from the town out towards Pearl Harbor itself, and the swarms of Japanese at work in them, the small trucks in which they took their produce to market all tidily parked in lay-bys—it was to be very different on that Sunday morning seven months later.

It was foggy when we steamed into San Francisco, so that we did not see that wonderful approach. Owen had gone to the purser's office to settle his bill, and Kate and I were sitting after breakfast in a large lounge, I finishing my coffee, when suddenly seven or eight men marched in, chanting, "The Press has come aboard!" The Embassy in Washington had sent a special message to Owen in Tokyo, instructing him to tell all his party that they were to "lean over backwards" to be helpful and accommodating to the press when we reached the States, so when one of these worthies came up to Kate and me I told them, apologetically, that they would find my husband in the purser's office—and took another sip.

"Hold it! The Ann Bridge cawfee-cup!" one of the men exclaimed, as a bulb flashed—word of this habit of mine of sipping coffee at all hours had evidently reached San Francisco already.

IX

A Year and a Day in the U.S.A. I

From San Francisco we went down to Hollywood. None of my books had ever been filmed, and in our innocence we thought that talking to film magnates on the spot might help towards this desirable end; we had a friend in the film world, Lily Hatvany from Budapest, who was now working with M-G-M, and anyhow it seemed silly to be so near Hollywood and not see this fabulous place. So we went.

Of course from the point of view of getting a book filmed it was a complete failure—we did everything wrong from the start. We ought never to have gone near the place unless we could have stayed in some rich hotel in Beverly Hills, and hired a car with a chauffeur to drive us to the various producers—I realised that later; as it was, we stayed in a cheap hotel in Hollywood itself, and when I was summoned to see George Cukor or Darryl Zanuck, I went in a taxi. Fatal! But it was very amusing and revealing all the same.

Lily Hatvany was frightfully good to us. She, whom we had known in Budapest in the rather sober setting of the Hatvany Palace, a bit further along the Bastion from the Legation, a vast house full of a truly amazing collection of porcelain, was now settled in a charming little "patio apartment", built round a courtyard with a garden and a fountain, where she gave excellent parties, full of film-stars; she already seemed to know pretty well everyone, and bestirred herself to help, putting me in touch with an agent called George Marton, who made appointments for me to see this film magnate and that—quite a lot of whom were Hungarians too. And she delightedly arranged to spring a surprise on Owen.

When he and Jane were returning from Mexico in 1938 they had crossed the Atlantic in the *Aquitania* with a charming Swedish starlet called Gwilli Andre, and had made friends with her; in fact she made of Owen's actual arrival at Southampton a rather startling scene. Only half an hour before the ship docked he slipped a disk when pulling the luggage about, and was almost crippled with pain; Kate and I, waiting on the quay among the press photographers—all eager for a picture of Our Man in Mexico City—were amazed to see him crawling up the gangway on all fours, followed by a dazzling creature in a shrimp-pink crêpe-de-chine frock and coat to match, the coat with a border of shrimp-pink fox-fur a foot deep round the hem—we fairly goggled at this vision; so did the photographers. But she was a very nice straightforward creature; we saw something of her in London, where she created a fine sensation among the elderly gentlemen at one or two of my little weekly cocktail-parties in West Halkin Street—derisively known among my children and their friends as Old Boys' Days. In Hollywood Kate and I learned from Lily Hatvany that though Gwilli herself was away, she had a small part in a film about to be released—*A Woman's Face*—and without saying anything to Owen, Lily arranged to have this shown to a whole party of us one evening in one of those small theatres where films are tried out. The effect on my husband was all we could have wished—he jumped up, asking where she was, to everyone's delight.

I think it must have been through Lily that I met Charles Laughton—anyhow I did meet him, and he kindly invited me to spend a day with him "on the set", where he was acting a dying millionaire in *It Started with Eve*; Deanna Durbin was the hat-check-girl heroine. I found this whole business quite absorbing. They were doing the scene where, from his bed, the old man sends the girl to a panel in the wall and says "Press it"—hesitating a little, she does so; the panel flies open, revealing a safe; she starts back with a little cry—"Oh!" The director could not get this scene to his satisfaction; they went through it over and over again, at least fifteen times; I was greatly impressed with Deanna Durbin's patience and good temper—and with her simplicity. She had just got engaged for the first time, and whenever they knocked off for a rest and went and sat in armchairs, her dresser always came to take off her high-heeled shoes and put easy slippers on instead, to rest her feet; invariably the girl said, "Where's my brooch?"—and would not be satisfied till the dresser had pinned it on, a diamond sun-burst, a present from her fiancé; at the end of ten minutes the brooch had to be taken off again, since as an impoverished hat-check girl she could not wear it in the film. I thought this charming. By now, mid-June, the weather was very hot, and Laughton, in bed under an eiderdown, sweated profusely; the stage trained-nurse was constantly bringing him fresh hot-water-bottles, which in fact were filled with iced water. He was supposed to be a truculent patient, gruff with his doctor, and very disobedient; he was constantly lighting a cigar, which was forbidden; his old friend the Bishop at one point took this from his mouth, and went through a door, from which then came the sound of a lavatory flushing. Laughton told me later, gleefully, that this episode, the noise of flushing "off", had been deleted on the orders of the Hayes Committee, which acted as a Censor Morum for all films, as too indelicate!

We had lunch in Laughton's little apartment "on the lot"; it was really a small house with a bedroom, sitting- and dining-rooms, kitchen, etc.—his Negro cook gave us an excellent lunch. But before that he sat in a sort of dentist's chair in his dressing-room, while his English man-servant, with spirit, took off the rubber pouches under his eyes and jaws which in the film made him such a convincing old man; he invited me to watch this performance, and I accepted eagerly—I could not see too much of Hollywood behind the scenes. Over lunch Laughton talked freely and even eagerly about his work, which obviously absorbed him. He said he found making films infinitely more satisfying than acting on the stage, because with the microphone one could use one's voice so much more realistically, without the need to project it to carry to the back of the house. "In this film I can speak practically in a whisper when I am supposed to be having a bad turn, and everyone can hear me," he said—and later, in the afternoon, I heard him doing just that.

Altogether he was a most gentle, civilised being, and charmed me completely. But the great surprise was to find him an ardent botanist, with an exhaustive knowledge of the local flora, especially the cactuses; he could tell one exactly where to find a given plant. "About one hundred and fifteen yards beyond milestone 129 on Route 25, going east," he would say, "you will see a small turning on the right, just a sandy track; go down it for two hundred and fifty yards, and at the foot of a small rocky mound you will find"— whatever it was. And, invariably, I did find it. I was not greatly interested in cactuses, but I was struck dumb by the rest of the flora of Southern California, which, in early summer, with the delicious climate, turn the place into the Earthly Paradise. I remember a rocky glen up behind Alexander Korda's house, whose steep sides were clothed with the enormous white flowers of *Romneya coulteri,* the Giant Poppy; the air on the Kordas' balcony was heavy with its scent. There were the small wild lupins, orange and purple, and delicate lily-like plants—Laughton told me the name of the best wild-flower book, and I went and bought a copy; in the book-shop I met John van Druten, whom I already knew, and he asked me out to his date-farm on the Palm to Pines Highway. As luck would have it Charles Mendl was by now settled in his wife's great luxurious house in Beverly Hills; he had his own car and chauffeur, and as he was going to New York for ten days he lent me both for that period. We so often seem to have had a use for Charles Mendl's car! Kate and Owen had by this time gone on to Washington, so I could do exactly as I pleased—drive down to see my Day cousins at Laguna Beach, drive over to spend the day with van Druten, drive everywhere in pursuit of flowers.

Lady Mendl loved entertaining, especially film personalities, and could of course afford to do it on a scale which I found rather alarming. She was kind enough to invite me to a dinner-party one night to which eighty people came, including Charles Chaplin; it was given in a restaurant whose ceiling was covered with quilted beige satin to lessen the *bruit de voix,* and we drank Lanson '28 champagne throughout the meal.

But there was a lot that I found alarming about Hollywood besides Elsie Mendl's entertaining, and the longer I stayed—I was there five weeks altogether—the more frightened I became. The whole set-up seemed to have something fundamentally crazy about it; artificiality pushed, really, over the borders of sanity. The very jobs I was offered seemed to me quite mad. Jesse Lasky, who had bought the film rights of *Peking Picnic* for £1,000 nine years before, but had never done anything with them, offered me a very handsome sum to write the film script for him; he seemed quite astonished when I pointed out that I only knew how to write novels, and couldn't possibly do a film script. Another film company, M-G-M or Twentieth-Century-Fox, were doing a film about the flight from Paris in 1940; there was to be an English girl in it, who fled with a Frenchman, and they were ready to pay me $1,000 a week, for six months, to do the English girl's part of the dialogue. I asked who would do the man's part—it seemed to me important to know whom I should be working with. Oh, that hadn't been settled yet—but they were eager to book me there and then, for this fantastic sum, to start work at once: on half a dialogue, with the other half still in the air. And besides the craziness, I vaguely sensed the inhumanity underlying the whole film business, which Evelyn Waugh brought out so clearly in *The Loved One*.

There was one other aspect of life in Hollywood which was disconcerting—the exaggerated attitude of the ex-patriate British, again perfectly caught by Waugh. One Sunday I was taken to church to hear Nelson Eddy sing "There'll Always be an England" —which he did very well; but then it was repeated by choir and orchestra; and finally sung, *kneeling*, by the whole congregation.

Hollywood was full of Europeans, besides the expatriate English, and really I felt rather more at home with them. In Charles's car I was able to drive out to Santa Monica to look up Thomas Mann, with whom I had made friends in Arosa four or five years earlier; like so many writers I have known, including Sinclair Lewis, he always wanted to *talk* in the evenings—too tired to write, his eyes too weary to read, someone to talk to was an imperative need. I used to ski along to his hotel after supper, and we would chatter and argue for an hour and a half, all Frau Mann would allow him, in German and English: if he found something too difficult for him to express in English he would say it in German, which I could understand; if I found something which I could not express in German I would say it in English, and he would understand—we got along splendidly. We had tremendous arguments about prose—he didn't altogether share my admiration for Proust, and was very indignant when I taxed him with using long, complicated sentences—"*Ich, verwickelte Sätze?* You do not mean like Henry James?" Yes I did— quite as bad. He liked to come to the tea-dances in the hotel and watch all the young people circling round after skiing; he could not take his eyes off Kate—"Die reine gothische Linie! Die wahre gothische Linie!" he would exclaim rapturously; I never knew if it was her profile, or her slim figure in the little black ski-suit, which afforded the pure, the true gothic line. He amused me about Auden. He was planning an article on young English writers who might be setting a trend, and asked me for names; when I suggested Auden he roared with laughter. "Ach, der Auden! Der ist bloss ein netter, typischer Englischer Bursch!" (Auden is just a nice, typical English lad!) But in California I found the old man a good deal aged, and felt that he was less at ease than in his beloved Switzerland.

Someone who seemed perfectly at ease, however, in Hollywood was Erich Maria Remarque. He had a villa with a pleasant garden and a swimming-pool on Hilts Avenue, and there were some nice things in the house, too. I was glad to meet him, not only on account of my enormous admiration for *All Quiet on the Western Front*, but because of what he had done for the expatriate Germans before and during the early part of the war. He had then had a villa on one of the Italian lakes, Lugano, I think, only it was actually in Switzerland, and therefore a safe neutral hide-out—the town close by was full of German-Jewish refugees, mostly artists or musicians or writers. I had heard all about this aspect of Remarque's life from Ike Mohrenwitz, my continental literary agent, who had had to leave his pleasant flat in Frankfurt-am-Main, his lucrative job and cheerful musical circle, and flee to Switzerland, like so many others; I eventually managed to get him to England, where he stayed for some time, and gave me a vivid picture of Remarque's generosity. This group of exiles were all deadly poor; a cup of coffee or a glass of wine was a thing they could only afford once or twice a week; six or seven of them would form a group and take it in turns to stand the coffee all round, "to preserve the illusion of hospitality", as poor Ike said. But in Remarque's beautiful villa, full of fine pictures and glorious rugs, hospitality was no illusion. Once a week, at least, he had them up to dine, when they could enjoy a proper meal, with excellent food and wine; and at least twice a week they were asked to spend the evening with him, when coffee and cognac flowed, and conversation too—the musicians were invited to play, the poets to recite. Mohrenwitz had made clear to me what an oasis of pleasure these evenings, in ultra-civilised surroundings, were to the poverty-stricken group of exiles. And when I met Remarque and talked of Ike he spoke so nicely about him, wanted to know how he was getting on in England, and said how much he regretted that in the end he himself had felt it wiser to close the villa and go to America.

As my mother was an American, and one of a large family, I had relations scattered more or less all over the United States, and I wanted to take the opportunity to visit as many of them as I could, and above all to see the places which had formed the background of my mother's childhood and youth—to her, as to me, places had always meant at least as much as people; but since she and I were both seventh children, naturally no one was left but those of the second or even third generations. I made first for New Orleans, her birthplace; but since my route led practically past the Grand Canyon, I stopped over there for a night. I found it most beautiful, especially at sunset and dawn, when the gigantic cliffs were of an even deeper red than by full daylight, and the vast chasm between filled with blue shadow. The hotel arranged a bus-drive out into the desert, which I loved: I kept stopping the bus to pick quite a new set of wild-flowers, and on the return trip got out a couple of miles short of the hotel to walk home, so that I might find still more; my fellow-passengers, though puzzled by this eccentricity, were surprisingly good-tempered about these delays, which might well have enraged them.

In New Orleans I was put up by some Glenny cousins, who were endlessly good to me—most of them had stayed with us in England when I was a girl. Cousin Emma Glenny was a very good person to introduce a stranger to New Orleans; in her youth Morgan Whitney had been a great admirer of hers, and when he died he left her all his albums full of the superb photographs he had taken of the wrought-iron work—doors, gates, balconies—which are a unique feature of the beautiful city; escorted by Cousin Emma I was allowed to see even inside features, not visible from the street. And Lucius, her brother, drove me to the old market in the early mornings, to see the Acadians, that strange ethnological group, descendants of the French-Canadian founders of the place, bringing in their produce in horse-carts, the women still wearing their pretty traditional costume of print dresses and shady cotton sun-bonnets; or he took me out to see the places where my mother had gone riding with my father when they got engaged, seventy years before. A girl called Hazel MacKinley had furnished me with introductions to various artists and people with collections of pictures; one lot of these actually lived in Pontalba Buildings, the great square of brick-built Spanish baroque—here too I was able to get inside.

Of course I had to lecture, to the Red Cross and so on; naturally, in my mother's home town I asked for no fees—to the great subsequent annoyance of Colston Leigh, the lecture agent, when he came to plan tours for me—and I had to give one or two press interviews. This led to my first experience of the idiosyncrasies of American taxi-drivers. In New Orleans in 1941 there was a special cheap rate for a fare inside the city limits, provided one drove straight from point to point. One day I was going out to lunch with Dorothy Spencer, telephoned for a cab, and gave her address; there was a post-office right on the avenue, and when we came to it I asked the man to stop while I posted a letter. As I got in again he said— "That'll mean the full rate, y'know." I fairly exploded. "Well for God's sake! Do you mean to tell me you want to ask double the fare because you pulled up just to post a letter? I never heard" . . . and so on and so on, at some length. He slowed down. "Hey, you're British, ain't you?" He turned and took a good look at me. "You that British writer that got out of some place in Europe?" I told him yes, and that at no place in Europe would a taxi-driver behave so. He drove on then, chuckling a little; we had a long conversation about conditions in England, about which he couldn't hear enough, and when we reached my destination he refused to take any fare at all!

I loved New Orleans, as any civilised person must, I think; I even loved the heat. The cousins took me out to some lovely plantation houses, such as my mother had described to me; the most beautiful of all was Oak Allee, with its deep arched verandahs round all three storeys, and the marvellous avenue of huge live-oaks, nearly a quarter of a mile long, but only eight trees to a side. So flat, so green, somehow so gently calm, almost sleepy, the Louisiana countryside—the greatest possible contrast to the dazzle and hurly-burly of Hollywood.

After a few weeks I went on to Washington, where Owen was doing some temporary job in the Embassy; he and Kate were staying in a rather dreary hotel, but the sinuses had been put right at Johns Hopkins, thank goodness. We settled that I should try to get some lecturing arranged and if successful that I should stay on in the States and maintain myself, since Owen was now practically on the dole. So I pushed on to New York. My kind relations had got me elected as an honorary member of some women's organisation, which meant that one could stay in certain specified hotels at practically half-price—a great help.

I hated New York. For one thing the height of the sky-scrapers gave me a sort of phobia, a funny ailment for a mountaineer. I was so terrified that I would throw myself out of the windows in my sleep that I used to pile the furniture against them every night. Then I hated having to telephone for everything—I was accustomed to ringing a bell and asking for what I wanted. And morning tea, on which I was very dependent, was of course undrinkable when the tea-bags, horrible things anyhow, were only put in *after* the teapot had been carried along the corridor.

I didn't really like Colston Leigh, the lecture agent, very much either. Matson, my literary agent, said he was the best, and as Leigh acted for Mrs. Roosevelt, no doubt he was right. There is a lot of rubbish talked and believed in England about lecturing in the States; unless one is someone tremendously important, it is by no means the gold-mine that people suppose, and it is very hard work indeed. Leigh's terms were that he made the engagements, paid the railway fares, and took 50 per cent of the fees; this left you to pay for your own taxis and hotels out of your share. He made it clear that he could not do very well for me because he had not had long enough notice; the whole autumn and winter programme had been arranged six months earlier, and all I could do was to fill in gaps— anyhow I had spoilt the market by giving those free lectures in New Orleans. In the upshot, over some nine months I just about broke even.

From New York I went up to Boston and stayed with Ellery Sedgwick and his delightful English wife—Owen and Kate came up too, and when Owen went back to his job in Washington Marjorie Sedgwick first arranged for us to take a flat in Ipswich, Massachusetts. That was a fascinating experience. The flat was on the first floor of a wooden house with the date 1614 over the door, and the rooms were large and shapely; it had all mod. con. as well, and Ipswich was a charming small town, with one of those beautiful New England churches of white painted wood, huge elms drooping over it, and a graceful spire. Across the river were some brick-built factories dating from the very early nineteenth century, and quite beautifully proportioned; they were still in use, with a labour-force consisting largely of Greeks and Poles. Ipswich was not very far from the sea, and there was a lovely walk down to Little Neck, where the clams come from, but I was rather aghast to see baskets of these delicacies waiting on the quay-side in a broiling sun, opening and oozing; I felt they would soon die and then become lethal.

Ipswich had a strong English flavour, too. Charles and Julia Bird lived in a large house in a park full of horses, and he hunted with the Myopia Club; on Sunday mornings there was beagling around about, with hunt servants in green coats and white breeches—all very homelike, except for the unfamiliar hazard of poison-ivy, *Rhus toxicodendron*, as one ran through the undergrowth; I got badly stung on my legs before I learned about this. People were very kind to us—not only the Birds, but the Wolcotts, the Raymond Everetts, and Isadore Smith, in whose pretty house above the saltings we spent many happy days and delightful evenings, always in excellent company.

At one point Kate scalded her foot, and had to go into hospital. This made the flat in Ipswich too remote; some kind person, probably the ever-helpful Marjorie Sedgwick, arranged for us to borrow the Langdon Warners' house in Cambridge, Massachusetts, and we settled in there. That was another very beautiful house, also wood-built, in a huge garden; we moved a bed downstairs for Kate, to avoid going up and down, and by day she would lie on a *chaise longue* on the deep verandah, looking out across the lawn to the huge plane-tree that stood in the middle of it. It was a very tranquil, happy time. When her foot was quite recovered she and Owen went down to Baltimore and flew back to Shannon, and so home. By then Colston Leigh had come up with a programme of lectures, spaced rather far apart, it was true, but lasting right into the following spring; I had become so attached to Boston and Cambridge that I was delighted to be allowed to stay on at 63 Garden Street—now in a big sitting-room on the top floor, with a small bedroom opening out of it, and the use of a bathroom across the landing; I shared this with Germaine, Loraine Warner's French niece, and another lodger. This became my base for the rest of my stay in America, and very pleasant it was.

It was an ultra-cultivated household. Beloved Langdon Warner—

on whom be peace—was in charge of the Oriental section of the Fogg Museum in Cambridge; his wife, born a Roosevelt (but she could not endure her cousin F.D.R.), was a fine musician, and conducted a small orchestra; her daughter Margaret played the cello (or was it the violin?) and Germaine was training for a professional singer. The house resounded with music from morning till night, and well into the night: the scraping of Margaret's strings, the repetitive bangings of the orchestra, Germaine's head-notes coming through my bedroom wall—luckily I can ignore noise, for when not lecturing I was hard at work finishing *Frontier Passage*. And of course I spent a lot of time, most enjoyably, seeing people—I managed to get a telephone installed in my bedroom in no time at all, so that my calls were no bother to the Warners.

One of the most interesting groups, to me, was the students, for the light they threw, all unwittingly, on American education. There were two links with these: Patches Damon, Kate's school-friend, and Kevin Andrews, whose educational story was particularly illuminating. His mother, Roy Chapman Andrews' wife, had been one of our dearest friends in Peking; when her marriage broke up she brought Kevin to England, and he went to school at Ripley Court, only a mile or so from Bridge End; from there he got a scholarship to Stowe—he was a gifted child. In 1938, when war threatened at the time of Munich, she took him back to the States and sent him to Exeter, one of the big American equivalents of our public schools. It so happened that I gave a lecture at Exeter, and dined with the Headmaster; I enquired about Kevin, and learned that he had just gone up to Harvard. But the Headmaster was rather funny about him. To find out what form to put him into, the boy, then aged fifteen, was given various examination papers appropriate to various stages—he sailed through them all; at last, in despair, the school gave him the current entrance examination for Harvard—he sailed through that too! So, to use the Headmaster's own expression, he simply "kicked his heels" at Exeter till it was time for him to go up to Harvard.

There I made contact with him; he used to come round to Garden Street in the evenings, and play his recorder: in a house anyhow so full of sound this bothered no one. Presently he began to bring his friends, and they in turn brought theirs, till I had quite an acquaintanceship among the Harvard undergraduates; by no means all first-year students. Those who were "majoring", as they called it, in English Literature occasionally consulted me, as a writer, about their essays. These sometimes left me practically gasping. I remember one delightful creature in his fourth year, who was doing a thesis on Kipling for his final school, and asked me to read it; I did so. It was the sort of thing that Patrick at Radley, or Jane at Hawnes, and their contemporaries would have produced at about the age of sixteen; I made a few quite minor suggestions—it would have been unfair to do more—but he wrote to me later in England that it had earned him a *magna cum laude*.

Of course the really magical thing to see in New England is the "fall colours"—they are unbelievable. I got a first glimpse of them when I went up to stay with some old cousins who had a house by the sea near Cape Neddick in Maine—mostly rather low shrubs of an extraordinary shade of carmine. But everyone told me that to see them properly one should go at least one hundred miles from the sea and one thousand feet up. I did not see how I was to manage this, but Fate dropped the opportunity into my lap. One morning at Garden Street some friends of the Warners' came in bringing a most beautiful little boy of three or four—when I asked about him they referred to him as Machado. I said the only person I had ever known of that name was a boy called Minton Machado Warren, whose father had been a professor at Harvard—I had met him in Switzerland as a girl. "Why, this little boy is Minty's second cousin!" they said. I remembered Minton as a very intelligent but exceedingly ugly little boy of about sixteen; he was undersized, and his parents, on Professor Osler's advice, had brought him to Europe for a year: he was to do no lessons, but to take a lot of exercise, in the hopes that he would grow. My sister Cora contributed to the exercise part by taking him, with me, for a lot of splendid mountaineering expeditions, some of them quite long—he had the makings of a first-rate climber, and was as sure-footed as a goat on really dangerous things like steep grass; we had a marvellous time. He and I corresponded for two or three years, but then that faded out. Now I asked if he had in fact grown. No, they said laughing, not upwards! —he was still the same short little Minty, and still mad on mountaineering; he was married to a terribly nice girl. They let him know that I was in Cambridge, and presently he rang up from New York to say that he would be having a long week-end off for some public holiday in October, and would I like to come up with him to the White Mountains and climb Mount Chocorua?—he had his own house there, and there was a guest-house where I could stay.

So I went. And I was perfectly right to do so. Minton's people had owned their house under Mt. Chocorua for ages, and he had spent most of his childhood and boyhood there; he knew every nook and cranny of the district, and could show me the place on the river where the beavers used to build their dams, and the cliffs where the falcons nested. We went up Chocorua in record time the first day, and afterwards drove about. He took me to call on George Washington Brown, a famous local character, whose great-grandmother had been a full-blooded Indian; old George had a lot of the Indian knowledge and skills; he made the best axe-handles in three states from ash he cut himself, bred marvellous hounds, as they were called—really a sort of pointer—and had spells to charm away rats and hornets, and even to bring clouds over the moon. He was a most beautiful figure, with long grey hair and a fine, intelligent face, and full of a natural dignity and courtesy that completely charmed me, as they did everyone. George Brown was extensively written up in folk-lore magazines after he died, only three or four years after I met him.

As to the autumn colours high up in the White Mountains, I find it impossible to describe them in a way that will be credible to those who have not seen them. Their intensity has a positively explosive quality. Rounding the shoulder of a hill, one comes on an isolated maple standing on a grey slope—it is like a gigantic bunch of daffodils; further on a group of oaks is exactly the shade of a bouquet of dark-red roses; lower down, deep in the woods, one moves in a world completely golden—a golden floor below, a golden canopy above, vistas of gold ahead, to right, to left. There can be nothing else in the world the least like it—and all seen through brilliantly clear, cold air, lit by brilliant sunshine. I was very grateful to Minton Warren.

X

A Year and a Day in the U.S.A. II

One of the pleasant features of diplomacy in the old days, say thirty years ago, was that even internationally the whole thing was on such a small scale that pretty well everyone came to know everyone else; the grapevine spread right round the globe, and diplomats were always more or less *au courant* with one another's movements. You might go to the ends of the earth, as we had gone to China in the 1920s, and make friends in the corps there; if you fetched up in the States fifteen years later you would certainly re-encounter some of those friends. It happened so to us. Of course our flight from Budapest was soon known to our former colleagues from Peking, and then the fact that we were in America—and, most kindly, they sought us out and made contact again.

The two who afforded me the best times in the States were Ferdy and Katie Meyer. When we were all in Peking he had been Counsellor at the American Legation; afterwards he went on to Japan for some considerable time; finally he became Minister in Haiti, and then retired. They lived in a charming house in Vermont, near the Green Mountains, in perfect comfort, beautifully looked after by three French-speaking Haitian maids whom they had brought back with them from the Caribbean—pale coffee-coloured, those maids were, with slender wrists and ankles, and exquisite manners. With the Meyers I could get a taste of country life, long walks and finding wild-flowers, and I often went up to them for the week-end; also with them I felt much more safe and at ease than was sometimes the case—they were old friends, staunchly pro-British, and eager for America to come into the war—they were sensibly, not hypersensitively, anxious to do all they could to ease and smooth Anglo-American relations.

With this end in view, they asked to dinner one night a gentleman who was on the Committee which diligently and generously shipped sporting rifles to England to arm the Home Guard. The whole American nation had been shocked to the heart to learn that when Hess stepped out of his Messerschmidt in Scotland in May and gave himself up, the Home Guard to whom he addressed himself was armed with nothing more lethal than a pitch-fork—and to Bundles for Britain were promptly added Arms for Civil Defence. But now trouble had arisen. The Committee had despatched as a gift to Hess's captor some quite superlative sort of rifle—it wasn't actually of solid gold with a diamond trigger, but it was the equivalent. They had expected to receive rapturous pleasure and gratitude, and an account of the presentation, practically accompanied by the town band—instead, a polite note of thanks from the London end, and then—silence. Ferdy and Katie told me that this had created a very painful impression, and I really must do something about it.

After listening sympathetically to the wounded Committee-man, I got the address of the person in London who distributed the arms, and promised to write to enquire. When I had got the rather embarrassed reply I telephoned to Ferdy, and arranged to go up again and give the explanation—it would be all right, I assured him. It was. I explained to the kind but injured gentleman that the farm-hand who had taken Hess prisoner was a Scot; no one could hold a sporting rifle without a licence, and a licence cost twenty shillings a year—the farm-hand was no sportsman, and had flatly refused to accept this ruinously expensive gift; I managed to make the man see that this was really rather funny. I heard later from Ferdy that his Committee had seen the joke too—so that particular menace to Anglo-American relations, that prop to isolationism, had been disposed of.

In fact America was about to be pushed into the war, whether she liked it or not. I had promised to spend the first week-end of December with the Meyers, but at the station it was Katie who met me with the car. Ferdy was terribly sorry, she said, but he had suddenly been summoned to Washington—the State Department had called him and said he was wanted to help in the talks with two important Japanese who had suddenly turned up to discuss affairs in the Pacific; he knew the Japanese so well that his presence would be useful. So he had had to go—it was too bad.

It was—much too bad. This was the last neat piece of pulling wool over American eyes that the Japanese had thought of, to cover their impending move. Next day Katie and I were sitting at luncheon when the telephone rang—a neighbour called "Put on your radio! The Japs are bombing Pearl Harbor!" We did so, and for the next four or five hours listened, incredulous, to that terrifying story of surprise, confusion, and destruction. To me the confusion was almost the most frightening part. At one point the radio was switched on to the Press Room at the White House, and various newsmen came to the microphone—they were incoherent with rage and distress, and the background noise was like the howling of wolves.

Later I was able, from various sources, to piece together rather more of the course of events in Hawaii than appeared in the Press at the time. Patches Damon was one such source—her family had sold Hickham Field to the U.S. Air Force; another was a Boston taxi-driver who had been in the Navy and spent much of his term in the Pacific. It was he who told me how skilfully the Japanese had chosen their timing, early on a Sunday morning. They knew perfectly well that the officers of all three services made a habit of going in to Honolulu on Saturday nights and hitting it up there—they seldom returned to their ships or barracks till next day, "around noon". On that ghastly morning, awakened by the sound of shattering explosions, scrambling sleepily into their clothes and going dazedly to find their cars, when they set out to drive back to their ships and planes, smoking and flaming ahead of them, it was almost impossible to get along—the small vans of the Japanese truckers, instead of being parked neatly in their lay-bys, as we had seen them, were out all over the road, causing more delays, confusion, and frustration. The Japanese had thought out every detail, with diabolical ingenuity and thoroughness.

And I think it was from Patches that I heard the extraordinary and desolating story of the radar-station. Up on the mountain above the town there was a monitoring establishment, manned by technicians, for tracking planes—and I think ships also—by radar; I was never clear to which of the armed services it belonged, or whether they pooled it. In any case, interested amateurs were allowed to go occasionally and be given a course in radar, and on that Saturday night a small group went up and received instruction. When the session ended, near midnight, and the amateurs departed, one asked if he might stay on, as he found it so fascinating; the sleepy official said he might, if he didn't interfere with anything, and went yawning off to lie down. About 5 A.M. he was roused by the zealous amateur, in a high state of excitement: he said that an enormous number of planes, three hundred or more, were coming down from the North, and begged the technician to come and have a look. The technician told him to go jump in the Pacific. Two hours' warning wouldn't have been a lot, but it would have been something; at least some of the planes, packed wing to wing on Hickham Field, might have taken off, and had a go at the raiders, instead of being burnt on the ground.

Long afterwards, at Sissinghurst, Harold Nicolson told me how horrified he had been some months earlier to see them parked so, and how offended the American officers were when he suggested, mildly, that in Europe we should be afraid not to have more of a dispersal area—he made himself very unpopular, he said, with his sophisticated little smile.

I had often looked out last thing at night from my bedroom window at the Meyers', and seen, with an astonishment I could never quite get over, lights burning down in the valley—I did so that night, and thought what a worry it was going to be for the Americans to organise a black-out over their vast continent; it was nuisance enough in little Britain.

Next morning I left early for Boston. I had promised to have lunch with Christine Marquand—she was a niece of Ellery Sedgwick's—and go on to a meeting of some women's discussion group in which she was interested. I had been a little nervous about this, and reluctant to speak, because the question before the meeting was to be "Should America enter the war?"—an awkward topic for an Englishwoman. However, it had now become academic, and I willingly gave hints and tips about home black-out for as long as they wanted. But before that, just after lunch, there occurred the famous spoof air-raid warning which caused so much confusion at the time, so much anger and recrimination afterwards. Some bright spirit decided that it would be a good idea to try out the sirens all down the East Coast, to see if they worked; the police were informed in advance, but not the public. When, as we were sitting in Christina's pretty drawing-room drinking coffee, that loud and menacing wail broke out, rising and falling, it caused something like panic. I got up and went to the window—the house stood high, and commanded a view of the road down the Bay, a busy traffic-way. "Can you see the planes?" several voices asked anxiously.

"I'm not looking for them—we shouldn't see them. I'm watching the traffic. It's flowing steadily, so it can't be a real alarm."

And I remembered the business of the play about a London air-raid in New York; Thomas Lamont took me and a whole party to see it not long before Pearl Harbor. It was quite a pleasant little comedy about a bargee down by the docks who was having a row with the authorities over how much he was to be repaid for the petrol he had used in his launch, bringing troops back from Dunkirk; it opened charmingly with a small boy trying to fasten a gas-mask onto his dachshund. But the main sensation, the real draw, was the scene of the bombing of London: not only the stage but the whole theatre was blacked out, while incendiary bombs exploded in the living-room of the launch-owner's house, to the accompaniment of a real sound-track of the bombing of the East End—the whine of the dive-bombers, the deafening noise of bombs exploding, the crash of falling masonry and the roar of flames. Mr. Lamont told me what a job he had had to get seats—the house was packed out night after night. Less than a week after Pearl Harbor, the play was taken off for lack of support.

A day or two later I had to go down to New York for a lecture, and had lunch at the Yale Club with John Farrar, of Farrar and Rinehart, Steve Benét, Walter Millis, and several other journalists. They spent most of lunch discussing what could be done to present to the British public a proper assessment of America's reaction to being at war—I sat rather quiet, amused: this was my work during the first months of the war in England in reverse. Eventually it was decided that an English writer ought to do it, and we trooped off to the telephone to ring up John van Druten out in California and ask him to take on the job. He turned it down flat. Discouraged, we trooped back again to our coffee. Then someone said, "Why we're crazy! Here we have Miss Ann Bridge right here among us!"—and they asked me if I would write the piece they wanted. Of course I agreed. It had to be done fast—John Farrar was going down to Washington next day, and as I insisted that whatever I wrote must be submitted to the Information people at our Embassy, he wanted to take it with him. After my lecture that evening I sat up most of the night writing it, and next morning took it round to Carol Hill's office; one of her girls typed it out there and then, with a covering letter to A. D. Peters, and John came and fetched it from my hotel. He read it through quickly, and declared himself delighted—it was graphic, accurate, amusing, and above all sympathetic, he said. I later rang up Captain Cotton-Minchin in Washington, and he too professed himself delighted, so off it went.

I had suggested in my letter to Peters that he might manage to get it into *Time and Tide,* or possibly even *The Spectator,* and had written it at what I thought would be a suitable length for either. Peters, however, had other ideas. Having read it, he took it straight round to Printing-House Square, and next morning it appeared on the leader-page of *The Times,* under the amended title "America Goes to War", over the name Ann Bridge. In England it was received with interest and appreciation: Owen even wrote to say that people in the Foreign Office seemed quite pleased. Alas, in the States the reaction was very different. When copies of *The Times* reached Boston, some time in January, there was a tremendous outcry; not less than thirty-two people rang up the Consulate, demanding that I should be deported—so I was told eventually by the Vice-Consul. Now this young man happened to have a hatred of war almost as deep and pathological as that of the Americans themselves, and never read any newspapers. When he finally told me about these complaints I asked him whether he had informed the people who made them that the article had been commissioned by a group of highly reputable Americans, and passed by the Embassy. No—he didn't know that. Rather indignantly, I suggested that he might have rung me up at once and found out, so that he would have had an answer for any further objectors—and he agreed in the end.

This painful little episode throws a certain light on the average American attitude at that time. I had tried extremely hard to be fair, and even, as John Farrar said, sympathetic—and in his opinion had succeeded. But the shock and surprise had so inflamed the normal

American hypersensitiveness to any breath of criticism that some people really almost lost the use of their eyesight. I had written, I believe truly enough, that Americans had come to regard war "as a disfiguring and rather shameful disease, like ringworm or impetigo, which nice clean nations simply don't get." Furious voices told the wretched Vice-Consul down the telephone—"She says we have impetigo!"

However, I persevered with my lecturing, which enabled me to see so much of the country, and to meet all manner of people, including my relations. Leigh had arranged two or three talks for me in Pittsburgh, and I was glad of that, as I remembered a charming cousin from New Orleans, Marie-Élise, who had married a man called Snyder and lived just outside Pittsburgh on Sewickley Heights; and I had long heard of Frank Leovy, who lived *in* Pittsburgh, and had married one of the Glennys, as a perfect angel. This was true; when I wrote and told him that I was coming he booked me a room in a nice hotel and filled it with orchids—he couldn't put me up, as he had illness in the house—and showed me the sights of his town, including the astonishing university building, a gothic skyscraper some forty storeys high, which strangely enough is rather beautiful. It has one charming feature: Pittsburgh is a town of many races, and on the ground-floor of the huge building is a series of rooms, one for each of the local immigrant nationalities, with its national emblem incorporated in the scheme of decoration; I was delighted to see the tulip, carved in wood, all round the Hungarian room. Cousin Marie-Élise presently took me up to stay in her spacious house, standing in what was practically a park, with wide views over the city lying far below; at night one seemed to be looking out over a burning landscape, with all the steel furnaces blazing in the dark.

Once or twice I had occasion to go down to Washington, where Angus Malcolm of Poltalloch, an old friend from Argyll, kindly put me up; he had a nice little house and, at first, an excellent Negro cook. Jeanne Malcolm, his beautiful mother, had stayed with him for some weeks to settle him in, and had trained the cook, leaving her a book of recipes in manuscript. Alas, this treasure left, and her successor was not nearly so good; on my next visit Angus announced that he had arranged a luncheon-party for me, but would I mind helping to cook it myself? Otherwise he was afraid it would be a flop. Helped by Lady Malcolm's admirably clear and detailed directions, the cook and I produced quite a tolerable dish of partridges on braised cabbage; Per Jacobson praised it highly, I remember.

There were other old friends in the Embassy at Washington— Jean and Roddie Barclay; and Sir Ronald Campbell, who had recently left the Legation at Belgrade—where he had been such a kind host to me on my forays to feed the prisoners of war—to become Minister in Washington. The Ambassador was Lord Halifax, and one got the impression that both he and Lady Halifax were not wholly at ease in what was still, for them, a relatively new post. He was following Lord Lothian, who had been adored by the Americans for his accessibility and easy manners; accessibility is not an outstanding characteristic of Yorkshiremen, and Edward Halifax had as little of it as any of them. Moreover, whether or how far he was responsible for Munich or not, he was given the full credit, or rather discredit, for it in this new assignment, which is anyhow a fearfully taxing one, even for a much younger man. For all these reasons they seemed somehow to shrink into themselves; they dutifully carried out their formal entertaining, but it remained extremely formal—something Americans very much dislike; and whenever they could, at week-ends, they escaped into the country.

So it came about that at the time of which I am writing, 1941 and 1942, more and more what would normally have been the functions of the British Embassy devolved on the Australians, Dick Casey (now Lord Casey) and his wife. I daresay they might have liked a week-end in the country now and again too; but they realised that half the most important part of diplomacy—the informal meetings, the casual-seeming encounters, the chance introductions—can, in Washington anyhow, only be conducted *at* week-ends, when the ceaseless round of official activities eases off a little. And with a dedication which was beyond all praise, month in and month out, the Caseys were regularly At Home on Saturday evenings, from 6 P.M. onwards—at home in every sense of the word, in a warm and welcoming atmosphere, with good strong drinks, and cheerful gaiety, and no hint of fatigue—on the contrary, an eager interest in everything and everyone. If it was important that someone in the Pentagon should meet, say, Sir John Dill unofficially and privately, or an isolationist Senator be brought into contact with some ultra-persuasive English journalist practically by accident, Casey had only to be told, and the thing was brought about—with the lightest touch, the happiest ease. The English cause in the United States owed more to that gallant and devoted couple than has usually been recognised.

Another friend from Peking days whom it was delightful to meet again was Henrik de Kauffman, who had been appointed Danish Minister in Washington two or three years earlier: he was now married to an American wife, and they both reminded me that I had chaperoned them at his temple in the Western Hills during the week-end when they became engaged. Henrik had become quite famous in the meantime, on account of his spirited action when the Germans, without any warning, occupied Denmark in April 1940; all communications with Copenhagen being cut, he set himself up as a government in exile, and from Washington radioed orders to the entire Danish merchant fleet to make for British, French, or American ports, which saved his country's not inconsiderable mercantile marine from falling into German hands. He was as good-looking, lively, and friendly as ever.

Early in 1942 I was asked to give a lecture in Montreal by the Canadian P.E.N. Club, and went; on our journey home from China I had seen nothing of Montreal but the station platform. A friend put me up, and the Club paid part of my fares. That trip was great fun. The lecture went with a bang, because in the middle of it a post-boy walked onto the platform and handed me a telegram. It was from Pauline Vanier, asking me to go on to Quebec and give a lecture to a women's club there two days later. Since there was a reply-paid form attached I felt obliged to explain to the audience, who were goggling with excitement at this unwonted interruption, what it was all about, and to ask their permission to scribble my reply—which was of course a delighted acceptance. But my fun in Montreal was by no means over yet. The Chairman of the P.E.N. there was a Judge of the High Court, and at dinner after the lecture we made friends; he kindly invited me to attend his Court the following morning, and have lunch with him afterwards. The Court was already sitting when I arrived, but a messenger took me in, and to my embarrassed astonishment led me right up to the dais on which the Judge sat, and told me to mount the steps. As I did so the Judge rose—the whole Court rose too; when I sat down on his right, he re-seated himself, and everyone sat down again. However I soon got over my embarrassment in the interest of hearing all the pleadings made both in English and in French; the evidence of witnesses was similarly repeated, if necessary by the interpreter, which made it all go rather slowly.

The first case was nearly over. When the next one came on the Judge explained to me what it was about. A firm in New England was suing a Canadian company for infringing its patent rights in some way by selling a brand medicine, made by the plaintiffs, without leave, or due acknowledgement, or something. When the defence lawyer got up to make his speech he made great play with the fact that the remedy in question, "Grove's Bromo-Quinine Laxative", was an obscure product, manufactured on a very small scale in a remote country town, hardly known outside the borders of its own state. I pricked up my ears at this, and rather nervously twitched the Judge's sleeve; he bent over to me. "That's all lies!" I muttered in his ear. "It was on sale in the two European chemists' shops in Peking in 1926." Too late, I began to be afraid that I might be put in the witness-box, but my friend was much too kind for that; in his summing-up he mentioned that to his knowledge the subject of the action was on sale as far afield as China; the Canadian lawyer looked aghast, and his client company was duly ordered to pay damages.

Quebec under snow was even lovelier than I remembered it in late spring; all the old part of the city was like a succession of silverpoint etchings from some late French Book of Hours. The final touch to my pleasure on this trip was given when I came to re-enter the United States. It seemed that the residence-permit, or whatever it is called, stamped on my passport when we landed at San Francisco the previous June, had run out, and on the Canadian border, without Owen, there was no red-carpet treatment at all; I was no longer a V.I.P., but a wandering British lecturer, who had already done wrong by staying in God's Own Country beyond my permitted time. The immigration officer was very tough with me, and presently announced, menacingly, that I should have to have my finger-prints taken.

"Oh, shall I really? How *lovely!*" I exclaimed—being finger-printed was an experience, like pulling the communication-cord on a train, that I had always longed for, hitherto in vain. Rather taken aback, and scowling at the stifled mirth of his underlings in the background, the officer afforded me this peculiar pleasure—I must say the black took a lot of getting off.

On June 2, just a year and a day after we had landed in California, I flew home. About three weeks before, I heard that the *Chicago Tribune* had bought the serial rights in *Frontier Passage* for $2,500. I hurried down to New York, bought two steamer trunks, and then spent most of the Colonel's good dollars at Macy's and elsewhere, filling them with all the things which I thought would be most appreciated at home, after two years of clothes-rationing; the delicious cheap American summer frocks, so well cut and so practical; the equally delicious undies—people at home had never seen cobweb-thin seersucker petties; dozens and dozens of nylon stockings, also then a complete novelty in England; even shoe-laces, which I knew were hard to get—and eau de cologne, and nail brushes, and masses of lovely soap.

The flight across the Atlantic was one of the most splendid journeys I have ever made. In those days it was by no means the commonplace that it has since become; three big seaplanes made the round trip once a week, and only more or less official passengers could get onto them. The flight began at Baltimore; there was a touch-down for lunch and re-fuelling at Gander, then the long hop to Shannon, and on to Bristol. Ireland was then strictly neutral, and had made the concession of the stop at Shannon on condition that *no* passengers should disembark and stay in the country. The flight out from Gander over the Canadian coast revealed a most sinister landscape—the northern horizon filled with long lines of greyish-white drift-ice, the black capes and islands below us each with a strange white rim along its northern edge, where the ice had piled up; here and there a huge iceberg had stranded and lay canted over sideways, like a vast white wreck; they reminded me of the *Normandie*, lying forlorn on her side in New York harbour. Further out, now nearly a mile up, we flew in brilliant sunshine; the cloud-floor below us looked perfectly solid, like a polar landscape in Greenland—with rolling plains, hills, and ridges, there blue with shadow, here golden in sunlight. It was hard to believe that it was not the solid earth over which our shadow sped bird-like, keeping us company—our sole companion in those celestial wastes. Looking out on this scene, the thought came to me—since the earth cooled to its present temperature, for tens of thousands of years this cloud landscape had been spread out here, summer after summer, season after season, but till, say, twenty-five years earlier no human eye had ever looked upon it; unseen, this beauty stretched beneath the indifferent sky; and even now, what a tiny fraction of the eyes of all earth's millions of eyes had ever beheld it. I was glad that my eyes were included in the fraction before, flying eastwards, we flew into the night, which rose, shadowy and immense, to meet us.

Our landfall was a group of mountains, standing up into a rose-red sunrise above clouds; we found a hole in the cloud floor and dived through it, down, down, down—here was the Shannon, broad and shining, here were houses and fields; here was Ireland. I was surprised at the strength of the emotion that overtook me as I stepped out onto the pontoon wing that morning. The air was sweet with a familiar sweetness that took me back to childhood—the last of the hawthorn-blossom, the first of the elder-flower; home birds, thrush and blackbird, piped and whistled songs I had known always, and my heart sang with them. I was home at last.

And oh, the good breakfast at the little inn—the bacon and eggs, the sweet butter and the strong tea. And the soft-voiced helpful Irish, so sympathising, so friendly. The post-mistress opened up her office fifty minutes before time, so that I could telephone to Owen, up in the County Mayo; the post-mistress there sent a message to him at the pub, and he ran down the street in his dressing-gown to speak to me and urge me to come up to Newport and join him, to see how Rockfleet, the Regency ruin we were restoring, was getting on. When I pointed out that this was against the regulations—"Ring up Maffey in Dublin, and get him to arrange it," Owen said blithely. Again the telephone girls, with gleeful chatterings to one another in Irish, helped my communications with the capital. Sir John, the U.K. Representative to Eire, was in his bath, but through his secretary agreed to do his best, and the young RAF officer—I used his telephone this time—allowed me to give his number, and wait in his office for a reply. His precious dachshund was very sick, with a temperature—its little nose was like a hot black coal; I had a tube of sulfa-pyridine tablets in my handbag, and dissolved one in milk, which we fed to him through a fountain-pen filler; in half an hour the creature was already better, and feebly lapping milk from a saucer—and the young officer was practically my slave. But time was running out—unless permission came I should have to go back

129

to the airport on the coach, rejoin the plane, and be carried on to Bristol. At last I had to go, and was walking dolefully down the road with the other passengers to where the coach waited when a shout from behind halted me—"Mrs. O'Malley!" It was the Flight-Lieutenant, running. "Bristol says the Foreign Office says the Colonial Office says you can stay," he panted out—Sir John Maffey had evidently been very energetic. So I went back to the airport, but only to get my luggage off the plane; then, somehow, I got myself conveyed to Limerick, where I spent the night in blissful comfort in the hotel, and next day I went on to Newport.

Travel in Ireland in 1942 was not really complicated, but it was a bit uncertain, and rather slow. The distance from Limerick to Newport is some 85 miles; it took me just sixteen and a half hours, whereas the previous day I had come nearly 2,000 miles in twelve hours. The contrast was charming. It was the hottest and loveliest of spring days, and the sun turned the pale stone of the field-walls to a tone between milk and silver; all through the pastures and along the banks the hawthorn stood white above the starry whiteness of the daisies; in the standing hay the moon-daisies shone like silver suns. And it was all so delicately small, the detail of the landscape so perfectly finished, so rich and yet so neat, after the vast monotonous empty spaces of those other continents that I had been seeing—the monotony of plain and steppe and prairie and desert. Here the hand of man had wrought for centuries, in patience and in love, and his spirit filled the land; the land had responded and now gave out faith and peace, sweet as the breath of summer in the meadow. Who then could complain of slowness, of long halts and delays? Certainly not I.

The train started at 8:45, a bare fifteen minutes late, and chugged gallantly through this lovely countryside on its composite war-time fuel of turf, beech-blocks, and coal-dust; we reached Athenry only forty minutes behind time. There I made enquiries. 'Twould be best, they said, to wait for the 2:30 and go on to Claremorris on that, and wait there for the Dublin train, which would carry me to Westport "some time". Sure the Newport bus would wait on the train; wasn't it that it came to meet? Reassured, I went to the inn, across the road from the station, to have lunch. I then noticed that I was short of money—I had expected to fly straight to England, and there be met. I consulted a total stranger—he cashed me a cheque on the spot, refusing even to look at the visiting-card I proffered him. Then I had lunch. It was fair-day in Athenry, and the inn was full of young women and cattle-dealers; one of the young women, sitting by me, turned her empty tea-cup upside down, and I asked if she wished her fortune told. She did, and for an hour I told the girls' fortunes from their tea-cups. So enthralling—and apparently so alarmingly accurate—were my predictions that when I went out to sit in the garden the cattle-dealers came sidling up, one after another, to have their fortunes told too. "Sure, you have no need to be cashing cheques and fretting over money," observed my recent benefactor; "with the gift you have there you could travel the breadth of the country and lack for nothing! They'd be paying you a florin apiece for those fortunes."

The 2:30 left at 3:50. It was very hot. I sat in a carriage full of school girls going up to the nuns in Sligo, noticing their clear grey eyes and the extraordinary whiteness of their skins; their arms, under the cheap blouses, were like milk or moonlight. They all smoked all the time. We got into Claremorris soon after 5:30, parked our luggage by a seat on the platform under a hedge of roses in full bloom, and then enquired about the Dublin train—"There's no word of her yet," a porter told us, so we went and drank tea in the refreshment-room. Still it was very hot, and now I became amazingly tired; but that peace and serenity, that profound satisfaction of being at home again still held—I have seldom been happier. We went back and sat under the rose-hedge by our bundles; "she" had now passed Athlone, and might be expected "anny time". "Anny time" stretched out to an hour or more; the sun stooped westward into those spaces where forty-eight hours before I too had ridden like Phaëthon in the heavens; the air cooled, deepening the scent of the roses. At last the train came; we bundled in, sat motionless for twenty minutes, and were off again.

Jolting on towards Castlebar, I knew the very place where I should first see Croagh Patrick rising blue and pointed over the lower land—and there, sure enough, it was, the Reek, the holy mountain, a lofty slender cone. And now in the deepening dusk we drew into Westport—and there was the bus, and the station-master bidding the conductor give me a nice place; and we all crowded in, and swayed and bumped along the familiar road, between the sweet soft moulding of the land, till the bridge came in sight, and the river, with the white houses beyond, and the great tower of the church on the hill above—and in the market-place by the scales the bus drew up. There was quite a little crowd in the street, including the garage proprietor and the inn-keeper. "Mr. Kelly! Mr. Devine! But where is my husband?" "Right here he is, ma'am—we have him here for you! You're heartily welcome; you will have had a grand trip."

In which of course they were perfectly right.

XI

Turkey I

It has been explained in an earlier chapter how I came to go to
Turkey in the late summer of 1940—to find fresh sources of supply
for food and clothing for our prisoners of war. But I soon found
myself involved in a far more fascinating search—for all the facts
which lay behind Mustafa Kemal Atatürk's revolution. In 1940
Atatürk had hardly been dead two years, and the men who had
been his earliest and closest adherents were still alive: among them
Fethi Okyar Bey, Ismet Inonü, and Ruşen Eşref Ünaydin. Ruşen
Bey was taking two months' sick leave after a serious operation in
Budapest, and was spending it on Büyük-Ada, one of the group
of islands in the Sea of Marmara known collectively as The Prince's
Islands, or to the English as Prinkipo; he had a villa there.
Büyük-Ada was anyhow a favourite resort, and since, owing
to the war, it was impossible to go abroad, most of the Turkish
Ministers and officials were spending the summer there too, away
from the blinding glare and relentless heat of Ankara, Atatürk's
new capital up on the Anatolian plateau—down among the soft
sea-breezes, and the shady pine woods which covered, and scented,
the whole island. There, by a strange chance, they were all congre-
gated, those men who had shared Atatürk's trials and struggles and
triumphs; and there, in the Ünaydins' pretty white villa, with its
façade like a small Greek temple, by incredible good fortune I spent
six whole weeks—during which, except when I went in by the little
steamer to the Embassy at Istanbul to cash a cheque, I never saw a

European face, or heard a European voice. For those six weeks of August and September in 1940, I lived a completely Turkish life, among Turks—something, they said later up at the Embassy in Ankara, that no Englishwoman had done since Lady Hester Stanhope's day.

Now Turkish life, though immensely civilised, has certain rather unusual features, one of the most notable of which is their passion for talking. They practically never play any active games, like golf or tennis, and very little bridge; their recreations are reading and conversation. This last, with Turks, is an astonishing experience—the care with which they formulate their ideas, the wit and elegance with which they express them in quick easy language, add up to something that in its way is as much an artistic performance as a violin solo—or rather duet. Two or three Turkish men will settle down after breakfast to talk about some subject which interests them; they will break off for luncheon and the siesta, and then settle down again to talk—on the same subject—till dinner; after dinner, with any luck they will continue talking till midnight. Unless they decide to visit a beauty-spot; at Büyük-Ada we often did this in the evenings. No cars were allowed on the island; we drove out in a cavalcade of small two-horse carriages, along the sandy roads through the pine woods; on reaching the desired spot all pulled up, and we walked about, making suitable quotations concerning the bay, or hill, or tower that we were looking at. Men and women alike spoke beautiful French, and most of them could, and did, quote freely from Rimbaud, Verlaine, or what have you; if, as often happened, the most appropriate quotation was from one of the Persian poets, the speaker would make a rapid and graceful translation into French for my benefit—when I was with them they talked French all the time.

Now this passion for conversation was exceedingly fortunate for me, for the subject uppermost in all their minds at that time was Mustafa Kemal, whose loss was still most deeply felt, his memory fresh and warm in their hearts—Kemal, and Turkey; what he had aimed at doing for Turkey, how he had set about it, what obstacles had stood in his way, what frustrations had most exasperated him. Sitting on a cushion against the low parapet overhanging the sea, under a stone pine, I would listen by the hour while Ruşen Bey, lying in a deck-chair, told me about Kemal; at the Okyar villa, up the hill, I would listen to Fethi Bey's accounts of Kemal, sitting on the balcony of his house. Certain things stood out. Atatürk's clear recognition, from the outset, that if he was to realise his ambition of turning Turkey into a modern nation, it could only be done by making her a European one; he could not hope to drag his countrymen from an Old Testament civilisation into the twentieth century in any other way. Hence his romanisation of the alphabet; people would have to learn to read in lettering which opened up European literature, as well as their own—which really included Persian—if they were to become European-minded; he insisted on Western numerals too, and reformed the calendar to bring it into line with the Western world. Hence his breach with Islam, which he saw as an ossifying if not indeed a fossilising influence. Education was taken out of the hands of the old "Ministry of the Culte", which taught only the Koran; the *medresses* or religious schools were closed, and secular ones opened; for use in these he had translations made of all the great European writers, from Sophocles and Aeschylus down to Dickens, for whom the Turks have a passion, and more modern writers too.

Hence his proscribing of the fez—if men wore a headgear which set them apart from the rest of modern mankind, they would not easily come to share their way of life. And hence his determination to set up his capital in Ankara, a new capital for a new state; he saw plainly enough, and rightly, that down in Istanbul, steeped in its imperial traditions, the forces of inertia, corruption, and reaction would be too strong for any major reforms. It was with an astounding passion that these men, Ruşen and Fethi and the rest, spoke of their beloved leader—his tireless energy, his unremitting work, his remorselessness, as well as his vision and his idealism. This was a very different picture from the drink-sodden womaniser portrayed in *Grey Wolf*, a book which angered literate Turks deeply, and to me it was a credible one; much more in keeping with the historical facts of Atatürk's achievements than the other. What struck me so much was how intelligently selective the man had been over the work of modernisation—looking for the "meat" of modern civilisation not in America, but in Europe, where it began—caring little about the outward trappings of modernity, the cars and telephones and other gadgets (except in so far as they were required for efficiency), but driving hard and straight for the mental and psychological fundamentals.

He was really *very* intelligent. Surely it is remarkable that a man brought up a Mahomedan should have seen instantly that in order to change the way of life of a whole nation it was essential to alter the habits of the women as well as those of the men. But he was far too astute to attempt to do anything with women by decree, as he did in the matter of abolishing the fez. Oh no—this must be done by persuasion and example; very gradually and carefully. He began by coaxing and persuading, individually, the wives of his staff to come to little dinners at his house in Ankara without even the *peçe*, the short piece of silk stretching from below the eyes to the chin, and only wearing a light piece of tulle over their hair. Now this, for women who had never confronted any man except their fathers, brothers, or husbands with an unveiled face—who had been told by their old *dadis*, the Turkish equivalent of English nannies, that they would burn in hell if they showed their hair after the age of thirteen —was asking quite a lot; however, nervous and embarrassed, one by one they came to do it, for the sake of the worshipped leader. And where the wives of the important men led, gradually the lesser fry followed.

Presently he had a modern hotel, with a restaurant, built in Ankara, in which he could entertain the European diplomats who, with the utmost reluctance, were forced to open embassies and legations up on the plateau, since Kemal refused to transact government business anywhere else; and here, at one point, he gave his famous ball, where for the first time the wives of deputies came with their husbands to a public function, and a few respectable Turkish women appeared in something approaching a décolletage, and danced with foreign men. In fact exactly five women did this; a dozen or more were urged to do so, eight agreed to, only five had the courage to go through with it. I knew them all well; and sitting in their cool rooms at Büyük-Ada, so many years later, I could hear the personal dismay in their voices as they described the agony of that evening. "*Je me entais toute nue!*" one of them said, shivering a little at the recollection.

They told me, too, all these women, how hard the going had been in the early days, when they had followed their husbands up to

Ankara, to live in old furnished houses in the Citadel. No electricity, only oil lamps—when there was any paraffin, but only two lamps to a house at that; when the paraffin ran short they used candles. Ruşen Bey, at Kemal Pasha's desire, translated the whole 700-odd pages of Emil Ludwig's *Life of Napoleon* into Turkish by candle-light in *four months;* usually after a fourteen-hour day in Kemal's bureau. No water, except what was drawn from the well in the courtyard and carried into the house; at first no servants, except their husbands' batmen, who could draw water and chop up wood for the small iron stoves which were the only form of heating, but were capable of little else. After a time most of these devoted wives managed to get hold of a woman apiece to help in the house; but they were peasanty creatures, completely untrained, who had to be taught to shake the rugs *outside* the door, not in the rooms, and to put the slops and rubbish down the open drain in a corner of the court, not scatter them all over it. But all the cooking, washing, ironing, and pressing of their husbands' suits had to be done by their own hands. Now these young women—most of them were little more than girls when they went up to Ankara—had been brought up in a fantastic degree of dependence and helplessness: attendants gave them their baths in the *hammam,* or bath-house; *dadis,* and later their maids, dressed them and did their hair; they never went out-side their gates without a female escort unless, again, accompanied by a husband, father, or brother: they had never so much as washed a pair of stockings in their lives. Now they had to go down to the market below the Citadel, and choose and buy meat, bread, rice, and spices, bargain and argue—milk, eggs, chickens were brought to the door, and once a week a loud cry in the narrow cobbled alleys announced that a log of wood was being dropped at each house. Hard going indeed, but somehow they managed; they described their struggles, in retrospect, with a certain humorous relish—what was clear was that much the worst part, what they had really minded, was appearing in public without the *peçe* and *sans tulle*—without some form of veiling on their hair.

And one and all, they told me how they were inspired and stimu-lated by the example of the peasant women, who played such a notable part in Atatürk's military successes. Although the Baghdad railway ran past Ankara, it was of little use as a supply line; the southern end was in the hands of the French, still at war with

Turkey, and the northern, at Istanbul, under the Sultan's Government, which had proclaimed Mustafa Kemal a rebel and a traitor, and put a price on his head. Supplies, but above all munitions, could only come through the Black Sea ports. Smuggled out of the Allied arms-dumps near the capital, or sent by sea from Russia, they were landed on the beach at Samsun or Inebolu, nine or ten days' march away—mainly at Inebolu; and the route for the first five days, over three ranges of mountains, was too steep and rough for heavy wheeled traffic. Over this section the shells, the boxes containing machine-guns, the bundles of rifles and the slingsful of ammunition were carried, and carried on women's backs, since all the men, and the mules, were at the front. My friends also came via Inebolu, and saw this fantastic form of transport; for five days, driving in light open carriages, which could negotiate the inadequate road, they watched, day after day and mile after mile, the endless line of women walking in single file, bent under these unwonted loads. Many carried a baby in their arms, more had a child or two tagging along behind; now and again a woman would fall out, sit by the road-side to give her infant the breast, and then shoulder her load again and take her place in the line once more.

Once up on the plateau, where the road was better, and there were no more of the appallingly steep slopes, the loads were transferred to *cagnés*, low country carts with solid wooden wheels, for the next six days' haul on to Ankara; the carriers turned round, babies and all, and foot-slogged back over the mountains to Inebolu, to begin all over again. But it was women, still, who acted as teamsters to the stolid oxen which drew the *cagnés*, tugging and prodding them along, while children ran alongside; many a load of shells had a baby perched atop. "The Road of the Revolution"—the Turks still call it that, with a ring of pride in their voices; and these delicately nurtured girls, seeing what the splendidly tough Anatolian peasant women were doing, all decided that, in so far as other, different tasks were in their own power, they would do no less.

Of course as the years went on everything grew easier; houses and flats were built in Ankara, electricity came, and piped water, and plumbing of a sort; even the strangeness of going unveiled, and wearing a hat instead of the muffling, anonymous black folds of the *çarsaf* in the street, even meeting strange men gradually lost their terrors. By the time I met them these women had all become experienced and completely *mondaine* hostesses—Paris frocks, of course, they had always worn, just as they had always read and spoken French with their French governesses. But as I sat with them, talking and listening, hearing of the ultra-civilised but completely sheltered, almost hidden background from which they had so rapidly and so roughly emerged, into a life at first harsh by any standards, I realised that this was one of the great stories of the world, and decided that, come hell and high water, I would tell it—in a novel; and at the same time would give the fiction-readers of the West a truer picture of Atatürk than had been vouchsafed to them in *Grey Wolf*.

To this end I asked, now, endless specific questions—about Mustafa Kemal mostly from the men, though the women had plenty to say about him too: his quite enormous charm, which could turn in a moment to abruptness, even anger; his love of music, and how he would sit at the piano, improvising, or making variations on an air fresh to him—he would accompany a new song, after the first few notes, simply by ear. The men were apt to lay more stress on his chivalry, so curiously combined with ruthlessness; on his extreme astuteness, always knowing when to stop and when to drive ahead, whether in diplomacy or in battle, which made him such a brilliant general and such a successful diplomatist and leader of a poor, ignorant and backward country. They spoke much of his love of the common people—marching, often, with his men, chatting and laughing; or in times of peace strolling alone about the countryside, talking to the men and women at work in the fields, cracking jokes with the old people in their houses. This brought a fantastic response, of course: his troops would all have died for him, as so many did.

The men, too, were rather amusing about his one failure. With his great idea of "Europeanisation" in mind, he wanted to turn the Turks into a nation of drinkers—of spirits as well as of wine; he started vine-growing and wine-making on a big scale, and in fact Turkish wine is now extremely good. But though his immediate entourage learned to drink heavily, and keep him company in his bouts, it never caught on. Secular education, even throwing off the veil, was one thing; defying the Prophet to the point of drinking spirits, and even wine, was another. At the tables of his former comrades-in-arms, those who were now, like Ruşen Bey, diplomats, wine might be served at dinner; but those marathon conversations, continuing sometimes till two in the morning, were conducted entirely on coffee and iced water—given the high intellectual level of Turkish talk, at least one European found this something of a strain!

From the women I sought, and got, detailed accounts of their upbringing, and the mode of life in those great Turkish households in the days of the Sultanate, especially in the *yalis*—the houses, often built out over the water, along the Bosphorous, to which the aristocratic families repaired in summer: the *selamlik*, the public or male part of the house, which the women only entered on formal occasions such as weddings or funerals, and the *haremlik*, the women's sphere, into which no men save close relations ever came. Each had its own garden, separated by the house itself; the dining-room was a sort of neutral zone, where both sexes, if members of the family, met at meals. Invariably, in such households, there was a French governess, usually a very high-class one; most of my new friends were thoroughly grounded in French literature, and the latest French books and magazines lay about on their tables. But behind the high walls which screened their separate gardens, and in the sheltered apartments beyond the dining-room, the older women exercised a surprising sway, even over their menfolk; their advice was sought and taken, their opinion deferred to, in spite of the professed duty of absolute obedience to their husbands. The portrait of Réfiyé Hanim in *The Dark Moment* is a portrait from life, at second-hand—Saliha Ünaydin's account of her own grandmother; and I myself met one or two elderly Turkish great ladies who resembled her in every particular. It was all very unlike the ideas of Turkish family life then current in Europe; the very idea of any but a monogamous marriage was horrifying to people of the type I was meeting.

From Büyük-Ada I went up to Ankara, and with Lady Knatchbull-Huguessen dealt with the affairs of the prisoners of war in Germany; but apart from the journeys up and down in the train I did little sight-seeing—we were too busy. However I made friends with Lady Mary Walker, whose husband was at the Embassy; she had been trying vainly for a long time to find another person who wished to visit Broussa, and still more Nicaea; when she suggested this to me I agreed eagerly. Neither of us spoke Turkish, but we hoped to manage somehow. But Lady K.-H. was not so sure; she thought we might get into difficulties and cause embarrassments, and therefore deliberately betrayed our plan to Admiral Sir Howard Kelly, who was, she knew, also eager to visit Broussa. Sir Howard was that naval officer who, in the little *Gloucester*, had chased the mighty *Goeben* and *Breslau* all down the Mediterranean in the First World War, in an endeavour to intercept them before they got into the safety of the Dardanelles and Turkish waters. He failed, but it was a very gallant act, and on the strength of it, a quarter of a century later, he had got himself attached to the Embassy as a sort of honorary Naval Attaché. He was a huge man with a brusque manner and a main-top voice, and like all his family a tremendous martinet; I knew about Kellys because before my marriage I had worked under his sister in the Soho office of the old Charity Organisation Society—Mary and I were greatly dismayed at the prospect of his coming with us. She moaned to Lady K.-H. that the Admiral would treat us like naval ratings, as indeed he presently did; but the Ambassadress was perfectly within her rights in doing as she thought best where the propriety and well-being of staff wives was concerned, and anyhow once Sir Howard knew that we were going, nothing would prevent him from coming too.

We went by steamer from Istanbul to Mudanyeh, on the Marmara, whence a small train took us up to Broussa, an exquisite little town lying on the lower slopes of that mighty mountain Olympus-in-Asia, and looking out over a flat valley covered, as with a green quilt, with mulberry-trees. Broussa is, and has been for centuries, one of the great silk centres of the world. Its Silk Exchange must be almost the most charming commercial centre there is—balconied buildings three or four storeys high enclose a paved square, with huge plane-trees shading it in the middle, and of course the inevitable fountains; outside the doors of the various silk-merchants, each with its brass plaque, stand high open baskets filled with the cocoons from which the raw silk will presently be unwound—when we were there elderly Turks were pausing to pick some of the cocoons up and finger them, gravely and appraisingly.

Mary Walker had looked out a fairly inexpensive hotel for us in a rather out-of-date *Guide Bleu*, which promised *confort modeste;* and modest the comfort proved to be. It was a regular old-fashioned Turkish hotel, in which one paid, not by the room, but by the bed;

there were four beds in our room, and we each had to pay double in order to have it to ourselves; the unfortunate Admiral had to pay for three for his privacy! Our room had a fitted basin into which cold water dripped ceaselessly from a single tap; the beds were hard, but the sheets clean. The manager spoke a very little, very bad French; the rest of the staff apparently only Turkish; we envied Sir Howard his little note-book with one hundred useful Turkish phrases neatly copied into it. And then Mary Walker made, quite by accident, the astonishing discovery that the waiter spoke Spanish! She herself, having spent much of her youth at La Roque, the Bute property in southern Spain, spoke it as easily as English. The waiter's Spanish was rather archaic, in fact she recognised it as sixteenth-century; and subsequent enquiries revealed how this phenomenon came about. At the time of the Inquisition there was a great exodus of persecuted Jews from Spain; many of them were silk-weavers, and these made their way, naturally, to Broussa, taking their language with them—but it was fascinating to find quite a high proportion of the twentieth-century population there still using their ancient tongue.

Everything in Broussa was interesting, and most of it beautiful— many of the mosques more beautiful, we thought, than the renowned Mosquée Verte. But we soon ran into trouble with the Admiral. He wouldn't do this, we ought not to do that; this was too far, that wouldn't be interesting. He was of course old enough to be our father—or at least Mary's, if not mine; but the real difficulty was a difference in the matter of our insides. We young women had excellent digestions, and adventurous tastes in food; we enjoyed odd new dishes in even odder little restaurants. Sir Howard hated them, and always wanted to get back to eat in the hotel, where the food was dull enough to seem safe to his ultra-Anglo-British tastes. Actually from his own point of view I am afraid he was right, for after an enforced meal in a restaurant on some expedition, he did go down with quite a sharp gastric upset, and was out of action for two or three days. Which was how Mary and I came to have the adventure we did in Nicaea, whither we went by ourselves.

For this expedition we chartered a taxi through the good offices of the new, big, expensive hotel, which had a European manager; we stipulated for a reliable vehicle and a trustworthy driver, who could speak some language other than Turkish. The man they sent was sound enough, as was his car, and he spoke odd but fairly fluent German—this was to prove our undoing. We set off early, drove south along that mulberry-quilted valley, with Mount Olympus rising higher and higher behind us; then struck east over a low range of hills, till we came in view of that amazingly blue lake lying below us, and at its end the City of the Creed, Nicaea.

So many famous places seem, when one reaches them, to be disappointing, hardly worthy of their great past renown—but no one could possibly feel that about Isnik, as the Turks call it. Like the New Jerusalem it lies four-square, still within the beautiful walls, brick-built, but footed and topped with creamy stone, with which Justinian enclosed it, all in a rare state of preservation; it is full of ancient churches, huge plane-trees cast shade over the open spaces, and water, still brought in from the hills along Justinian's aqueduct, flows in open channels beside its streets. It is quite perfect: down on the shore of the lake which bears its name white marble quays abut on the blue water, the marble bollards still *in situ;* all deserted now, and overgrown with pink hollyhocks—a dream-like place. Strabo, the Greek geographer, was so impressed with the intense blue of the lake that he actually mentions it in his account of that part of Asia Minor; it was nice to think that the colour of this stretch of water had been admired for 2,000 years.

But we only saw the quay and most of the town later on. As we drove in through an arched gate-way in those elegant walls our driver turned round and suggested that we should first see the Kinema, which was *sehr schön;* we had no great appetite for a cinema, but he drove there anyway, and we presently found ourselves admiring the curved rows of marble seats of Justinian's amphitheatre! The central space was grassed over, with sheep and goats grazing, tended by Turkish children; there were also some soldiers strolling about, who naturally came up to have a good look at us—we learned later that they were in charge of an anti-aircraft post installed at the further end. Now the Turks had suffered greatly from coming in on the German side in the First World War, and to their natural xenophobia was now added a violent hatred of the Germans. One of the N.C.O.'s knew enough German to recognise that we were speaking the hated language to our driver, and reported it instantly. As we made to drive away a Turkish officer came up in a car, put two soldiers in ours, and forced our chauffeur to drive us to police headquarters; there we were taken upstairs and locked in a room. More officers came and nattered at us in Turkish, but that got them nowhere; Mary and I kept pointing to our mouths and saying In*gles,* Fran*ces,* and at last the penny dropped—a stout civilian was fetched, who did speak a very little French; the *Kaimakam,* or Mayor. To him we showed our passports, and explained that we were the wives of diplomats, come *en touriste* to admire the unparalleled beauties of Isnik. The Kaimakam studied these documents doubtfully; at last, holding mine, he said—"Vous, mari, ambassadeur anglais, Budapest?" pointing a thick finger at me incredulously.

"Mais oui, mais oui, monsieur—c'est mon mari à moi!"

This fascinated them all, two live English diplomats' wives, here in Isnik. We were taken into another room, and the schoolmaster, who spoke fluent French, was sent for, to act as interpreter; to him I had the happy idea of mentioning that I had just been staying on Büyük-Ada with Ruşen Eşref Ünaydin, a colleague and friend of my husband's in Budapest—I knew that Ruşen Bey had a considerable reputation as a writer in his own country. "Ah, notre grand poète!" —the schoolmaster was delighted, and passed this extra evidence of our respectability on to the military.

Then, suddenly, our arrest turned into a party. We were taken downstairs and went out, officers, schoolmaster, Kaimakam and all, and drank coffee at a small restaurant just up the street; we sat at tables on the pavement, under one of those immense plane-trees, near one of the city gates: a runnel of water flowed past its foot in a cobbled channel, and the peasant women, coming in from the country with baskets of grapes on their heads, paused in the shade, set down their loads, and washed first their feet and then their goat-skin sandals in the running water, before going on to the market. Several times a flock of goats came in, herded by wild-looking children; they all stooped and drank together.

But we had not come all the way to Nicaea to be entertained by Turkish officers, however gallant and lively, and presently we told both the schoolmaster and the Kaimakam that we desired urgently to visit the Basilica of the Creed, La Petite Agia Sofia, as it is called locally. I had a special reason, over and above its religious and historical importance, for wishing to visit the building in which the Nicene Creed, at the close of the Council of Nicaea, was given its final form. In the year 1900 my father-in-law was the British Judge of the Supreme Court of the Ottoman Empire and Egypt, with a circuit which extended from Adrianople to Khartoum and from Benghazi to Baghdad; he was a great sight-seer, and went to Nicaea. A French architect was engaged in restoring the little church; some of its mosaics needed repair, as they were loose, and he had "spares" for the purpose; he gave Sir Edward a couple of handfuls of the *original* ones from the niche in the apse in which the Patriarch's throne had stood during those mighty deliberations. On my very first visit to Denton, before Owen and I were engaged, Uncle Edward presented me with two or three dozen of the tiny opalescent glass cubes, some of them with faint traces of gilding on one side—I was immensely startled at finding myself suddenly in possession of such unusual relics, for if walls have ears, these small objects, embedded in the apse of that primitive church, had heard the first pronouncement of the great and final statement of the Christian Faith.

Years later I had some of them set as a Maltese cross in the lid of a silver ciborium, and presented it to the parish church of Lecanvey in the County Mayo, with the stipulation that it was always to be used for the administration of Communion to the pilgrims on the summit of Croagh Patrick on the occasion of the annual pilgrimage; I asked Stephen Gaselee, the Foreign Office Librarian, who so often had to toil through my books in typescript, if he would compose a Latin inscription, giving their history, to be engraved on the bottom. Fortunately he had, so he said, "a passion for writing epigraphic Latin", and produced the following:

> *Audoenus et Maria O'Malley me fieri fecerunt et dede-*
> *runt ecclesiae Sancti Patricii apud Lecanuiensis. Lapillos*
> *incrustatos adsportaverat Edwardus Audoeni Pater ab*
> *abside basilicae Nicaensis ubi muris auritis symbolo*
> *Nicaeno primum intonato interfuerunt.*

Which I find masterly. The "interfuerunt", solemnly tolling at the end of that string of ablative absolutes, has a resonance almost worthy of the "symbolum" itself.

But of course all this was of no interest to our Moslem hosts. They were, however, eager to show us La Petite Agia Sofia as yet one more example of Greek criminality; we piled into our car with the schoolmaster and the Kaimakam, and, the officers following in jeeps, we drove to the spot. Alas! alas! The tiny basilica—we were astonished by its smallness—lay in ruins, its central dome split in half, the little apse tilted to one side, the side walls lying flat; immensely strong the mortar must have been, for all the wreckage lay in these large pieces; there was hardly any rubble. The schoolmaster told us the story. After Atatürk's defeat of the main Greek Army in 1923 at Dumlupinar—the Turks still call it "The Battle of the Commander-in-Chief"—the Greeks had to withdraw from all the area round Broussa and Nicaea, but before leaving they blew up the so holy Basilica of the Creed to prevent it from falling into infidel hands! Since it had survived unharmed in those same infidel hands for close on five centuries, and had indeed been carefully repaired while in their custody, as I had the best of reasons for knowing, we shared the indignation of our hosts for this idiotic and wanton act.

Having mourned over the basilica, the Turks took us to see one or two mosques, as an antidote—there are some very lovely small ones in Isnik—and then gave us lunch, again at an open-air restaurant in the shade of a giant plane-tree, with water flowing past. It was the schoolmaster who insisted on our walking down to see those marble quays at the waterside, and he agreed that most of the ecclesiastical dignitaries who attended the Council would almost certainly have stepped ashore there, since in Roman times the main access to Nicaea was by that cerulean water, rather than over the rough tracks inland. At last we parted, with warm farewells all round, and drove back to Broussa, after a most magical day, with Olympus-in-Asia towering ahead of us against the sunset.

I spent a few days with Mary Walker and her children at her little villa on Prinkipo, and went across to lunch with some American diplomats from Peking who had a house on the Anatolian shore—they kindly sent their launch for me. As we pulled out from the Islands I saw an astonishing sight: an enormous pyramid of white birds wheeling above us in circles over the sea; it was at least half a mile across at the base, and rose to a thousand feet or more, narrowing all the time—from the top single birds peeled off and flew steadily to a point a little west of south. I strained my eyes to see what they were, and presently recognised them as storks; gulls joined, screaming, in the pyramid, but only the storks headed away. I realised at last that what I was seeing was part of the autumn migration of European storks to Africa—it was now late September. But why they chose to mass for their departure over the south-east corner of the Marmara I had no idea; still less could I guess why the gulls, who were not leaving, should insist on joining in.

The luncheon was an immense affair, and had a tragic sequel. I sat next to Sir Denison Ross, the Persian scholar, whom I had known in London for a long time; he was then in Istanbul, editing from the old Embassy a news bulletin on the lines of our bulletin in Budapest (as described in *The Tightening String*), only with three times the staff, and half the circulation; he was a little vexed when I told him our figures. We ate out of doors; it was a very hot day, and the lunch was long and rich, with iced Bulgarian champagne flowing freely. When it was nearly four o'clock I murmured to my neighbour that I thought we ought to go; other people were making a move. "I seem to remember, Sir Denison, that at those Book Society sort of parties in London, you and I were so often among the last five or six to leave."

"As far as I remember we were generally among the last two to leave!" the old man replied cheerfully, with his jolly laugh; but he got up. He was going back to Haidar Pasha by train, a rather slow local train, and across to Istanbul on the ferry; the local train will certainly have been very hot, after crawling for hours round the Marmara in the blazing sun, and the ferry almost certainly chilly—there is always a sharply cool air at the entrance to the Bosphorus, where the currents run strongly; probably he caught a chill. Anyhow he was taken ill in the night, and hurried to hospital; three weeks later he was dead. I could only be glad that at the last party he ever went to, he had been so characteristically happy and gay.

Before returning to Hungary I spent a few days at the Park Hotel in Istanbul, completing some contracts for figs, sultanas, and wool for the prisoners of war and, at last, doing a little sight-seeing—I had done none in Istanbul so far; Saliha Ünaydin came across from Büyük-Ada to help me with both. She took me to several *yalis* up the Bosphorus, many in private hands, which strangers never see, so that I should be able to describe them in my book; and she took me to Hagia Sofia itself. That was a memorable experience. Old Dr. Tom Lattimore, from New England, was still doing his wonderful work on restoring the great mosaics, some of which had been loosened by earth-tremors; Saliha knew him—he was immensely popular with the Turks, among whom he had lived so long—and he came down off some scaffolding and pointed out to us, first, how marvellously the light from the highest windows had been arranged: the windows themselves one hardly saw, but when the main altars had been in position, light from the sun itself had been introduced to contribute to the ritual of the liturgy.

Then he showed us how the work of restoring the mosaics was carried out. Working from a careful drawing of the original design, when the loosened lapillos, the coloured cubes, had been moved and spread, in sections, in flat containers, the whole of the old perished mortar was scraped off and replaced by fresh, into which, section by section, the mosaics were put back while it was still moist enough to take them—a laborious task, requiring skilled and patient craftsmen. But there had to be, inevitably, a border several inches wide extending beyond the pattern of the mosaic itself, to hold it firmly to the wall, and this had presented him with a troublesome problem. Left alone, it stood out whitely against the ancient stonework. He tried painting it in shades of grey, but the paint, however carefully chosen, had a glossy finish that spoke of modernity. The solution he finally hit on was, to me, infinitely ingenious and charming—to cover the still damp mortar with layers of dusty cobwebs! After an initial experiment he collected scores and scores of empty matchboxes and handed them out to the children of the district, with instructions to fill each box with cobwebs, the dustier the better, for some minute payment; much of Istanbul is still built of wood, and he now had an ample supply coming in regularly. He showed us men carefully patting the grey films on, layer after layer; the result was of course perfect. To Saliha he talked in French, which he spoke very well; when she praised the effect of his *toiles d'araignées* he replied—"Mais oui, madame; c'est le couleur de l'âge même."

XII

Turkey II

My new friends on Büyük-Ada had all been enthusiastic when I announced my intention of writing a novel about Mustafa Kemal Pasha's transformation of Turkish life, especially from the women's angle, and Saliha and I planned to come back together the following summer, go by steamer from Istanbul to Inebolu, as she and a friend had done in 1919, and motor over the Road of the Revolution, following in the footsteps of the horses which drew her open carriage—in winter. But that did not happen. I had resolved to write that book "come hell and high water", but quite a lot of hell, and many, many high waters, were to intervene before I saw Turkey again. By the summer of 1941 the Germans were in Budapest and I was in the States; in 1942 I was in Scotland being ill; early in 1943 Owen was made Ambassador to the Polish Government in London, and I was really needed at home, if only to do the cooking when he gave men's luncheons at the flat in More's Garden, which was all we had in the way of an ambassadorial residence, though he had a small office in Lowndes Square. In 1944, to our great delight, Ruşen Bey came to London as Turkish Ambassador, and by the time he and Saliha left we had gone to the Embassy in Lisbon, where we remained till the spring of 1947; when Owen left I stayed on to collect material for *The Selective Traveller in Portugal*, which a publisher had already asked me to write. In 1948 Owen and Jane settled in at Rockfleet, our house in the West of Ireland, where I soon joined them and set about making a garden; it was only in the early autumn of 1949 that, at last, I felt free to return to Turkey and pursue my researches into the Atatürk revolution.

By then Ruşen Bey had been sent as Ambassador to Athens, which, owing to the emergent crisis in Cyprus, was already becoming a tricky and important post; he was also quite unwell, and it was impossible for Saliha to leave him and come with me to Inebolu and Ankara, as she had hoped to do—in fact I got ill myself. I caught a chill up on the Parthenon, in Athens' treacherously cold wind, and had to be put into the British Military Hospital at Phaleron. However, we turned the three weeks I spent there to good account. I told Saliha that before I went to Turkey I must have the plot of the book worked out thoroughly, so that I should know what to look for in the way of *mise-en-scène;* and together, in that hospital room—it was a maternity ward, fortunately empty at the time—we arranged the whole thing, I propped up in bed making copious notes, she sitting beside me, frowning with concentration, while we planned the dramatis personae, the unfolding of the plot, and above all the names for all the characters. This was something I could never have done alone, with any real *vraisemblance;* the book is really as much Saliha's as mine. How could I have known, for instance, that the gate-keeper in a big Turkish house was always given the title of "Agha" after his name? Or the curious position of the *dadis*, generally impoverished female relations, who acted as nannies to the children, waited on their mothers, and yet lived as members of the family? Saliha agreed with me that to interpret, as it were, this totally unfamiliar way of life to English and American readers we must have both a male and a female English character, so Fanny and Dr. Pierce were invented; and we also agreed that Fanny should come to Turkey first as a child, to see everything with a child's sharp clarity of vision, and to slip into intimacy with a Turkish family in a way that would be almost impossible for an adult—except as one of the Mademoiselle Marthes who abounded in Saliha's childhood under the Sultanate.

Saliha was so good, too, about giving me all the proper forms of address: the Pasha calls Rafiyé Hanim, his mother, "Ané"; Féridé, my principal heroine, her grandchild, calls her "Niné". There are the pet-names—"My Two Eyes", "My Sweetmeat", and "Dji-djim", meaning "darling"; when Féridé wishes to cajole her father she calls him "Baba-djim", and her Grandmother "Niné-djim". Both the servants and the *dadis* address Rediyé Hanim as "Hanim Effendi". All these details are not, perhaps, essential to the plot of the book; but it did seem to me that to use them helped a great deal to give the Western reader the sense of being in a far country; and of course to the Turks who later read it, usually in a French translation, they were a delight.

We had to find an excuse for Dr. Pierce being in Turkey so often, and I made him a student of Turkish folklore—Ruşen Bey was greatly interested in this, and knew a lot about it; he taught me several Turkish folk-songs, including the one given in the book, "I Launched my Falcon in Flight". Indeed I had intended to call the book *The Falcon in Flight;* but my American publishers, when it was already being advertised under that title, told me that it must be changed, for a peculiarly dotty reason. An American radio character called himself "The Falcon", and threatened to sue them for libel because, he said, he had never been in flight from anyone. Apparently it never occurred to him that the words might mean airborne.

This time I went to Turkey by boat, which is far the best way to approach Istanbul, with that wonderful profile of all the domes and minarets of the mosques standing out against the sky behind Seraglio Point, Hagia Sofia shouldering up among them, and the battlemented mediaeval walls of the city running down to the water in front. I stayed this time at the old Embassy; Sir Noël Charles had brought part of the great building, a copy of the Farnese Palace in Rome, back into commission again. We ate in the dining-room, which in 1940 had been crammed with crates, full of the silver from all the Legations in South-east Europe, including ours from Budapest—it stayed there, in neutral safety, until it could be shipped home. Sir Noël took a kindly interest in my project, and told the Turkish Government about the book; they expressed the utmost enthusiasm, and promised to put a car, a chauffeur, and a French-speaking courier at my disposal to take me wherever I wished to go. This was fine—but of course it was essential that I should have another woman with me, for long journeys and staying in hotels, and I determined that this should be a Turkish-speaker, and preferably a Turk. By the greatest good luck I got hold of Nermine Okyar, Fethi Okyar Bey's daughter, and persuaded her to come along at my, or rather the Turkish Government's, expense; the Turks of course realised the absolute necessity for this arrangement, and readily agreed to it.

I took a second look at some of the *yalis*, and decided which one I must use for the Pasha's house, Féridé's home. Unfortunately this particular house was on the Asiatic side of the Bosphorus, and for the purpose of my and Saliha's plot it had to be on the European shore, so in the book I simply transposed it—rather reluctantly, but as it was in private hands, and in any case, I had "composed" it out of two or three *yalis*, I didn't think this would matter much; only one or two of the more learned Turks were likely to spot it. How wrong I was—a fellow-countryman spotted it instantly. One day at lunch at the Athenaeum, soon after the book appeared, Field-Marshal Montgomery of Alamein accosted my husband with—"Read your wife's book about Turkey. Tell her she's put that *yali* the wrong side of the Bosphorus. Know the place well."

I think it was Sir Noël who said that I ought to meet Halidé Edib, the woman who had been a sort of "La Passionaria" of the Atatürk revolution, throwing off the veil from the outset and riding about dressed like a man; my Turkish friends took rather a dim view of her, and when the meeting had been arranged I saw why. Obviously she could have told me a great deal about Mustafa Kemal Pasha, but she only wished to talk about Halidé Edib. So that was not much use. And presently I got on the train and for the second time made the fourteen-hour journey up to Ankara, to begin three or four weeks of high-speed *reportage*.

Some blessed person introduced me to a woman Deputy, Madame Tezer Tashkiran, and she was so pleased at the idea of the book that she put herself entirely at my disposal for as long as I wanted—incredibly kind she was, and clever too. With some trouble I extracted the promised car out of the Ministry—the official I spoke to looked aghast when I told him that it was to be outside my hotel at nine sharp every morning! Turks, even if enthusiastic in theory, are apt to be lethargic in practice. Not so, however, precious Tezer Hanim; she was always there on the dot. Together we went and inspected the old Assembly Building, where Atatürk so often imposed his will on the timid or recalcitrant Deputies; the children's school-desks which they originally used in 1920 and '21 had been replaced by something more modern, but the hideous chandeliers, originally for use with oil lamps, were still in place. We went to the ugly villa close to the station, in 1921 practically the only modern private house in Ankara, where Atatürk took up his residence when he stopped camping in a Wagon-Lits coach drawn up in a siding; this was where Féridé first went unveiled to those little dinners of his. We drove out to Kalaba, the old Agricultural College outside the town, where he had his military Headquarters, and saw the very room on whose walls hung the maps on which he planned his campaigns, and the actual table, with curious bulging legs, at which he and Ismet Inonü sat to discuss them. We went up to Çankaya and saw all over the Kiosk, as the Turks called the villa on the slopes above the town, shaded with poplars and by a musical spring, in which he eventually went, with infinite relief, to live; it was in fact Saliha Ünaydin herself who came on it on one of her walks, and told him about it.

Tezer Hanim took me up to the old Citadel, and into several of the houses built half in, half on the city wall; they were charming externally, half-timbered, with red tiles set on a slant in plaster between the silvery-grey beams; each had a well in the courtyard, with a row of water-jars standing in the shade, and most of them a tree too. Inside there was a curious mixture of furnishings: hard stuffed divans under the windows, covered with gay embroideries and woven stuffs, usually a modern sideboard, and of course a brass bed—in bourgeois Turkish houses the "best room" always had a bed in it; a stone-floored *cabinet de toilette* for washing opened out of most of them, but of course there was no sign of a fitted bath. Immediately inside each front door stood a set of open-fronted shelves, four or five of them; outdoor shoes stood on the lower ones, indoor slippers on the upper; even near the middle of the twentieth century Turks still thought it excessively unhygienic, not to say dirty, to walk through the house in shoes worn in the street, and changed into indoor ones the moment they got inside the door.

Tezer did all this quite beautifully. We were taken to the first two or three houses by an old servant of hers, who had friends living up there; after that we were handed on from one house to another; in each Tezer introduced me to the mistress of the house as Bridge Hanim, a writer whose books were read by everyone in England and America, who had come to Turkey on purpose to describe, in a book, the War of Independence and the wonderful deeds of El Ghazi—by now the Turks had begun to call Atatürk that—and the gallant actions of Turkish women in those stirring days. Then, over coffee and sweetmeats in silver dishes, an indispensable start to a social occasion, I asked questions of her in French, which she passed on to the rest. I particularly wanted to get from the older women their personal recollections of the Greek War in 1923, with all its fears and privations: of the tidal wave of wounded, and how they washed and cooked for them, and *what* they cooked—and as my questions were put to them, their vivid faces lit up, their talk ran like a river. It all had to be translated, of course, but often I could tell from their gestures what was being said—they would rise and push me to the window, pointing and exclaiming: "There!—and there!"—they could not be saying anything else. And I would look out from those swallows'-nests of houses on the Citadel wall over the wide valley floor, now fast filling up with a modern city, and try to imagine it pale and empty, as it had been twenty-six years before; and stare and stare at the ridge of hills away to the west, and seek to realise what it had been like to see the sky behind it angry with a glare of burning homesteads, and lit with the flare of bursting shells —while Tezer tried to pass on to me that spate of information. If we asked, we were shown all over the house, from the upper attics where strings of herbs and vine-leaves, hung up to dry, looked like grey-green marabout boas, to those ground-floor kitchens, often hollowed out in the thickness of the Citadel wall itself, giving onto the high-walled courtyard—with the earthen ovens for baking and the charcoal for grilling and brewing coffee. After two days of such visits it was really easy to visualise, and describe, my two heroines, Féridé and Nilüfer, wrestling with the anyhow unfamiliar tasks of cooking and housekeeping in these rather primitive surroundings, especially after Saliha's vivid accounts of her difficulties; and from those women in the Citadel, and their behaviour, I was able to pick out enough to create the characters of Sitaré and Gula, the Thorny Rose, their respective landladies.

At my request, Tezer took me along the dusty path running round below the Citadel wall to the spot from which one can look down on the station, where Orhan and Féridé, homesick for the lights of Istanbul, used to walk at night to gaze at the six oil-lamps with their tin reflectors which illuminated it, then Ankara's only form of public lighting—Ruşen and Saliha, as they told me, had often done just that themselves. Indeed most of Féridé's activities were based on

Saliha's own experiences. She had herself run down during the Battle of Sakarya, when it seemed certain that the Greek troops must reach Ankara, to ask news from the Red Crescent—so of course we had to find the old building, at the bottom of the Karaoglan Çarsisi, the big street running up from the town in the valley to the Citadel. Tezer Hanim was a champion at ferreting out places, and people too; she soon found an old man who remembered the battle, and the noise of the guns, and where the Red Crescent's first office had been, behind the Zincirli Kami, a big mosque—he led us to it, a tiny building in a narrow alley, which had reverted to its original use as a stable. This old man, and some of the officials who had earlier showed us over the National Assembly buildings, readily came out with stories about Atatürk—exactly how he had stood at his desk on the dais, the gestures he used, how he shouted at the Deputies.

But one thing amused and interested me particularly. On my first visit, nine years before, Atatürk had not long been dead, and the legend about him had not crystallised, so to speak; now it had, and to begin with the stories told to the stranger were always the same—about eight of them.

Tezer kindly gave a tea-party for me one day—all women, and it gave a measure of how far and how fast the women had moved in Turkey since the days which Saliha had so vividly re-created for me. There were sixteen guests besides myself and they included a barrister, two solicitors, a judge, a surgeon, two doctors (one a specialist), two heads of colleges, and more Deputies.

By the time Nermine came up I was ready for the long drive over the plateau and down to the Black Sea coast. Out on the plateau itself I saw things that my Turkish friends had not described: the whitish hills full of gypsum, some capped with a layer of red soil at least 300 feet thick; there had been rain in the night, and this soil, washed down, had turned the rivers a brilliant red—the sight of flocks of the silver-white Angora goats, drinking at those crimson waters, was breath-taking. At one point, before reaching the valley of the Devrez-Çai, we crossed a belt of rolling downs, thickly set with a scrub of dwarf oaks which I recognised as a variety of *Quercus toza*, familiar from Hungary; the white goats were here too, browsing on the shrubby growth. It was now autumn, and I should have to translate all the scenery I passed through into winter's end, and the beginning of spring, in the book; it was a piece of luck for me to know that the first spring foliage of *Q. toza* is pink to carmine, covered with a silvery down—so that when Nilüfer and Féridé passed that way they would have seen those goats, silver-white in a pink-and-silver landscape.

We spent the first night at Kastamonu, the Byzantine *Castamon,* now the seat of a Vilayet, which means of a Vali, or provincial governor. We could not resist doing a little sight-seeing, and looked especially at the beautiful old houses along the embankments on either side of the river which runs through the town—plaster below, silvery-grey wood above. Except on the embankments the streets were narrow, cobbled, and very steep, and beautiful as the carved balconies and recessed arches of the houses were, our feet soon ached, and we went to our hotel. This, as was so often the case in provincial Turkey, served no food, and after washing we went out to dinner at a restaurant. It was very full, but entirely of men; we were the only women except the waitresses.

Nermine rang up the Vali's daughter, with whom she had been at school before she went to Cambridge, and told her all about our journey to Inebolu, and why we were making it: so that Bridge Hanim, the authoress, could see the whole Road of the Revolution, from its start on the Black Sea coast to its termination at Ankara, and describe it all in a book so that English and American readers could learn of the great deeds of the Turkish people under the Ghazi; especially getting the ammunition ashore and up to the front. The Vali's daughter passed all this on to her father, with splendid results; he became enthusiastic too, and himself telephoned to the Kaimakam at Inebolu, warning him of our arrival and telling him that every facility was to be given us.

We went to bed. The *confort* was even more *modeste* than at Broussa nine years before—I doubt if foreigners often visit Kastamonu.

Next day we drove on, across two more mountain ranges, heavily wooded near their summits with fine stands of pines which I later learned were *P. nordmanniana;* lower down these changed to sweet chestnuts, with a thick undergrowth of hazels and the wild azalea, *R. mollis;* of course these were not in bloom, but their leaves, pale pink and primrose yellow, were very lovely—and strangely, the air was full of the spicy aromatic azalea scent. There were plenty of things I needed to see on the way, but I had already decided to do that on the return journey, so as to get everything in its proper order of progression—we hurried straight on. The road ran down out of the mountains into a valley thickly set with hazels, here cultivated— something like half the hazel-nuts used in chocolate-making throughout Europe come from the southern coast of the Black Sea; and there, too, on the very shores of the Pontus Euxinus, I saw with rather sour amusement that detested shrub, *Rhododendron ponticum*, the bane of Scottish gardens, growing wild on its native heath.

At Inebolu we were expected, and greeted warmly at the hotel; there was also a message from the Kaimakam inviting us to luncheon next day in the Municipal Building. The hotel, however, was in some ways even more primitive than the one at Kastamonu— fringed woollen draperies swathed the windows, very hard divans covered in more bright woollen stuffs ran round the walls; the modern dressing-table in our bedroom had a jug and basin perched on it in front of the mirror; there was a single chair, and no table. Nermine Okyar was rather shocked—she was learning more about the hinterland of her own country than she had ever known before, I fancy. But thanks to the Kaimakam's injunctions her urgent demands for at least two tables and four more chairs were promptly met, brought in by two chambermaids draped all over in various shades of pink, and wearing one of the two delicious local forms of headdress—a huge white veil with a very narrow border of tiny black flowers, which they somehow twined all round their heads, faces, and shoulders. The other headdress, which we had noticed some women wearing on the road as we drove in, was a big headscarf patterned in plum and beige, very beautiful; our courier told us that we could buy plenty of these in the market; but when we went to do so we found that the modern ones were aniline-dyed, with hideous crude blues and yellows added. I bought one with the greatest reluctance. However on our return journey I managed to exchange it with a woman by the road-side for her own, one of the beautiful old ones, which incidentally threw an interesting light on the *mores* of the peasants. Anatolian country-women don't worry at all about showing their faces to strangers, but to change from one *basortü* to another involved uncovering the hair, which in 1949 was still quite a different matter; that young woman ran two or three

157

hundred yards uphill till she could find bushes thick enough to screen her while she exposed her head—actually in a clump of the ponticums.

The Kaimakam of Inebolu did us really proud. Next day, after a prolonged luncheon with various officials—no other women, of course—we were taken down to a small newly completed jetty, got into a launch, and steamed a couple of miles out to sea, so that I could get the look of the coastline as my heroines had seen it when they came in on their ammunition-boat on a fine winter's morning—with all the officers, who had come aboard disguised as ragged working-men, making the deck glitter from end to end with uniforms, shining buttons and medals, and gold braid on epaulettes and collars. Of all Saliha Ünaydin's admirable descriptions her account of that transformation-scene, in the bright early sunshine, remained the most vivid in my mind. But when she arrived at Inebolu twenty-eight years before the jetty had not been built; passengers and ammunition alike had to be discharged into big chunky boats, rowed ashore, and hauled up the bare shingle by ropes attached to primitive capstans, three or four small tree-trunks set in a wooden drum, and pushed round by men chanting a loud song. This part, too, the Kaimakam had taken care of: some of the capstans were still in position, and he had actually assembled several of their original crews—grey-haired men now, they bent to their old task with a will, hauling empty boats up the shingle, still singing their old shanties. It was an inspired thing to have done—one could see what a terrific task it must have been with heavily laden boats; and the old men's faces, bright with excitement, re-created for us their earlier sense of joyful effort and triumph.

We spent a second night at Inebolu, and set off in good time the next morning, for I knew I should want to stop frequently on the way. I looked carefully at everything we passed, recording it in my mind—a really acute visual memory is such a boon to a writer—and, as I went, translating the scenery from autumn to the end of winter. The first pass, over the Küré Dagh, rises to nearly 6,000 feet; through Nermine I had made enquiries of the Kaimakam and his colleagues, and learned that in early March the snow would lie at least as low as 3,000 feet, and might be as much as seven or eight feet deep on the top. Here, then, was where Saliha had seen the patriotic inscriptions scratched on the vertical banks of snow through which the road had been cut: "Ismir [Smyrna] shall always be ours!" "Not a foot of our soil shall be lost!" We paused at the small wooden inn on the summit, where Saliha's open victoria had stopped to rest the horses, and she had talked to the woman ammunition-carrier who sat on her load in the snow to give the breast to twins. Then down into the next valley, by a very steep road whose hairpin bends made it rather frightening even with its new modern surface, and up the further side to the substantial village where they had lunched in the Han, or Inn.

But what I had got at all costs to see was the Ecevit Han, which became a legend for its comfort and the splendid food produced by the landlord, Ismail Agha, to all who travelled by the Road of the Revolution. It stands just below the village of Ecevit, by itself—a long low building of silvery wood, with ten windows looking out onto the road, and ten more across the open valley, full of immense cherry-trees; but it was shut! Ismail Agha was long since dead, and travellers in cars no longer required an overnight stop between Inebolu and Kastamonu; it did not pay to keep it open, our courier said. We told him to ask in the village for the key—that would be useless, he replied, shrugging; it was never opened. While I remonstrated and argued with him Nermine, good girl, was poking round the old building; presently she came back and led me to the far side, where one of the silvery boards in the wall was loose. "If we gave that a good pull, could we not get in?" We could, and did; squeezing through the gap we found ourselves in semi-darkness, but with some light coming through the cracks in the walls; as our eyes grew accustomed to this twilight we saw that we were standing in what had been a stable. We pushed open a door at one end, and found ourselves at the foot of a handsome wooden staircase; we went half-way up it and threw open the shutters, letting in a flood of light onto the half-landing. At the top we opened more shutters, and then explored the place thoroughly. For a remote country inn it was very well arranged: a wide central corridor, with rooms leading off it on both sides, each room with the usual cylindrical iron stove for burning wood, a raised sleeping-bench, and even brackets to hold an oil-lamp on the walls—the plaster above these was still darkened by the smoke from the paraffin. The furniture had all been removed, of course, but it was easy to imagine how pleasant it had been with curtains and cushions at the windows and on the sleeping-benches, and it was splendidly built; the floor was of beechen planks, twenty inches across, still retaining traces of polish. On the plastered walls, as well as the discolouration from the lamps there were numerous inscriptions, some in pencil, some scratched with the point of a knife, both still legible—Nermine translated some of them for me. All were in praise of the Han, of Ismail Agha and his wife, and of the wonderful, wonderful food!—it was rather touching to read them, so long afterwards.

Saliha had particularly mentioned to me, as the final wonder in such an isolated place, that the Ecevit Han boasted an indoor lavatory—we found it too, on the landing half-way up the stairs. Before leaving we carefully closed all the shutters again, and pushed the loose plank back into position after we had squeezed out. Then we went on, through lower country, till we reached the village of Seydiler Köy. I had to have a good look at this, as it had been the terminal, so to speak, for that human chain of women ammunition-carriers; it was at Seydiler that they dumped their loads, which were then transferred to the ox-drawn *cagnes*. A long straight street, overhung by trees here and there, a very tiny *han;* we examined this too, and then drove on to spend a second night at Kastamonu—but this time, before dinner, I went and took a good look at the old brick-built *han,* the main one in the city. I also noticed how on the approach to Kastamonu the Ilghaz Dagh, the last big range of mountains between the coast and Ankara, stands up against the sky beyond the town—this was where Saliha had had an adventure that would have to be placed carefully, and it was useful to know how menacing the mountains looked from a distance.

Next day we drove over the Ilghaz Dagh and down onto the open plateau to Cankiri. Here Saliha's very detailed description and my own insistence on seeing *exactly* what she had seen brought me a great piece of luck. The *han* at Cankiri, like most of the larger ones, was built round a square courtyard, with two storeys of balconies above giving onto the bedrooms; Saliha had told me that her room was on the top floor, and how she had leaned from the window, at sunset, looking westwards along the valley towards Ankara, rejoicing in the thought that one more day's drive would bring her to the capital, and her husband. Nermine had shown astonishing patience and tolerance about my endless pauses and inspections, but she was getting tired, and at Cankiri she protested that surely a first-floor room would do?—no need to climb another flight of stairs to the top. I told her to wait, and climbed to the upper storey. Several rooms were shown me, at first not looking westwards along the valley; all had the customary mixture of Western and Eastern furnishings: the inevitable brass bedstead and mahogany sideboard-cum-mirror, with gay local folk-weave for cushions and curtains. But in one room, looking north, my eye was caught by a perfectly charming rug hanging on the wall—rugs are often used as wall-decorations in Turkey; it had a deer and a fawn on it, and two trees, each with a large parrot a-top; the general colour was creamy beige, with warm red in the border, and hints of faded blue and coral—enchanting. At the time I went on endeavouring to make the courier get me taken to a room with a view to the west, and at last succeeded; I too leaned from the window, noting the orchards immediately below, with their pisé-de-terre walls, and the long vista of poplar-bordered river along the valley. But on the way back to the staircase I went into the room with the rug again, and told the courier to ask the landlord if he would sell it, and for how much. He asked what seemed to me a huge sum, 500 Turkish lira—I shook my head, laughing derisively, and went on downstairs to rejoin Nermine.

But it was a *very* pretty rug, and as we were walking out of the front door I took 150 lira in notes out of my purse and told the courier to offer them to the landlord, who was following us with a faintly regretful expression. Instantly the son was sent flying upstairs to fetch the rug; it was quite a big one, and had to be rolled up and lashed across the car roof with cords. Back in Ankara I showed it to Godric Muntz, who was rather knowing about rugs; he said he thought it was a Kayseri one, about a hundred years old, and asked what I paid for it. I told him. Now the pound sterling stood rather low at that time, one only got about seven Turkish lira for it; the dollar, on the other hand, stood very high; and in order not to be short of ready cash, and to avoid all bother with the English Exchange Control, I had caused my American publishers to put a thousand dollars to my credit at the Ottoman Bank in Istanbul. It was with some of these dollars that I bought my lovely rug, for something under £9. It lies in front of the drawing-room fire now.

My job in Turkey—all of it that I had time for, anyhow—was done, and I was anxious to get home to say goodbye to Patrick before he went off to South Africa. Down in Istanbul again it was fairly easy to book a passage from the Piraeus to Marseilles on a boat which would do it in time; but there was not a berth to be had on any of the ordinary steamers from Istanbul to Greece. Rather doubtfully, the shipping-agent mentioned to the young Consul who was looking after me that there was an Italian tramp-steamer, with a cargo of hazel-nuts, leaving for the Piraeus next day, which had a spare cabin and occasionally took a passenger; but she wasn't much of a boat, he said, and he was afraid the lady might not be very comfortable. The lady, however, took the chance; I still spoke some Italian, and it was only for forty-eight hours anyhow.

That was a most peculiar trip. She was not much of a boat, true enough. There was a curious structure forward, a sort of glassed-in bridge with a table, where the Captain and I ate our meals; below this two fair-sized cabins, his and mine—mine, certainly, was full of bugs till I shut the windows and stuffed newspaper under the door, and then used the American Army "bug-bomb" (an early form of aerosol insecticide) which Godric had kindly armed me with. Every morning the ship's cook stepped across from the galley wearing, instead of an apron, the filthiest kitchen cloth I have ever seen tied round his waist, and asked if I should like what he proposed for lunch and dinner. In fact the food, though full of garlic and dripping with oil, was rather good; I like lower-class Italian cooking. But my cabin, even when bug-free, was ill-lit and very uncomfortable; I was glad to think I should only have to put up with it for forty-eight hours. This consoling thought proved to be an illusion. Once out through the Narrows it began to blow, and presently one of those savage storms which occur at certain seasons in the Aegean blew up from the north-west, dead in our teeth; hazel-nuts are an extremely light cargo for their bulk, and the wretched little ship rode very high in the water—she was flung "every which way", as we say in the County Mayo; also it was very cold.

The Captain began to get worried—I think not without reason; presently he came banging on my cabin door, and demanded that I should go over with him to the wireless cabin amid-ships to translate the weather report. For some reason which I never fathomed, this, in the autumn of 1949, was best heard in the Eastern Mediterranean in English. Can we still have been operating the Cairo transmitter? Anyhow I duly pronounced "Forza sette", "Forza Otto", "Forza Nove"—and that the outlook was that it would get worse. I think the skipper would have run for shelter if he had thought he could get there, but his wretched craft was so unhandy that he concentrated on keeping way on her, and just butted into it. How the cook managed to bring our meals across that tilted, drenching deck I can't think, but he did, and I continued to eat them with relish; the Captain thought this very amusing, patted my back, and plied me with rough red wine. He got me out once in the middle of the night, when the gale was worse than ever; in fact I had decided not to undress, just in case, but it would have made no difference if I had been in my nightgown—very determined that Captain was.

After more than forty-eight hours of this the gale took off; we reached Piraeus two days late. Even so, I had nearly a week in hand before my next boat left for Marseilles; I didn't want to foist myself on the Nortons at the Embassy again, so I went to the big hotel, and there reported to Saliha Ünaydin all that I had seen and done. With friends, the Pawsons, I did some real sight-seeing, in the way it should be done: in a small party, with people who knew the inhabitants as well as the country, and spoke the language—they were both completely fluent in Demotic Greek.

That was a marvellous time for me. We went to Corinth and stood in the little ruined market-place, where they showed me the very steps on which St. Paul stood, because he was so short, to preach to his flighty converts. Then we drove on into the Peloponnese, where the landscape changed from the pale gold-and-ochre made familiar by Lear's water-colours of Greece to sombre granitic mountains, dark with heath, along the splendid American-made road; below it the little train chugged on its way—it was not so long, David Pawson said, since they had stopped having a truck full of hay pushed in front of the engine, in case the line was mined. At Mycenae we turned down to the left to the small local inn, La Belle Hélène; the old proprietress came out and hugged and kissed Pamela, her three sons greeted both her and David with cries of joy—they were called Orestes, Agamemnon, and Kosta, and ran the hotel between them: one cooked, one waited at table, the third made the beds and swept the house. Fresh from the Italian boat, I made discreet enquiries as to whether I should need to use Godric's bug-bomb? Oh no, the Pawsons said—another useful thing the Americans had done, besides road-making, was to sprinkle DDT so thickly over the whole of Greece that there was hardly a fly or a flea left in the country, let alone a bug. After an excellent dinner, cooked I think by Orestes, the local school-children were brought up from the village to sing folk-songs to us, and show off their dancing; we all had to take part in a particularly pretty dance called the Samiotika, where the complex inter-weaving chains were formed not by holding hands but by holding handkerchiefs.

But before that we went up the hill to the ruined palace of the Atreidae; Pamela said that sundown was the best time to see it. That is a haunted place. We walked between massive walls in the grass-grown spaces where those fated rooms had been; some of them had stone-built channels for water running through them, and one at least must have run with blood. Beneath us the Gulf of Nauplia lay spread out in the evening light; below the steep hill where Argos stood a flat stretch of green was touched by the last rays of the sun, a surprising sight in that sombre rocky landscape: one understood in a single glance why the Argolids had had horses —they had some grazing. But the astonishing thing about Mycenae then was that nothing in the surroundings had changed in the least since the days of Clytemnestra. Sheep, baa-ing, were being driven home for the night along the track at our feet, just as she must have seen and heard them, evening after evening. She had breathed the strong scent of the thyme that filled the whole air as dew began to fall; up on the dark heathy slopes above little points of light sprang out as the goat-herds, camping out for the night, lit their evening fires—so many times she must have seen them too. But most of all there was the Gulf below, pale and empty in the fading light; once she had seen it full of ships, some day she would see it full of ships again—and what then? It was frightening to be brought so close to the past; I was glad to get back to the lights and cheerfulness of the inn.

Next morning, although it was now November, we had breakfast out of doors in front of the hotel, in warm sunshine, and then drove down to the Gulf and along the eastern shore to Nauplia. On the way we stopped to look at Tiryns—and once again the past was brought hard up against the present. The old Mycenaean fortress stands on, in fact practically covers, a low mound rising barely a hundred feet above the flat coastal strip; but it is the only point which now, as when it was built, commands the coast road and the southern approaches, by sea and land, to Mycenae and the pass behind, leading through to the Isthmus of Corinth. And during the

German campaign in Greece Tiryns was again put by the Germans to its original uses. They dynamited the entrance to make it large enough to get their lorries through, and parked them inside; they built gun-emplacements on the old fortifications—the rotting sand-bags were still sticking up through the grass and fern when we walked round. It was startling to see with one's own eyes the relics of a twentieth-century war superimposed on a military installation 7,000 years old.

I got back to London in time to say goodbye to Patrick, and then went on to Rockfleet. I had completed my on-the-spot investigations in Turkey, but there was still quite a lot of work to be done to get the historical facts absolutely right, and the events in the novel in the correct relation to them. Two books I found invaluable—Winston Churchill's *The Aftermath,* and the official Turkish history of the War of Independence, which described World War I from the Turkish point of view and was full of actual dates and details of small incidents: like the fact that at Kastamonu, where for the first time Atatürk appeared without the tarbush, he elected to wear a Panama hat! But the books did not tell one everything—and then I had to write and make enquiries.

All this took time; it was only after eight months of solid research that I was able to sit down and write the book, which did not appear till 1952. But all these enquiries put me in a position to use for the first time what I now call "acknowledgements minatory", which have a markedly inhibiting effect on over-critical reviewers. At the time I didn't think of that, but quite simply and honestly began my paragraph of acknowledgements with the words—

> The author desires to express her indebtedness and grate-ful thanks to the following:
>
> To the Foreign Office, the Admiralty, the War Office, and the Royal United Services Institution for questions answered and information supplied; to the officials of the Turkish Foreign Office for assistance and facilities afforded . . .

When the book appeared more than one critic actually said in their reviews that they would have taken issue with some of my statements but for the "formidable array" of authorities mentioned. A very useful arrangement.

XIII

An Embassy at Home

In February, 1943, after a year and nine months without a job, Owen was appointed Ambassador to the Polish Government in London, headed by the delightful Prime Minister, M. Mikolajczyk—a government in exile, but much more representative of the hopes, ideals, and aspirations of the Polish nation than the Russian-appointed "Lüblin Committee", composed of renegade Poles and semi-Poles, which professed its authority among the ruins of Warsaw. It was a sad, thankless, and really hopeless assignment. If anyone cares to know, a quarter of a century later, just how sad, thankless, and hopeless it was I recommend them to read Chapter 21 of my husband's autobiography, *The Phantom Caravan*. England had gone to war in 1939 for the defence of Poland; three years and five months later the British Government, out of deference to the ignorance of one of our two belated Allies, and the intemperate greed and hostility of the other, was actively engaged in selling Poland down the river—and this while Polish men, on land and in the air, were fighting and dying beside Englishmen for what they still, despairingly but optimistically, believed to be our common cause, the cause of freedom. It was a wretched, heart-sickening task, and had to be carried out in inconvenient and difficult circumstances. Usually diplomatists live in a large house, with the best of the local servants, and ample offices for the Chancery and its staff. We had our flat, fortunately fairly spacious, in More's Garden on Chelsea Embankment, and Owen was provided with a very small office in Lowndes Square; he was also allowed petrol for his car, and when on long official trips, like visiting the Polish troops re-forming in Scotland, or their airmen in East Anglia, with an official car and a girl chauffeur (a F.A.N.Y.) as well. But all we had in the way of domestic staff were two charwomen, who came in the morn-ings for two or three hours four or five days a week, Mrs. Holmes and Mrs. Hoare; they could clean the flat and wash vegetables and peel potatoes, but neither could in any way be described as a cook. Moreover food of all kinds was strictly rationed: half a pint of milk per person per day, a minute scrap of butter, two ounces a week, and what amounted to one good chop in the way of meat; two eggs weekly, if one was lucky, and a tiny helping of jam—sugar, half a pound weekly.

When an Ambassador is appointed he is summoned to "kiss hands" with the Sovereign—i.e., to talk to him alone for anything up to twenty minutes. This is not, or used not, to be the case with a Minister, who only represents the Government; but an Ambassador represents the King in person, and so must meet his Ruler—and an Ambassador's wife is sent for to see the Queen. Owen duly went and had his interview with King George VI, but I could not obey my summons to see the Queen (now the Queen Mother) when I was first summoned, as I was lying flat on my back with a slipped disk in a nursing-home in Edinburgh; it was only in May, when I was back in London, that I paid my call at the Palace.

I had of course made it my business to learn in advance what the drill is on these occasions. Prepare to arrive a quarter of an hour in advance of the appointment, in case of accidents; royalty works so hard, and to such a tight schedule, that any delay would be as inconvenient as it would be unpardonably rude. On no account to initiate a subject oneself, but in reply to any question to make as ample a response as possible—carry the thing on, as it were—to save hard-worked royalty the trouble of thinking of a fresh topic; and at the smallest hint of encouragement, enlarge on any theme already embarked upon. In fact, in a modest way, to make sensible conver-sation.

I was struck at the outset by two things about the Queen: how pretty she was close to, with her lovely complexion; and by the extreme common-sense of her first questions—Didn't I find it rather difficult to manage any sort of diplomatic entertaining in London, with the rationing? And what had we got in the way of servants? I told her about Mrs. Hoare and Mrs. Holmes, and how helpful they were—"But the one thing they won't do, Ma'am, is to empty the pig-bucket into the pig-tub."

The Queen looked surprised—but did we keep pigs in Chelsea?

Not the O'Malleys themselves, I told her; but Chelsea Borough Council had started a war-time piggery in Battersea Park, and on the corner of Beaufort Street, just outside the flats, was a special galvanised tub for clean scraps for the pigs, alongside the ordinary rubbish bin—so of course I emptied the pig-bucket myself every day. Her Majesty laughed a little at that; encouraged, I pressed on and told her how sometimes when I came back into the flat I would hear the telephone ringing, and, setting the pig-bucket down smartly in the passage, would run to the telephone, to hear a very respectful voice ask—"Could I possibly speak to Her Excellency?" At that she laughed.

In fact the business of entertaining was rather complicated. We did very little indeed, but there were occasions when it was much more convenient, not to say more prudent, for my husband to have one or two Polish Ministers and anyone he wished them to meet to luncheon quietly at home, rather than in the expensive publicity of a restaurant. For these luncheons I did the cooking, and borrowed Bush, old Lady Gosford's butler, to wait. When Lady G. had suffered for years from thieving butlers who drank her brandy, I sent Bush to her; it was a blissfully happy arrangement: he stayed with "The Lady" till she died. They were both so grateful that neither mistress nor man minded in the least that I should borrow him when I wanted.

And with a little ingenuity one could contrive quite nice food. My nine months of illnesses proved a boon in one way, because my doctor had no hesitation in prescribing me a pint of milk a day, and any amount of glucose and black-currant purée; the glucose alleviated the sugar shortage, and as I took my daily pint in Jersey milk it was possible actually to save some quite good cream off the top. The Poles always had the same pudding at those luncheons—black-currant ice-cream, made with the medicinal purée, real sugar, and a week's cream hoarded in the frig; for a main dish, in the summer, I usually managed to twiddle a sea-trout out of one of the fishmongers in the Kings Road, and if I had been frugal with my invalid eggs, to provide *oeufs-en-cocotte* for the first course. In winter I often got game, by a lucky chance. In the autumn of 1943 I went down to Charlbury to get in my sister-in-law, Eva O'Malley's, apple-harvest for her; I stayed at The Bell, but they put me out to sleep, and my room was in Foster, the butcher's, house. We became tremendous friends, and after I went back to London, Foster used to send me a parcel up once a fortnight: a couple of rabbits, or a hare, or—best of all—a brace of pheasants from Cornbury Park. These were not poached, as they would have been in Ireland; Foster bought the hares and rabbits from the farmers, and the pheasants, quite legally, from the Cornbury keeper—but they made a great difference to the housekeeping.

And bit by bit, as I got to know the Chelsea trades-people, I found out all sorts of ways of alleviating the severity of rationing. Any form of fat to cook with was one of the worst shortages, but I soon learned that the Chelsea butchers had great difficulty in disposing of what the meat-trade used to call "flank of beef"—i.e., the animal's belly, which like streaky bacon is composed of alternate layers of fat and rather coarse meat; I could get five times as much of that as of any ordinary meat for the same number of coupons. It was marvellous—with a sharp knife I would separate the meat from the fat, which I rendered down into dripping; the meat bits, with plenty of vegetables added, made a splendid casserole. As for cows' heels, they were not on the ration at all, but when the butcher found that I would actually pay for them he skinned them for me—and there was not only a splendid strong broth, but the basis for aspic as well. For aspic, though, one needed tarragon vinegar, and that had disappeared from the London scene; however in one grocer's I found some bottles of plain white vinegar, and bought them all; André Simon brought me up some plants of tarragon from his home in Sussex, and told me what to do—heat the vinegar, put sprays of tarragon in the bottles, pour the hot, not boiling, vinegar on top; cork, and leave for six weeks; then remove the tarragon and recork. So in six weeks I had tarragon for salads and aspic.

There was a lot of talk about "digging for victory" during the war, and the tenants in More's Garden were not only allowed, but encouraged, to dig up part of the open space between the flats and Crosby Hall next door, and grow vegetables in it; it was poor dry soil, full of brick-bats and mortar rubble, and the tenants' vegetables were not a great success. Unconscientiously I decided to dig for

luxury rather than victory, and planted thyme, tarragon, and chives
—all from André Simon, of course—and sowed parsley and chervil;
after all one can't really cook without herbs, and they all throve in
the lime-y ground.

Owen's position as Ambassador to the Polish Government of
course involved me, once I was back in London, in a certain number
of activities connected with the Poles—besides cooking for their
Cabinet Ministers when they came to lunch—and the one which
occupied most of my time and energy was an excellent little organisation called the Polish Children Rescue Fund; it had been in
existence for some time, and I was co-opted onto the Committee. Its
raison d'être was to do as much as possible to help the 100,000-odd
Polish civilian deportees whom the Germans, with diabolical craft,
had uprooted from their homes in Poland and planted down in the
eastern provinces of France, from the Belgian border to Verdun,
from which they had previously removed the local population—the
idea being that strangers, who neither spoke the language nor knew
the terrain, would be less troublesome along the frontier than a
bitterly hostile population who knew every hide-out and rabbit-run
which might be useful to any resistance movement. These deportees
were mostly women and children, with a sprinkling of old men; 45
per cent of them were children. Some were in villages, some in
improvised camps; all were short of food and clothing—many of the
children had no shoes of any sort, and in winter ran about with bits
of board tied to their bare feet; perhaps worst of all, like everyone
else in France they were short of soap, and the Quakers and the
Polish Red Cross in Paris reported fearful infestation with vermin
among them—also the children, in particular, were suffering badly
from lack of vitamins. SHAEF in Paris was being very co-operative
about shipping over anything in the way of clothing and supplies
that we could raise, and the Quakers were helping the Polish Red
Cross with the distribution.

But in the winter of 1944/45, after five years of extremely stiff
clothes-rationing, and considerable losses from the bombing of individual homes, there was not so very much spare clothing left in
England. As a nation, we were immensely helped by the "Bundles
for Britain" from the United States; and, indirectly, these bundles
eventually helped the Polish deportees too. The Committee which
supervised the unpacking and distribution of the American clothing

soon came to know which places in America—and they were in the great majority—sent absolutely first-class stuff, which could be sent on, unexamined, to the district committees to be handed out; but presently they could also recognise, from the place of origin marked on the outside, which cases would contain underwear which hadn't been properly washed, stockings with holes in them, and—most disagreeable of all—garments, especially jackets and cardigans, from which the buttons had been frugally nipped off before despatch! For these there was no use whatever, and they silted up in an empty Mayfair mansion. This seemed a great pity; if only the stuff could be washed and mended, it would be a godsend to the Poles. I made some enquiries locally, and presently learned that in Chelsea there was a former factory which had been requisitioned early in the war for a gas-decontamination centre; six baths had been installed in the basement; there was lighting, heating, water, cupboards and shelves and trestle-tables—in fact everything necessary for our purpose; moreover it had a yard at the back into which lorries could drive to unload, and turn round.

The Polish Ministry of Social Welfare came and inspected the premises, and undertook to bear all expenses incurred; the Committee of the Polish Children Rescue Fund rented them and the Chelsea Borough Council let us have the place at a modest rent for our charitable purpose; public sympathy for the Poles was very strong. But the Borough Clerk warned me that we should have to have a night-watchman, or the clothing would certainly be stolen, the shortage was so acute. On his advice I went to see the Chelsea Civil Defence people, and we "borrowed" two of their Heavy Rescue Squad, hefty men who worked at the Post just across the Square —their times of duty were forty-eight hours on and forty-eight hours off, and they took it in turns to come to the factory, stoke the boilers, bring the cases upstairs, open them, and generally do all the heavy work; we fitted out two little rooms for them with borrowed furniture, china, and so on, and a very small electric cooker, so that they could eat and sleep in comfort. We got a permit for soap flakes out of some Government department, and acquired a hundredweight; and by all passing the word round among our friends we got together a team of voluntary workers.

This was not so easy; practically every woman in Britain who wasn't physically crippled was doing war work of one sort or another; but a surprising number of ladies managed to pinch out two or three hours, twice a week, from between their other jobs, and came to help. Of course they came at all sorts of odd hours, some early, some late, some in an extended lunch-hour; to ensure that there was a full work-force of twenty-five women working all day, six days a week, involved most elaborate calculations and the keeping of a complicated staff-roster—this, like so much besides of the organisation that kept the little place running smoothly, was carried out by blessed Eileen Ellis-Rees, who in the end gave up most of her time to the work. Thanks to her, it *did* run: packing-cases came into the factory from the yard at the back, were opened by the Heavy Rescue men, and carried upstairs; the contents were sorted, washed, mended, ironed, and made fit for use, and then repacked (carefully listed) to emerge at the front door, and be collected by a firm who pressure-baled them in sacking—SHAEF insisted on this—for shipment to France. Besides the night-watchmen we employed a secretary for the endless lists and general correspondence, otherwise all the work was done free; two well-wishers gave us £350 towards our expenses, the Polish Ministry advanced us £600—and away the little enterprise sailed on its short-lived course.

Because of the factory, as we called it, I was brought into frequent contact with various Polish departments—like the Army and the Polish Red Cross—besides the Ministry of Social Welfare, and began to realise some of the difficulties, for blunt Anglo-Saxons, involved in any dealings with Poles. Against their blazing enthusiasm, reckless generosity, and crazy courage, there had to be set an extraordinary fecklessness about practical matters; they were almost as indifferent to detail or routine as they were to danger, which is saying something; they forgot appointments, and they quarrelled—*how* they quarrelled!—among themselves. The religious festivals of the Roman Catholic Church were a further obstacle; I was not then a Catholic myself, and was constantly frustrated, on ringing up some Ministry or other on a week-day, to find it closed.

The Polish Red Cross now began pressing me to procure, specifically, two things for the deportees—DDT, and some concentrated form of vitamins for the children. DDT was then still something of a novelty, and could not be bought on the open market, but I managed to coax two kilograms of the pure stuff out of the Hospital for Tropical Diseases; this, it was explained, must be mixed with talc powder, in the proportion of one part to ten. As for the vitamin concentrate, rose-hip syrup was being produced in England in quantities, and I presently found a firm somewhere down in the East End who, on hearing of the plight of the Polish children, offered on the telephone to sell us one hundred ten-gallon carboys of syrup at below cost price. This of course was marvellous—it would suffice to give reasonable doses to all the 45,000 children in France; but how was it to be got there? Large carboys of sticky fluid were the most fragile and awkward cargo imaginable. SHAEF, as always helpful, agreed to fly it to Paris for us; but the deportees were not in Paris, they were miles and miles away, near the German frontier. The Polish Red Cross said that if I could get the stuff flown to Verdun, their branch there would be able to decant it and send it in small manageable lots to the camps and villages; but they were themselves so short of transport—and petrol—that they could not possibly get it there themselves.

I now began to pester everyone I could think of about that rose-hip syrup. My husband, painfully familiar with my one-track mind and persistence in pursuing any object I happened to have in view, tried to restrain me from making a nuisance of myself to the authorities. And so there came about a charming little episode which I have always secretly regarded as a small miracle, probably the handiwork of Our Lady herself—the Poles certainly thought so.

Owen and I had been bidden one day to a luncheon with the Polish President Raskewic; I went up to Lowndes Square to meet Owen at the office and be taken on in the car. As we drove off he said to me—"Charles Portal and his wife will be at lunch." (Sir Charles was then either head of the RAF, or very high up in it.) "And I forbid you to say anything to him about your miserable syrup. In fact, unless you give me your solemn promise not to, I will pull up and let you get out, *now*." Miserably—oh what a golden opportunity lost!—I promised, and we drove on. Arrived in Portland Place, we entered a room full of Polish Generals and Air Marshals, and shook hands with the President—but no Portals! And then, after a longish pause, who should be announced but Sir Archibald Sinclair, the Head of the Air Ministry, and his wife! Owen started making his way purposefully towards me, but the room was very full; I edged away, and hid behind a very stout Polish General—I managed to keep out of my husband's reach till luncheon was announced, and we all went in and sat down at table. I sat on the President's right, Lady Sinclair on his left; and during luncheon I again pitched my woeful tale of the Polish children walking in the snow with boards tied to their naked feet to her, across Raskewic— to such effect that before the meal was over that kind, sensible woman said to me:

"Write all that in a letter to *me*, saying exactly where the carboys can be picked up in Paris, and who they are to be delivered to in Verdun—I will see that my husband gets it, and I am sure he will have it done." The President of course was delighted to learn of these efforts being made for the relief of his dispersed and suffering nationals.

But if the whole thing was just another example of Polish imprecision, it was very fortunate for us. Lady Sinclair was as good as her word—I was amused to learn years later, from my son-in-law Paul Willert, who was Air Attaché in Paris at the time, what an absolute curse getting those hundred carboys flown to Verdun had been to everyone concerned.

It presently became evident that someone would have to go to Paris to supervise the distribution of the clothing, infant foods, soap, and other things which we had been accumulating for the deportees; and moreover someone in a position of sufficient authority to overrule the various rivalries and animosities which seemed to exist—not only inter-Polish ones—and to resolve the exceedingly varied problems which constantly arose; as the Ambassador's wife, I seemed a fairly obvious person. The Poles promptly made me an officer in the Polish Red Cross (I was already one in both the British and Hungarian Red Cross Societies) to give me full local status; the uniform, fortunately, was Air Force blue, so I was able to buy outsize WAAF skirts and shirts ready-made, and only had to have a tunic made to order—a shop in Bond Street supplied the high casque, which was the same for men as for women. My Hungarian sheepskin coat and high fleece-lined boots completed the outfit; my luggage was mostly filled with tea, coffee, and cakes of soap, and carrying my precious two kilos of DDT, I set off.

The first of the unanticipated problems I encountered even before reaching Paris concerned the DDT. On the train I happened to share a table in the restaurant car with three young French doctors, a woman and two men; we got into conversation, and noticing my

Polish uniform they asked a lot of questions, and were interested that I was going to work among the deportees. I in my turn asked them for the name of a firm from which I could buy my talc in bulk—I should want twenty kilograms, I said. They just laughed at me—there wasn't twenty kilograms of talc in the whole of France, they said; it had disappeared. Later in Paris, I learned from the Quakers that the American Red Cross at Rheims (known as Amcross) had plenty, but I had to go there to get it.

Paris in February, 1945, was an absolute jungle of organisations, official and semi-official, military and para-military. First and foremost of course was SHAEF; but even SHAEF was divided into sections—British, American, French, and Polish, all with different offices. There were also the various national sections of the Red Cross: American, British, Belgian, French, and Polish—the last known, naturally, as Pol-cross; it was with this that I was mainly concerned. There were the Quakers, calm, efficient, and benevolent; there was Entre-Aide Française, run by two splendid women; there was UNRRA; and so on down the scale to tiddlers like OSE—Organisation de Secours aux Enfants (juifs). There was a French Ministry of Deportees, run by a kind overdriven man called Frenay, which in fact counted for a good deal less than SHAEF. Through this jungle I began to feel my way, and in it I soon learned that among this welter of nationalities, committees, and commissions, my poor Poles were rather a Cinderella. For instance, while the British, American, French, and Belgian Red Cross Societies drew rations from a department of SHAEF called the *Intendance,* Pol-cross did not; and their ration of petrol for their anyhow pitifully small number of cars and vans was hopelessly inadequate. The rations I soon sorted out through the English section of SHAEF; then someone took me to a French official, the *Repartiteur des Carburants,* and he kindly quadrupled the Polish Red Cross petrol on the spot.

The acute shortage of petrol made getting about difficult even in Paris; taxis had disappeared off the streets, and incredibly ancient horse-cabs were the only form of transport besides the Métro, and anyhow they would not take a short fare—to get driven from my hotel, the Georges V, to dine at the Embassy I had to bribe the man with five cigarettes. The Georges V was where official visitors were put, because it was a "non-black-market" hotel; this meant that—though the furnishings were lovely and the public rooms full of white lilac—one nearly starved. It is perhaps worth mentioning what was served at the two main meals; it was the same every day. For lunch, which cost the equivalent of sixteen shillings—a bowl of vegetable soup, which had never so much as nodded at a bone or a piece of meat, very occasionally thickened with semolina; a small plate of macaroni, wholly innocent of oil or butter, over which was thinly sprinkled some sort of sausage, toasted and powdered, accompanied by one potato and a little boiled turnip or cabbage, followed by an apple or a pear. Dinner was the same, except that it cost a pound.

I used to ring for the *femme de chambre* first thing and hand her a couple of spoonsful of tea in an envelope with which to brew my morning tea, and later gave the *valet* enough coffee for my breakfast, which consisted of bread and rather sour quince cheese. So those dinners now and again at the Embassy were a godsend. How the Duff-Coopers managed I don't know, but there was always heaps of delicious food, which their famished guests fairly gobbled; and—so intelligent—though there was the splendid white-haired English butler (it always seemed to be the same one, over thirty years), the five or six footmen who waited at table were all in khaki battle-dress. All the men, except the Ambassador, were in uniform too, of course, and most of the women; I have never enjoyed Embassy parties so much as then, when my only form of dressing was to rub my shoes and put on a clean shirt. But Lady Diana added to everyone's pleasure by wearing quite lovely dresses—shining, trailing, giving an almost forgotten sense of luxury and repose.

The Poles soon provided me with a small car and a young army Captain as chauffeur, and our Embassy furnished me with an *Ordre de Mission*, specifying any places outside Paris I wished to visit—no one could move without one. I went first to Rheims in pursuit of that talc; both the Quakers and Entre-Aide were eager to begin using the DDT as quickly as possible. We set off on a slightly foggy morning, and spun across France. The long straight roads, bordered with trees, were damp from the dripping boughs overhead, and of course slightly whale-backed; I am always a little nervous when being driven by someone else, and my fear of a skid on the slimy surface was not diminished by the frequent large notices put up by the U.S. Army—"Drive carefully. Mines swept to ditches." My constant appeals to my Polish Captain to drive a little more slowly were received with the utmost politeness—and ignored. At last, really to take my mind off my own terror, I asked him what he was in civil life. "A dirt-track racer!" he told me happily.

A curious sight on our way was the pipes bringing petrol for the American troops; these, to save time, the Yanks had innocently laid on the surface of the dark wintry fields, a hundred yards or so from the road. But of course the ingenious French peasantry were out in their scores, piercing the pipes with any sharp instrument that came to hand, and collecting the jets or trickles of benzine that resulted in anything from jam-jars to buckets. "Où les Americains, là le marché noir!" said my Pole sardonically. In fact I was rather shocked by the goings-on of the Am-cross personnel at Rheims. I arrived at three in the afternoon, and was at once offered champagne—from a magnum—by the Colonel in charge. I was chilly after the long drive in an open car, and asked for tea—"Aw, have this! It's great stuff." He went on to tell me that the shortage of bottles in Rheims and Épernay was so acute that for three empties returned one was given a full bottle; to "help out" he had taken the trouble to learn where the bottles were made: "At Bay On, way off by the Atlantic Ocean, down in the South some place", and had sent "a cupla trucks" there to bring back new bottles. Recalling the desperate struggles of the Polish Red Cross to get enough petrol to take dried milk to half-starved babies at Nancy and Verdun, sending two lorries all the way from Rheims to Bayonne, not all that far from the Spanish frontier, just to secure his supplies of champagne struck me as rather irresponsible; especially when the good Colonel went on to boast that he had sent another truck to the district of Cognac to bring back another load of bottles, full this time, of brandy. However I didn't say what I thought, because I wanted my talc, and to me the Colonel was very kind—he gave me his camp bed, and slept all night in an armchair, snoring loudly; I went back to Paris next morning with my precious twenty kilograms.

Both ways, my driver and I had lunch in small country pubs, where to my astonishment we were served (at rather less than half the price of the wretched luncheon in my hotel) with a perfectly normal meal: an omelette, veal and salad, and compôte, followed by cheese and bread, and *butter;* the inn where we ate on the return journey was barely fifty minutes' drive from Paris. This led me to conclude that rationing, predictably, was not functioning as efficiently in France as in England.

One night I went to the Opera in Paris—*Samson and Delilah,* and the proceedings amused me very much. That vast and beautiful auditorium had known no heating for four winters, and it was icy; everyone sat in fur coats. The stage was just as bad, and the wretched chorus, whose actual costumes were minimal, wore long-sleeved combinations under their jewelled bracelets and brassières; the scruffy drabness of much-washed wool contrasted comically with their rather tawdry splendours; several of them, even so, were blue with cold. The temperature did not altogether surprise me; by this time I had already made two or three tours in the eastern region—to Verdun, and to Chaumont, where I went with Madame Sikorska, the General's wife; and I had found the same thing in the hotels where we put up. A French provincial hotel which has had no *chauffage* for four years is a pretty chilly place in February and March, especially as the Germans had removed all the carpets and curtains when they left. After 7 P.M. there was no hope of hot water, or even a hot drink—unless one bribed the *patronne* with a cake of toilet soap to brew up one's own Horlicks on her private electric saucepan. With Madame Sikorska we arrived in good time, and a hot supper was laid on for her; she was very lively and brisk, and made light of all discomforts, only concerned for her compatriots and their well-being. When I was by myself, as often as not we only got in after 9 P.M., cold, tired, and hungry, and we usually started off again about half-past eight in the morning.

I have always wanted to write a book about the Poles in France, but never managed it. Their courage, enterprise, and religious devotion were quite extraordinary. One of the difficulties we ran into with the clothing that was being distributed was that unless each child could be provided with *two* dresses or suits, the one given was kept to wear on Sundays, so that the child might go respectably— and respectfully—to Mass; this went for shoes too, even in winter! Out in the villages they always organised a school for themselves at once, in any barn or empty space available; and every yard of waste ground—*terre en friche,* as the French called it contemptuously— was dug and planted with whatever vegetables they could get seeds of: carrots and onions were coming up all over the place by the

178

beginning of April. The women sewed furiously, making appliqué table-cloths out of parti-coloured scraps, and selling them, or using them to decorate their miserable quarters. As always, everything was much easier and pleasanter in the country; in the towns many of the so-called "camps" were merely huge half-derelict buildings, disused barracks or factories. Even in these the exiles gallantly constructed little "homes" in the great draughty rooms, enclosing them with scraps of wood or corrugated iron, or even sacking, round the small stoves where they huddled with such bits of furniture as the French could provide—but at least preserving an individual entity, a family life. Indestructible people, Poles!

It was a strange experience, driving about day after day on the fringes of a war; often we could hear artillery booming in the distance, and more and more frequently, as the weeks went by, we overtook long files of German prisoners on the roads, being marched westwards into captivity. But the clothing, the baby-foods, the syrup and soap and DDT were getting distributed; the Polish Red Cross people worked like tigers. More and more help was coming all the time—with some American money the Rescue Fund bought ten lorries, which SHAEF brought over to France; Singers, appealed to, gave ten sewing-machines. It was lovely work to be doing.

But it was hard work too—long hours, exhausting days; in the end it proved too hard. On one of my returns to Paris to deal with matters there I went down with a bad cold and a shattering cough. I sent for an English doctor, but this was not a case for penicillin; with the minimum of delay he got me into the American Military Hospital at Neuilly—as a Red Cross officer I counted, it seemed, as military personnel. One of the young Embassy wives most kindly came and did my packing and helped me to dress; two orderlies arrived with a wheeled chair and took me off. Going down in the lift I saw myself in the mirror, and noticed with surprise that my face was almost exactly the same colour as my Air Force shirt—I was cyanosed, though I didn't know the word, let alone its significance, then. It was pneumonia. But some form of sulphonamide gradually did its stuff, and presently I was able to have a telephone plugged in by my bed, and could go on talking to SHAEF and Entre-Aide and the Pol-cross people as need arose.

I had one surprising visitor while I was in that hospital. The Polish Embassy telephoned one day to say that Cardinal Hlond, the

Patriarch, was in Paris, and proposed to come and see me. Well, a lot of odd things happen to one, but I must say I never expected to have a Cardinal come and sit by my bed; that, however, was what he did, and stayed for nearly an hour. He was a splendid figure in his crimson robes, with a noble intelligent face; he was also tremendous fun. We laughed a lot; my sharpest memory of him is leaning back in his wooden chair, rocking with laughter, and clapping his hand to his head to stop his little crimson skull-cap from falling off his silver hair—he kept on doing that. Before he left he gave me his blessing; and not only me. The nurses told me that when he left the corridor was packed; there were a lot of Catholics among the G.I.s, and they had waited outside to get it as he came out.

When I was convalescent Kate came over to look after me, and Duff-Cooper, angelically, put us up in the flat at the top of the Embassy—Lady Diana had gone to North Africa with her boy—till I was fit to travel home. It was May by then, and presently, as the flat was in its usual state of chronic stafflessness, I was sent down to an hotel in Sussex which specialised in giving convalescents meals in bed and general invalid care. Owen drove me down on V-E Day, through South London; I shall never forget the laughing, cheering crowds in the sunny streets, among the bomb-shattered buildings— so gay, they were, after their years of fear and danger.

But all these efforts for the Poles, in the factory in Chelsea, in Paris, and in eastern France, were nearing their end. In July the final sell-out took place—the British and American governments recognised a new Communist Polish government, spawned by the Lublin Committee, and withdrew their recognition from Mikolajczyk and the Government in exile. All the splendid people Owen had dealt with in London, even the tireless and dedicated Pol-cross officials who had been my friends and fellow-workers in France, became overnight stateless people, traitors and criminals in the eyes of the new regime. This bitter and cruel betrayal is one reason, I think, why I never wrote that book about the Poles in France—it was something that did not bear thinking on. Alas, alas, alas!

XIV

Portugal—Rois en Exil

In September, 1944, Mr. Anthony Eden, then Secretary of State for Foreign Affairs, had told my husband that it had been decided to send him as Ambassador to Madrid. We were delighted by this news; the taste of Spain which we had had at St. Jean de Luz in 1938, going in and out to Burgos, had given us a strong appetite for more—a couple of years in Madrid would be a marvellous finale to Owen's diplomatic career. But Mr. Eden added that it might seem slighting to the Poles if he were removed at once, so he must wait for a more appropriate moment. In March, 1945, Mr. Eden told Owen that it was still not considered advisable to remove him from his post with the Poles, but that it was impossible to leave Madrid any longer in the hands of a chargé d'affaires; so someone else was being sent there, and when the right moment came he, O'Malley, would become Ambassador at Lisbon. From the career point of view this was rather tough; Madrid ranked a good deal higher in the hierarchy of Embassies than Lisbon, and therefore carried a better pension on retirement—Owen naturally pointed this out to Eden, who said that when the time arrived he would see that that was put right, and he would also speak about it to Winston. But in May Eden collapsed with duodenal trouble, and by July, when the Polish government in exile came to an end, the Conservatives were out of power—so that was that.

However, in diplomacy, as in other spheres of human life, the grandest jobs are by no means always the most agreeable, still less the most rewarding; when we came to leave Portugal neither Owen nor I regretted for a moment that his last post should have been Lisbon rather than Madrid. I still can't quite put my finger on what it is that makes Portugal such a lovable country, and the Portuguese such lovable people. Portugal of course has a delicious climate, with oceanic mildness and moisture, but lying far enough south of the cyclonic zone to escape Britain's dreary weather, and to enjoy lovely warmth for most of the year; this gives it a flora of astonishing variety and beauty, and the coast is on the migration route for birds. (One morning in Lisbon Owen came into my room at half-past seven and said—"If you care to come out into the garden, there are 403 goldfinches in it; I've just counted them." Morning and evening are of course the best times to watch migrants, as they pause to eat.)

And Lisbon must be one of the most beautiful capitals in the world; like Rome it is built on seven hills, but Rome does not stand on a great shining estuary in which a whole fleet of battleships can lie at anchor without getting in anybody's way. As for the people—well, I disagree strongly with the school which holds that such things as "national characteristics" do not exist; I am convinced that they do, and the Portuguese national characteristics are mostly delightful. As a people they are cheerful, gay, and naturally good-tempered; the peasants are as hard-working as Chinese. But they don't take life too seriously; their sense of values is enormously sound, and they recognise the importance of fun and enjoyment, whether it is a matter of work or of religious celebrations; any job—like de-husking maize or scrutching flax or gathering olives or the vintage—that can be done communally is turned into a party, and ends in feasting and dancing; and religious festivals end in feasting and dancing too.

I think that possibly one reason why the British and the Portuguese get on so well together, and have done for centuries, is that our national ancestry is so similar. Both countries were overrun, and largely populated, by Celtic tribes; both enjoyed the enormous benefit of a prolonged Roman occupation; both, later, underwent a Teutonic invasion and settlement, their Visigoths matching our Angles and Saxons—Portuguese speech, especially in the country, is full of Germanic words. Of course we escaped the Moors, who left such an indelible mark not only on their architecture but on their social structure; and unlike us, in the whole course of their explorations and subsequent overseas settlements, whether in the New World or the Old, it never occurred to the Portuguese to exercise a colour-bar—hence the relatively easy racial situation in their African territories even today, except when disturbed by infiltrators, with their inter-marriage and shared education as the normal thing. "Integration", so laboriously being striven for now by the English and Americans, has never been needed by the Portuguese, because segregation was never allowed to happen. Anyhow, whatever the reason, they are simply one of the nicest peoples in the world.

I didn't get out to join Owen till nearly Christmas, after a great struggle with the Board of Trade over clothes-coupons. I had been warned that Lisbon was an ultra-well-dressed capital, and was enraged to learn that the extra coupons for taking up a diplomatic post overseas were one hundred for a typist, and one hundred and fifty for an ambassadress—which seemed to me rather out of proportion. The London shops, however, had an ingenious scheme by which frocks, coupon-free, were put into sealed parcels and only delivered at Victoria Station, or the docks, or whatever, on the point of departure, with an export permit attached—so we got by.

My first task, of course, was to call on the wife of the Head of State, President Carmona; this proved to be a very different proposition from calling on Madame Horthy in Budapest. The President, earlier in life, had married his cook; the Portuguese, who with all their good qualities are, like most traditionalists, snobs to a certain extent, had never accepted her, and she never went out in society. Like the Regent in Budapest, the President had an official residence, the old Palace at Belém, and there—as arranged by the Chancery—I betook myself at four o'clock one winter's afternoon. As we drove up to the pink building I looked at my watch, to time myself correctly—yes, exactly four. I need not have bothered. A rather scruffy little man in uniform met me at the door and led me upstairs to a small room where a stout middle-aged party stood waiting to receive me, wearing a hat and gloves—I didn't expect any halberdiers, of course, but there was no fire, and no sign of tea. Another man, in civilian dress, stood by her—to interpret, he explained in French. I sketched a curtsey and made some civil remark about how pleased I was to be in Portugal; he passed this on, and then said—"Madame la Présidente says she wishes you spoke Portuguese." "Tell Madame la Présidente that I have only been in Portugal six days, but that in six months I *shall* speak Portuguese," I said firmly. This too he passed on, with no better result—"Madame la Présidente is sorry that you do not speak Portuguese now." I praised the beauty of the Palace, and the old stone pines that stood in front of it; Madame Carmona continued to regret that I could not tell her this in Portuguese. Very soon she rose, and said goodbye. I bobbed, and left. As we drove out of the Palace gates I again looked at my watch; it was precisely six and a half minutes past four.

We were apt to foregather in Owen's study for drinks at about six, and there, that evening, in reply to his query as to how I had got on with Madame Carmona, I recounted what had happened—I thought it made rather a funny story. I was still, even in our last post, too innocent to realise that this ridiculous episode could be seen as, and indeed was, an international affront. Owen however was much sharper; he lifted his desk telephone and asked to be put through to Dr. Mathias, the head of the Portuguese Foreign Office, immediately. He and Mathias were already on the best of terms; but my husband now repeated what I had told him, in a very severe voice, and said that unless something was done he proposed to report the matter to the Secretary of State in London that same evening. I was aghast—Mathias, we gathered, was abject; anyhow we all went on drinking whisky and talking about other things till about 7:15, when we went up to dress. There on a table by my bedroom door was a square yard of mauve orchids, with a card—"Hommages et salutations respectueuses—A. O. de Salazar." Something had been done.

We were able to get our own back on poor Madame Carmona in a rather elegant way. Some months later the Home Fleet was to pay a formal visit to Lisbon, its first since the war; the Portuguese made a tremendous thing of it. There was to be a gala performance at the Opera, a State Banquet at the Ajuda Palace, followed by a reception for 2,000 people, a dinner at the exquisite little pink and white palace of Queluz; the Admiral—Sir Nevile Syfret—was to give a huge cocktail-party on his flagship, *Nelson,* and also a "men only" dinner for the President and the Cabinet. We had to do something too, of course, and decided to give a reception for about 350—all the Embassy would hold—of the *Sociedad,* Lisbon's high society, on the same night as the Admiral's dinner. And to this Owen determined to invite Madame Carmona. To handle all the social activities without making any howlers among the locals, he asked the Foreign Office to send out Marcus Cheke, who had worked at the Embassy more than once, and knew Portugal intimately—he had written books about it; and as to the *Sociedad,* as John Curle, the First Secretary, said, he knew the precise social status of every cat and dog in Lisbon. The Foreign Office agreed, and out he came.

I had been out that afternoon hunting for the wild paeony on the landward slopes of the Serra da Arrabide; I didn't find it, but I did acquire a baby badger, which I bought from some peasant boys who were taking it home to fatten up, kill, and eat, they said—it was so tiny that it came back to Lisbon curled up in the crown of my felt hat. When Marcus was shown into the study Owen was on the telephone to the Zoo, asking what infant badgers ate, and slept in—I was sitting on the floor in front of the fire, trying, rather successfully, to make the creature take milk diluted with warm water; I found it would suck it from the palm of my hand if it could tug at the loose flesh in front of the fingers, as a sort of teat. Owen waved a hand over his shoulder, saying, "Give yourself a drink, Marcus," and went on talking to the Zoo in French; I said—"Do please excuse me for not getting up, Mr. Cheke, but I'm just feeding this baby badger. We're going to call him Marcusinho, after you." Mr. Cheke showed no signs of pleasure at this compliment; he looked thoroughly disconcerted by the peculiarities of the O'Malleys. Owen got his instructions from the Zoo and ordered Martinez, the butler, to have a *deep* cardboard box lined with hay and put by the hot towel-rail in Her Excellency's bathroom. In fact Marcusinho soon settled the question of where he slept himself; he bleated and whimpered so pathetically that I couldn't sleep, and took him into my bed, where he curled up in the crook of my knee and slept as quiet as a mouse—and there, for the first few weeks, he slept every night. Badgers are intensely clean. If he wanted to do a duty in the night he would creep up and nip my elbow, and I would put him down on the floor; there he would run off the carpet onto the polished boards in the corner—always the same corner—and perform, and then trot back to the bed saying, "Aow! aow! aow!" and I would scoop him up and put him in again. At that stage he was no trouble whatever.

Owen presently told Marcus Cheke that we were going to have Madame Carmona as the guest of honour at our reception. Marcus was horrified, but in spite of his dismay the party had to go forward. She had already been invited; the Portuguese Government—probably quite as dismayed as Marcus, but flattered all the same—had forced her to accept; all that was left was to make it go as easily and gracefully for her as possible. In all this Marcus helped a lot. A "lady-in-waiting", who knew her way about socially, was produced for the poor old lady; Tony Wellington, the Air Attaché, who had been brought up in Rio, and spoke fluent Portuguese, was detailed to act as her interpreter and A.D.C.; Marcus, having settled the list of guests, went round explaining to the *Sociedad* that this was a political gesture, and that they would have to play, and above all arrive *punctually* at 10:30 P.M. Meantime I told the Embassy wives the drill. They would stand in a semi-circle at the near end of the long drawing-room, and of course make a bob when Tony introduced them—"and all wear a tiara if you have one, and of course long white kid gloves."

In fact it all went rather well. Having greeted our guests, at 10:45 sharp Owen and I and the three Service Attachés trooped down to the front door—Robin Drummond-Wolff immensely impressive in the full dress of the Black Watch, kilt, plaid, lace ruffles, and all. Remarkably, Madame la Présidente was on time—she was helped out, she came in, revealing her evening dress as a high-necked, long-sleeved affair of plum-coloured velvet, covered in soutache, in the fashion of twenty years earlier. Up in the drawing-room Owen led her round the white-gloved wives, Tony Wellington introducing each in turn, and each in turn making her much-practised bob, while the Portuguese notables, spread out up the long room, looked on, their eyes almost starting out of their heads with astonishment. Then she was led up through them to the pleasant "petit salon" at the far end, comfortably installed on a sofa, and given champagne; and Marcus and Tony brought in kindly souls, carefully selected, who *could* speak Portuguese, to sit with her and keep her happy. Presently supper was brought in from the buffet in the big ballroom, and she tucked into lobster salad and pâté-de-foie-gras and ices with relish; later, hearing *bruit de voix* from the ballroom, she insisted on coming through to see the fun, and ate a second hearty supper there. She really enjoyed herself very much, and I was so glad for the poor old thing.

The Portuguese are so fortunate, when they wish to lay on grand entertainments, in having such a succession of beautiful, or at least magnificent, buildings to hold them in. Queluz, where Dr. Salazar gave his own dinner for the Fleet and the British, is a quite exquisite little eighteenth-century palace, full of perfect contemporary things, especially the mirrors and chandeliers; the latter have never been converted to electricity, and the whole place was flooded with the warm soft light of hundreds of candles. Moreover, all the original liveries had been preserved, and we were waited on by men in red coats with white stockings, silver-buckled shoes, and white wigs! After the dinner a pavane was danced, quite beautifully, by a group of young people, also in eighteenth-century costume, to music by an eighteenth-century Portuguese composer. The whole evening, from beginning to end, was something quite out of this world. As for the Ajuda Palace, no one could call it beautiful, exactly, but it has a rather splendid Piranesi-like grandeur, and is so vast that even with 2,000 people in them, its immense rooms did not seem crowded. After the actual dinner the Carmonas, Dr. Salazar, and their guests processed through the main salon, already full of people, to the far end, where a space had been cordoned off for them, with chairs and tables; I was amused to see that the Embassy example was being followed—there was quite a lot of curtseying. Salazar of course is a man of enormous charm, and seldom seen in public; when we were installed in our enclosure all the beautiful young women pressed up against the cords to gaze at him. We had got on rather well at dinner, when I sat next to him, and I ventured on a tiny tease— "Excellence, je pense que c'est la première fois qu'on voit les houris au dehors du Paradis." He gave me one of his Red Indian glances at that, but consented to laugh.

Of course everyone had to call on everyone—the Admiral called on Owen, among others, and Owen returned his call to the flagship. I was determined not to miss this, and somehow contrived to get myself, Kate, and Patrick and his wife smuggled on board in advance. We stood at the rail while the naval barge bounced across the sunny water; as the huge guns, deafeningly close, boomed out the salute to H.M.'s representative, we saw Owen stand up, also saluting, swaying a little on the choppy waves, the sun glittering on his gold braid, the white plumes in his cocked-hat shivering in the breeze—a very pleasing spectacle for his family. For the gala at the Opera Giulhermina Suggia came down from Oporto and played

Elgar's 'cello concerto—an amazing piece of virtuosity, but rather tough fare for what was after all more a social than a musical occasion. I had met her before, at a farewell party we gave for Ashley Clarke and his wife when they left, and next day she came up to call, and we sat and chatted in my delightful sitting-room. She told me she was presently going to England for a concert-tour, flying both ways; she was, she said, terrified at the idea. Had I ever flown? I said yes, I had flown the Atlantic. And wasn't I terribly frightened? I said no—partly because the old Irish chauffeur of an aunt of mine in Boston had given me, expressly for that journey, a medallion of St. Michael, who protects travellers by air as St. Christopher protects those on land. I offered to lend it to her, and she was delighted; in the event she made the double journey quite safely, and with almost no fears, she wrote later. But nothing would induce her to return the medallion—I wrote and wrote, always in vain. In the end, when I was up in northern Portugal, I went to her little house, and collected it; it still lives in my despatch case, and has made many flights since then.

Portugal, with its equable climate, stable government, pleasant people and relatively low prices, was of course an ideal place for refugees from other, less comfortable parts of Europe; they came in large numbers, and either stayed in the many excellent hotels, or rented houses in the pretty resorts along the Tagus estuary, like Cascais or Estoril—and among them came, and remained, a number of royalties. There was Don Juan, the heir to the throne of Spain, and his wife and sons; there was the Comte de Paris, Pretender to the French throne, with his enormous family—ten or eleven children, I think he had; there were a couple of Hapsburg Archdukes, among them my old friends the Annas from Budapest; there was also King Umberto of Italy. Owing to some tedious scruples on the part of the Foreign Office, for which I never fully understood the reason, we were not allowed to have these people to the Embassy—not even Don Juan, who after all had an English mother, and looked and spoke like a British naval officer, which indeed he had been. But we met them all in the houses of other diplomats, whose governments had fewer inhibitions; and also, most frequently, in the two homes of an enormously rich Portuguese, a sugar magnate, who had the innocent foible of delighting to entertain princes of the blood—and a marvellous chef. It was at his Lisbon house that I first met Don Juan, who had a rather undemanding sense of humour and a main-top voice—which extended to his laugh; he was great fun, and we made a good deal of noise. Not long afterwards King Umberto arrived in Portugal, having abdicated, or whatever he did; the magnate lost no time in making his acquaintance, and soon gave a luncheon for him at his house near Estoril. As we drove out there my husband read me a little lecture. It was one thing, he said, to have uproarious jokes with Don Juan, or even to make the Comte de Paris giggle; they were, when all was said and done, only Pretenders. But Umberto was a real King, and he must be treated with proper respect; it would be highly unbecoming to make a lot of noise with him. I promised, meekly, to remember.

The magnate's Estoril house had a long sunny balcony, where cocktails were served; I made a proper curtsey to the poor ex-King, whose reddish face, understandably, wore a most melancholy expression—then our host led him to a comfortable chair, and beckoned me to take a seat beside him. I felt really sorry for the poor man, but stuck to the proper rules, and remained silent till he asked me, with an obvious effort, if I knew Italy at all. Very well, I told him; as a girl I had constantly stayed in Friuli in the house of my cousin Cora di Brazza. That rang a bell. Cousin Cora had been a lady-in-waiting to his grandmother, Queen Margherita, for years and years, and her husband, Detalmo, had been rather a card; his stammer and his absent-mindedness had become a legend. The King began to look noticeably less gloomy; soon we were capping stories about Brazza peculiarities—Detalmo was the eldest of seventeen brothers and sisters, each one odder than the next, and the tales about them were endless. All too soon—oh dear, oh dear—the royal laughter broke out, loudly. I glanced guiltily along the verandah—Owen was scowling at me reproachfully.

I wish here to enter a brief protest against the all-too-common practice, both in the press and on the radio—but especially on the radio—of making cheap sneers at dethroned monarchs. Not so long ago a phrase like shabby royalty was uttered, derisively, on the BBC by some individual who had never, I imagine, spoken to a King or Queen, on or off the throne, in his life, or been nearer to one than the wrong end of a camera. This image is untrue. These people are usually not rich, but they are not shabby; they live, in their place of refuge, modestly and acceptably, like ordinary gentle-people; many of them engage, unobtrusively, in charitable work.

The presence of the royalties in and around Estoril gave me part of the plot for *The Portuguese Escape;* there really was a royal wedding soon after we left, and the agitation to secure an invitation to it had already begun long beforehand, so that could be used in the difficult relations between Hetta Páloczy, my little Hungarian heroine, and her ultra-snobbish mother, to good purpose. But I really enjoyed much more the times that I spent staying in the country, with the Grahams up the Douro for the port vintage, and with the late Hubert Jennings and his wife at Vale de Cambra, where they had a sweet little house on the outskirts of a village, to which they retired in the summer. They both spoke Portuguese as naturally as English—Ruth Jennings, in particular, had got the peculiar flattened "a" of the speech of northern Portugal to perfection, pronouncing, for instance, the name Sarmiento "Surmiento", or something very near it; and both lived on terms of complete intimacy with the villagers, who came to consult Hubert about local disputes and difficulties, and his wife about domestic problems.

With her I was able to go into their houses, and watch the women weaving rugs from scraps and rags on their small hand-looms; she took me to the flax-scutchings, where the women and girls sat round beating the hanks of flax on cylinders of cork-bark; it was under her auspices that I attended esfolhada-parties, where both men and women pulled the papery husks off the maize-cobs. The fields came right up to their garden fence; from my bedroom window I could watch the girls reaping with their sickles, and later tying the hay up into tiny erections rather like sheaves of corn, but each with a little hood of grass on top to protect it from the rain, so that they looked like small green nuns kneeling about the meadows. And it was Ruth Jennings who took us to stay in the house on which, more than any other, Gralheira is based; its owner was not a duke, only a marquess, and the Gralheira in the novel, like the *yali* in *The Dark Moment,* is a composition of a number of large houses, in all of which all wayfarers were fed and housed, free, by the owners. But there, because Mrs. Jennings knew the people so well, and realised my appetite—greed, really—for the domestic details of daily life, I saw the kitchen and store-rooms, and the sleeping-places for the travellers, more thoroughly than anywhere else. Also it was exceptionally beautiful, and full of those Victorian peculiarities of plumbing—and there really were eight telephones on our host's desk, and the azulejo picture of the hunter treed by a bear in the garden.

The vintage at the Gerard Grahams' *quinta* was absorbing, too— the wine-treading at Gralheira described in *The Episode at Toledo* is in fact a strict account of the port-vintage, although Gralheira is not in the *pais do vinho,* the wine-country, which is confined to the Douro valley. Many wine-shippers make a tremendous social occasion of the vintage, inviting the fashionables from Lisbon to come and stay at their grand *quintas,* but at Malvedos it was not at all like that, thank goodness. No road approached the Grahams' simple, rather chalet-like house; we bundled out of the train at a halt—there wasn't even a siding—and some men and mules took our luggage up a dusty track too narrow even for the small country carts; there was a lot of luggage, as they had to take stores for their three or four weeks' stay. And while there we lived, perforce, mainly on Portu- guese food; dishes of rice or maize and bacalhau (dried cod), in various forms, plus fresh fruit; no spirits or sherry—we drank light white port before meals, water at them, and vintage port after- wards. The first evening Gerard Graham spent in his study with his local manager, discussing the state of the grapes at the various *quintas* from which wine would be bought; the room was rather like an army headquarters, with Gerard as the C.-in-C.—maps on the walls, which were frequently consulted, and pads on the big desk on which dates and notes were jotted. The upper terraces at Malvedos were ready, and next morning we were all out at seven to see the first bunch cut, a ritual occasion—I was even more excited by a pair of black stone-chats which had nested in the roof; lovely elegant black and white creatures, which I had never seen before.

I must mention that the Grahams indulged me to the point of letting me tread the wine myself—I longed to know what it *felt* like. So one evening towards the end of the first batch—it would be wrong to say "brew"—they took me down to the *adega* with a cloak over my bathing-dress while the *ranchos,* the real treaders, were away at supper, let me wash my feet and then step into the warm runny stuff and tread about; I had been afraid it would be slippery, but the granite floor of the *lagare* was rough and firm. It was a lovely experience—and Gerard kept some of that wine and bottled it unblended, labelling the bottles "O'Malley-Malvedos 1946"; he sent me two or three dozen to Ireland afterwards, and it was amusing to give guests port that one had trodden oneself.

I had wished to stay right through that first part of the vintage, from the cutting of the first bunch of grapes to the wine being run off into the huge *tonels,* and I had my wish. The last thirty-six hours before the wine is run off are very exciting; the thermometer and the saccharinometer are constantly being dipped into the "must" to test it for temperature and degree of sweetness; at exactly the right moment brandy is added to stop the fermentation—which is what makes port sweet—poured in from narrow wooden jars bound with brass, nearly a yard long, and each holding four litres. This is the critical part of the whole long, carefully watched operation, and at that time Gerard Graham's study became more like a military H.Q. than ever: youths on bicycles, on mules, or on foot came dashing up with scraps of paper giving the temperature and saccharinity of the wine in the other *lagares* operated by Grahams; and Gerard would study each, and then jot down orders on a pad for the boy to take back—"Brandy now," or "Give it another two and a half hours."

It was a feverish period. When the moment came, and the brandy had been added, a bunch of brush-wood was placed across the exit-hole to keep back the skins, twigs, and pips, a pipe was connected, the stopper removed, and away the wine ran, down into the *tonel* below. A year later, and later in the season, on my way by car up to Traz os Montes and Bragança, I saw the barrels of wine going down the turbulent waters of the Douro in thick-built clumsy-looking boats to Vila Nova da Gaia, opposite Oporto, where the long patient business of allowing the wine to "fall bright", refreshing it with more brandy, tasting, and blending goes on, year after year, to produce in the end that splendid thing, vintage port—which the Portuguese themselves don't drink! Part of the blending and maturing is done in enormous vats, almost the size of a small bedroom; at a later stage the wine reposes in outsize casks, one of which is known as "The Ambassador". When the current holder of that title comes up from Lisbon to pay his official visit to Oporto—as all must—wine is drawn off from it for him and his party to drink, there in the Lodge, and his name is then inscribed on the cask. We duly went through the ritual, more to my pleasure than to Owen's; he likes vintage port as little as the Portuguese do.

The Portuguese are extraordinarily hospitable. Not only do they open their country-houses to the traveller, but almost more than any other nation among whom my husband has served do they make the British representative welcome—and his staff and his wife too. As soon as I arrived, invitations began pouring in all over again—Owen had of course met most of the Lisbon people already—and one of the first was to dine with the Palmelas. Them we had already met in London, where the Duke was Portuguese Ambassador; of course we accepted. Oddly enough no *place* was mentioned on the card, only the day and the hour; we knew that they had houses all over the place, but assumed, foolishly perhaps, that they would be at their favourite holiday home, Calhariz, over on the Outra Banda, "the farther shore"—which before the Tagus Bridge was built could only be reached by crossing in the little car ferry. However to make sure I telephoned to the Duchess in the morning, and asked if the ferry at 7:45 would enable us to be there in good time—she said Yes, yes, perfect; the earlier the better—and how nice it would be to see us. We crossed the river in the fading light, and drove out in gathering darkness through the strange country of sandy heath and pine woods; Oliveira, the chauffeur, knew the place well, of course, and anyhow Portuguese roads are admirably sign-posted. I was just saying to Owen that we should be rather too early when the car swung down into the open space before the big white house; how odd, there were no lights in the windows. A horrid chill of doubt came over me, which turned to panic as our headlights caught the front door—the branch of a tree had fallen down and lay right across it. Oliveira got out, and rang and knocked; no answer. The place was empty!

Then *where* were we to dine? And how were we to let them know? Owen told Oliveira to try to find the steward's house, and after a lot of banging on farm doors we were at last directed to his abode; he had a telephone, thank goodness, and in any case knew that the Senhor Duque was in Lisbon, in the huge town mansion. Owen made the man do the talking, to save time and confusion—no, it did not matter in the least, we were to go straight back, it was not a party. Back we went, by this time cold and pretty hungry; Oliveira drove like Jehu. Luckily we just caught a ferry, and it was only a little after 9 P.M. when we drew up in the Rua Escola Politecnica—such an odd name for a street of great houses. The door was flung open instantly; the Palmelas were waiting on the threshold, and took us in, and gave us drinks. In the confusion of mutual apologies I said: "But dear Duchess—we are so terribly sorry—but I did ask you if the *ferry* at a quarter to eight would be in time." That one fatal little word had caused all the *confusão*, as the Portuguese so resonantly call it. "I thought," she replied sweetly, "that you meant the tram!" Her husband laughed out. "They have a car, you know!"

In spite of this disastrous beginning it turned into a very pleasant evening, with no guests beside ourselves; only a fair proportion of the family—the Palmelas had nearly as many children as the Comte de Paris—plus the chaplain, and the English nanny. Except for saying grace at the beginning and end of the meal the chaplain hardly spoke; the nanny however took a major part in the conversation throughout. With these dear people all was simplicity and ease, always—and this was just a family gathering in which we had been included. Owen was of course interested in the splendid English Chippendale, of most of which our host was rightly proud; after dinner he went round examining it piece by piece. My husband is in fact a first-class joiner, and knowledgeably turned small tables upside down, and opened cupboard doors, to satisfy himself, as he would when buying a piece in England—the Palmelas looked on, amused. At last—"That's a fake, you know, Duke," Owen said, indicating a small table; "and that tallboy is a married job." This expression was too much for Domingos Palmela's excellent English, as "ferry" had been for his wife's; Owen demonstrated, from the drawer-linings and something to do with the key-holes, that in fact the upper and lower halves of the tallboy had not been made for each other, and in the end convinced the tallboy's owner. This may seem rather undiplomatic behaviour, but it was right with those people, and on that particular occasion; it earned my husband the undying respect of his opposite number in London.

That was the first of many happy visits to that house, and it would be idle to pretend that the Lisbon home of the Duke of Ericeira in

The Portuguese Escape is not modelled on it. In the novel the Chancery itself, and the Embassy proper, were of course "drawn from life". One charming feature of the Embassy, to us, was the neighbourhood in which it stood. It was not in the least like Belgravia or Mayfair; still less like Kensington Palace Gardens, big diplomatic residences all in a haughty row. Oh no. The house stood on a corner in the angle between two very modest streets, one of which was purely "working-class"; the caller arriving on foot would often have to step into the roadway to avoid our neighbours' washing, which flapped above the pavement from strings propped out on sticks. Just under my sitting-room window, across the narrow street, were two or three little one-storey houses with cobbled courtyards, and since it was in these courtyards that the occupants spent most of their time, I was familiar with every detail of their lives: what vegetables were going into the mid-day stew; when the daughter was going out, and washed her hair and cleaned her white shoes in preparation for the event; when the husband tore the trousers of his suit, and they had to be patched; when the cat stole the fish, and was pursued with screeches and a frying-pan.

And in Lisbon, with the war over, a feature of Embassy life which we had missed in Hungary re-appeared—visitors; those who came to stay, or those who, in passing, looked in. This was delightful. Even more people came to Lisbon than had come to Peking; naturally, since it was so much nearer home—"handier", in fact—and with a large pleasant house and troops of well-trained servants, it was a pure pleasure to entertain them. Stuart Piggott came to look at prehistoric remains—we gave him the car for a day, and showed Oliveira on the map where to find the groups of tombs; when he went North to see the Citanias, the Iron-Age towns, I put him onto Ruth Jennings, who knew them intimately, so that he saw them all at speed, and lost no time in searching. The Salisburys came—well they were the Cranbornes then; they didn't stay with us, but she and I had some splendid times wild-flower hunting, and he was thrilled with the library at Mafra—though shocked by the incompetence of the librarian when his wife found a book on Rosicrucianism on the same shelf as some old books on roses.

The Portuguese, incidentally, got rather a shock over the Cranbornes. Owen told Dr. Mathias that the Portuguese Government ought at least to put a car at their disposal, as he held an important position—what position, Mathias wanted to know, though all eagerness to help. When Owen told the little man that Lord Cranborne was Leader of the Opposition in the House of Lords, and that his opposite number in the Commons was actually paid an official salary for being just that, Mathias was at first incredulous, and then gasped with astonishment—a *paid* Opposition was quite a new idea! However, he saw to it that the Cranbornes had the car. Sir Kenneth Clarke came to look at pictures; Prince Charles, then Regent of Belgium, came to enjoy himself—as he was a Regent we were allowed to have him to the house, and Owen borrowed a yacht and took him sailing; they were nearly wrecked, and had fine fun. Dear George Campbell came and spent a month staying with us, so that at last we were able to repay a little of his endless hospitality to the O'Malley family at Crarae over so many years.

And quite at the end, when Owen had already left for home, and I was clearing up with Mr. Brown, the Office of Works functionary, Rose Macaulay turned up on her way back from the trip round Spain which resulted in *Fabled Shore*, in a wholly characteristic fashion. She telephoned about half-past six from her hotel—no, she wouldn't come and stay, she was only going to be in Lisbon one night, but might she come and dine? Yes, eight o'clock would be all right. No, she didn't want the car sent; she would come in her own car. I made Martinez open the last bottle of good claret that was left out—most of our stores were packed—and awaited her in the eager anticipation with which her friends did await a visit from Rose. Eight o'clock came; 8:15; 8:30; still no Rose. At last another telephone call—perhaps the car *had* better come to fetch her after all, as her own was out of action. Oliveira was despatched at once, and in a few minutes she arrived, her apologies almost stifled by mirth. Her car had somehow gone on fire, standing in the street outside the hotel; the management telephoned for the Fire Brigade; Rose meanwhile quenched the flames herself by emptying all the decanters off the tables in the dining-room onto them. But what took so much time, she explained, was persuading the three fire-engines that their services were not required—"I felt just like Matilda's aunt," she ended up.

"And did you have to pay to get the men to go away?" I asked—I knew my Belloc too.

"Well only a little!"

Oliveira went down off his own bat to see if he could repair the damages to Rose's terrible old car—a typically Portuguese action; he returned triumphantly to report complete success, and waited, also unasked, to take her back at the end of our hilarious evening. No wonder people are happy in Portugal.

XV

Writing Thrillers—Julia Is Born

After writing *A Place to Stand,* which was published in 1953, I set to work on my *Portrait of My Mother* (in the United States called *A Family of Two Worlds*). This involved months of research, and correspondence with my American relations, known and unknown. For in the course of my enquiries I came on a whole set of cousins of whose very existence I was unaware, the descendants of my great-uncle Thomas Davis Day; half-way through the nineteenth century a breach occurred between him and my grandfather—I still do not know the cause of it—and the two branches of the family, from then onwards, ignored each other's existence till, first by letter, and then meeting face to face, in the mid-twentieth century they and I were happily reconciled.

I had to wait twenty years to write that book: till my husband retired from the diplomatic service I did not feel free to do so, after all the fuss about preserving my pseudonymity when I began to write. In fact I left it almost too late; by the time I started collecting facts my two eldest sisters, and all my American aunts, who could have told me so much, were dead. However, the few survivors rallied round nobly, and many other people helped; at one point I had paid researchers at work on local documents—in New York, New Orleans, and New London; I still have four or five huge files of notes and letters and photographs. But in the end I did get enough information, verified, checked, and re-checked, to make an accurate job of the American side of the family history. The English part was much easier, because my mother, herself a passionate genealogist, had put in an immense amount of research on her husband's family; when she died, many years before I started work in preparation for the *Portrait*, my sisters handed over to me all her notes—mostly in those curious linen-covered box-files, like dolls' chests of drawers, which the Victorians used for keeping their papers in. In fact I had a rough idea of the Sanderses and Brookings, my father's people, because as a girl I had often helped my mother, hunting through wills at Somerset House, and searching in ancient parish registers in country churches; the earliest ones were in a curious script related to "black-letter", which often the village parsons themselves could not decipher; but thanks to our German governesses, who had forced us to write all our German exercises in gothic script, I could usually read them without too much trouble. In fact they were less difficult than my beloved mother's own handwriting, which was the worst I have ever seen.

When that book was, at last, finished, and in the printer's hands, I felt slightly at a loss what to do next. I had no particular plot in mind for another "straight" novel, and felt that I had said all I had to say about love and marriage and serious human relationships; but I did not in the least want to stop writing—it had become a habit, and a pleasurable one at that; moreover, the money it so painlessly brought in was more than ever useful after my husband had retired. And then I had a bright idea. Sir Compton Mackenzie, after years of writing serious and admirable novels, had started, late in life, in quite a new vein—a series of light-hearted comics about absurd Highland lairds, which were having a great success; I knew all about their success because we were published by the same firm. Why should not I, like him, change my own more modest tune? Not to write about Highland lairds; I knew too many, and had in any case written an archaeological novel about the West Highlands, with several lairds in it, which wasn't particularly successful. No, but thrillers, at which I had never tried my hand; amateur detection, preferably abroad, with an amateur sleuth. I was rather taken with this notion, and began to tease away at the idea. Why not a girl sleuth—who looked dumb, but in fact had plenty of wits; and beautiful, of course. But what was she to sleuth *at?*

Fortunately, while I was cogitating over all this, it happened that some people in Ireland whom we knew slightly were worried about one of their sons who had been yachting in the Mediterranean, and failed to write home for weeks or even months; there was no urgent reason for his return, but there was the germ of a plot—the search for a missing relation. And so, most happily, and with amazing ease, *The Light-Hearted Quest* was conceived, and Julia Probyn was born. The missing man's family was switched to the West Highlands, the name Glentoran thought up; he was given an entirely different set of relations: his sister Edina, his tedious mother; and a really urgent need for him to be found was easily discovered.

Inventing characters is sometimes difficult, sometimes fairly easy; I cannot in any way account for the extraordinary ease with which Julia, who is a pure invention, sprang into being, and Mrs. Hathaway too. I simply went, mentally, to Glentoran, a patchwork of at least three West Highland houses, and somehow there they all were. As to where Julia was to sleuth, that all fell into place too. A year earlier I had been over in London on business and got influenza twice in five weeks; that was the winter of the smog, and the 'flu turned to bronchitis, both times, till at last my doctor told me, peremptorily, to take my respiratory tract to hell out of the metropolis—in fact out of Britain, and into the sun. By good luck I had a standing invitation to stay with our then Consul-General in Tangier, Godric Muntz, and his wife, so I sent them a cable asking if I might come at once, for a *long* visit—and got a welcoming reply.

But getting there was not so easy. The obvious way was to go to Gibraltar by sea and cross over to Tangier; but this was mid-January, and all the big liners which touched at Gib on their way to Australia and the Far East were fully booked till the end of March. Somehow I heard of a very small shipping-line which ran cargo-boats to Tangier, and would take the odd passenger; one was leaving almost at once, and I booked myself onto her.

That was an immense stroke of luck. All the absurd business of getting on board the S.S. *Vidago* in Chapter Two of *The Light-Hearted Quest*—the crane-driver helping with the luggage, the twenty-four hours' delay before the boat started, because the dockers had chartered a private plane to fly to Belfast for a prize-fight, the little office on the quay-side where the three men gave Julia tea—even the Captain polishing his tumblers before he gave her whisky in his cabin—it is all a perfectly straight transcription of what happened to me on that most engaging of trips. I was feeling intensely full of enjoyment on that voyage—the delight of convalescence, of escape to sun and warmth, the eager pleasure of seeing new things and new places—and that has somehow injected itself into the book, I think.

Unlike Julia, I had no idea that we were to call at Casablanca; there the reality was slightly different, to begin with. When we arrived the kind Captain had to go to call at the Consulate, and invited me to come with him "just for the drive"—I was delighted, of course. In the outer office he said I ought to send in my card, as a matter of courtesy, along with his—I did so, and out came dear Peter Pares, whom we had known in Hungary, and greeted me with the utmost warmth; he invited me to stay the night. Another stroke of luck, another gift; I went back with the Captain and packed a case, Peter's chauffeur picked me up at the boat, and took me on that extraordinary round of the Casablanca hospitals before lunch.

At Tangier I stayed at the Consulate-General with Godric and Marjorie Muntz. The mate on the boat had told me to go to Dean's Bar, as one of the sights of Tangier—and I went fairly often with June Robertson, Godric's secretary, just because it was such a nice place. Dean I did portray at full length as Purcell; eventually he became a key character in the book—but I was told that when it reached Tangier, and he read it, he was delighted with the *réclame* it gave his bar, as well as the affectionate portrait of himself. He is dead now.

And so it went on throughout my time in Morocco—everything I saw, everyone I met, every place I went to, fell into place like the pieces of a jig-saw puzzle when I came to write. The excavations at the Romano-Phoenician "factory" down by the shore were in fact conducted by a most elegant Italian princess, a distant connection of ours. But the site had to be described because it was so fascinating, and besides, a newly opened Phoenician grave was the perfect place in which to have Colin, the missing man, at last come on Julia, who had been searching all over Morocco for *him*. At Fez I stayed at the Consulate; I was to have gone in Godric's car, giving a lift to Alec Guinness, but floods had made the road impassable, so I had to go by train, and shared my supper, first with an American airman from Fort Lyautey, who gave me the idea of Steve, and later, after changing trains at Petit-Jean, with a very angry old Australian. The Consul and his wife showed me Fez, and took me to the antiquarian shop which in the book I have called Bathyadis'. After a few happy weeks in Tangier I went down to Casablanca again, and Peter Pares drove me to Marrakesh for two or three days; we had lunch more than once at the Café de France on the Djema el F'na, the great open square which the French used to call the "Place Folle", because of the wild non-stop entertainments which took place there day and night, so I knew the exact lay-out of the terrace where Julia and the Duke of Ross-shire are injured by the bomb intended for Colin and his boss.

The main problem about the book was *what* secret job Colin would be doing in Morocco with the blessing of the Bank of England, so that he was allowed to transfer his bank account to Casablanca—one of Julia's first clues; and the solution to this I got, not in Morocco at all, but in Ireland. Percy Le Clerc, of the Irish Commission for Ancient Monuments, had become a friend when he was restoring Carrigahowley, our ruined castle on Roigh Bay; he knew Morocco well, and had travelled down in the South where the chrome and other valuable minerals are mined; he suggested that British Intelligence might well be anxious to lay their hands on a certain quantity of something new and very rare—moreover, he put me onto all the activities of *Affaires Indigènes*, the government department which under French rule dealt, as its name implies, with local matters. But for Percy I could never have known that travellers with cars must have a *fiche*, an official document, to move from one place in Morocco to another; a curious little fact which enables Julia and Paddy Lynch, at last, to track Colin down.

It was of course important to make my imaginary mineral something probable, or at least possible; and here again Irish help was forthcoming. Our nearest and dearest neighbours on Roigh Bay were Roney and Rosina Jennings; their eldest daughter had married a professor of geology at University College, Dublin, and he was persuaded to describe to me a deposit, currently being discovered in the United States, which was almost pure uranium—it was in the fossilised remains of trees, and parts of it even showed traces of bark, he said. Moreover the geological formation of Morocco was such that it was by no means impossible that the same sort of thing should one day be found there. This was splendid; but of course it must have a name—and "Astridite" was coined.

How I enjoyed writing that book! I suppose it was because I

enjoyed Morocco so much; North Africa was a completely new part of the world, full of wonders unknown to me. On the way home I went via Spain and stayed in Madrid with Fina de Calderón, the folk-singer; we had made friends when she and Fernando, her husband, were staying at Bussaco, and I had gone up from Lisbon for a few weeks' rest in the very odd hotel there. When I went to Spain they were busy converting an old convent outside Toledo, "The Convent of the Guardian Angel", into a *cigarral*, and Fernando drove me down to see it, and showed me Toledo at the same time— marvellous place. Anyhow all that came in very conveniently when I wrote *The Episode at Toledo* some years later. I asked Fina if I might use the *cigarral*, and she was delighted with the end product when I sent her the book.

From Madrid I went on to Lisbon, and spent a few happy days out at Monte Estoril with Susan and Luiz Marques. Susan and I had collaborated in 1947 and '48 in writing *The Selective Traveller in Portugal*, and great fun we had doing it, driving all over the country in a minute car with a minute chauffeur, to see for ourselves that the compilers of both *Baedeker* and the *Guide Bleu* had made the same mistakes as *Murray's Handbook*, published in the 1870s; we uncovered some most extraordinary ones, none of our predecessors in the guide-book world having bothered, as we did, to verify their facts *sur place*.

While within easy reach of Lisbon I went and looked up two old friends—Martinez, the Embassy butler, who had retired soon after we left, and Marcusinho, the badger. Marcusinho we had had to retire while we were still in Lisbon; as his teeth and claws developed he became a rather difficult pet, and when he had chewed his way through the wooden gates outside the garage into the Rua Arriaga, and clawed his way through the brick and *pisé de terre* wall from the empty stables, where he was housed, into the kitchen of the adjoining gardener's cottage, to the outraged dismay of the gardener's wife, we offered him to the Lisbon Zoo, which gladly accepted him. From both I got a warm welcome. Martinez and his wife, whom I had never met, gave me wine and biscuits in their little flat. Martinez was a Galliego Spaniard and an ex-bullfighter, and had always continued, while in his official position, to wear his hair with the traditional fringe of pot-hooks across his forehead, to recall his glorious past; he must have dyed it too, for it had always been jet black—now the pot-hooks were gone, and the hair was sandy grey; he was more mellow than of old, and obviously delighted to be called on. So was the badger. When I went out to the Zoo and found the badger-house the keeper told me solemnly that I should not be able to see him—"They sleep by day, the Excellency understands." The Excellency, undeterred, stood and called loudly—"Marcu*sinho!* Marcu*sinho!* Marcu*sinho!*"—sforzando each time. And after two or three repetitions, and a few grunts from the little dark shed, Marcusinho came lumbering out across the small enclosure to where I stood by the wall, grunting eagerly. It was at least four years since he had seen me, or heard my voice; and although I had been, so to speak, his foster-mother, this seemed to throw a strong light on the intelligence, and the faithfulness, of badgers.

I decided that Portugal was a suitable scene for Julia's next activities, and since she was a free-lance journalist, I let her go to cover a royal wedding. It was Kate's idea to introduce that shrewd, difficult ingénue, Hetta Páloczy, fresh from Communist Hungary, as a sub-heroine, to point up the follies of her snobbish mother. For all the details of life in Hungary under the Communists I was indebted to my friend Mrs. Stenger, who had married a Hungarian, and stayed on to care for him till he died; when she came out she was able to tell me how lost the poor nuns were when ejected from their convents to attempt to gain a livelihood in a strange and bitterly hostile world—Hetta, in the book, had been left in a convent school when her parents fled in 1945. With all this settled, and the much-loved Portuguese background firmly in my head, I was well away on *The Portuguese Escape*—once more the book seemed practically to write itself. I had only to go back mentally to the familiar countryside, and the shops and streets of Lisbon and Estoril, and let my cast of characters rage about in cars or Land Rovers, pursued or pursuing.

So many people complained to me that Hugh Torrens, who had seemed so attractive in Morocco—indeed Julia was greatly attracted by him—should have turned into a bit of a bore in Portugal, that I thought rather hard about why this had happened; it had been quite unintentional. And the only explanation that I could think of interested me, because it throws a certain light on how characters shape themselves as one writes—I have always held, and said, that it is only when characters begin to "take charge", and develop on their own account, that they really come alive. Torrens seemed interesting in Tangier because I didn't really know him; like the reader, I only met him for a very short time, at Lady Tracy's cocktail-party and for the rest of that evening; and he was lively and striking-looking, and full of a fresh emotion which made him seem, at the time, a vivid personality. But he was always fundamentally a bit of a bore, and when I met him again in Portugal, and got to know him better, like Julia I liked him a good deal less. It is as simple as that.

It was my son-in-law who gave me the idea for Julia's next enter-prise. In the early summer of 1958 my husband and I decided to spend a few weeks in Switzerland. "Since you're going there, why don't you write about numbered accounts?" he said. At that time, in common with most people in England, I had never heard of num-bered accounts; Paul had to explain to me what they were, but I saw at once that there were all sorts of possibilities in the idea. Kate as usual had a contribution to make. She said that Julia had so far had a walk-over with too many men—Geoffrey Consett, Torrens, and Steve; this would put people off her if it went on too long. "Honestly, darling, this time I think you'd do better to let *her* fall for someone, and get the brush-off."

Well, there in the vaguest outline are the two main items in the plot of *The Numbered Account;* and that spring, for the first time in my life, I set off for a foreign country with the germ of an idea for a book of which the scene was to be laid *in* that country. We stayed first at Gersau with Dory Müller, whom I had known as a child when we spent summer after summer at her parents' hotel in Mürren; her delightful house served as a model for Herr Waechter's, admittedly a little bit touched up. At that time I had not less than three Swiss publishers in Zürich, and Dory drove me over to call on two of them—they functioned in just the same tree-shaded suburban surroundings as Herr Waechter's "Eden-Verlag". There I made some enquiries about numbered accounts, and both publishers urged me to go to Geneva and open one, so that my royalties might be paid into it, and I could come out from time to time "to eat them!"—thus avoiding British income-tax. Of course I couldn't do that, but in the course of conversation I uncovered the necessity for producing a death-certificate to get money out of a deceased person's account, and also the rumours about some Swiss Banks' earlier failure, for this reason, to pay over money deposited by Germans who later died in concentration camps—I learned afterwards that this had been put right by 1958. From Dory's house I telephoned to Herr Nüssbaumer, whom I had met in Moscow, and made a date with him in Geneva for a fortnight later.

From Gersau we went on to Beatenberg, where of course almost the first thing we did was to go up the Niederhorn on the ski-lift, swinging through the air in those little open twin-seats; it amused me as we went up to pass so close to the people coming down that, as Owen said, you could see the warts on their noses. Returning, we walked down to the half-way halt, and while we waited for an empty seat I chatted to the man who hauled the seats round to the lower section, and learned about all the water for the restaurant on the summit being carried up in milk-churns at night, after the lift was closed. Both these facts played a vital part in the book later.

I happened to have two lots of friends near Geneva, Tony and Honor Waterfield, and an English friend married to a Swiss pastor; I seized the opportunity to stay with both. Staying in Tony and Honor's delicious house on the lake shore I met a man who worked in one of the innumerable international organisations at Geneva, and he asked us all to lunch at the Palais des Nations, so that, like Julia, I was able to see what that surrealist place is like inside. In Geneva I called at the appointed time on kind Herr Nüssbaumer, and I was fascinated to see the interior of one of those grandiose establishments. I was actually given a number for an account—I have it still, but there is nothing in it! He filled in the information I had gathered in Zürich thoroughly, so that I knew all I needed when I should start my book, from the technical angle; moreover, he was giving a big dinner one night for the Red Cross, to which I was bidden, where I met a lot of bankers, and got an idea of how they talked. Then I went back to the Berner Oberland and joined Owen at Interlaken.

Not so many people as one might expect actually *stay* in Interlaken for any length of time; they dash through it on their way to somewhere else, or perch there for a night or two as a starting-point for excursions. This is a great mistake. Interlaken is a place to linger and dawdle in—to smell the scent of new-mown hay in the streets while one shops, to sit and listen to the blackbirds in the public garden, to idle along the path by the river and watch the swifts over the green water, and poke about in the curious narrow back streets. We stayed at the Hotel du Lac, the original of the "Fluss", where poor June and her criminal companions stopped till they whisked her off to the Golden Bear. Of course we made some excursions; we went up to Mürren, my old haunt as a child, and had lunch with Arnold Lunn, and he came down and dined and spent the night with us; we went up to the Schynige Platte and the Kleine Scheidegg. Most rewarding of all, from the point of view of *The Numbered Account*, we did the "Three Passes tour" on a coach, and also walked through that sinister place the Aares-Schlucht—Owen was fascinated by this, and insisted that I should use it somehow in the book; in fact it came in quite neatly for the rather vulgarly dramatic *dénouement*, when Antrobus, although he has just been shot in the leg, throws one of the thugs into the river racing past below. And, like Antrobus and Julia, we saw that fascinating bird the wallcreeper, fluttering like a butterfly over the grey face of the rock.

I began to write the book when we got home. By then we had bought our house in Oxford, and were having it done up; I stayed at the Randolph for much of the time to supervise the work, and in my pleasant bedroom there, and on a wooden bench in our newly acquired garden, I worked out the plot, and began to arrange all this material, trying to do so to the best advantage. But what I most enjoyed was describing the old Switzerland, ignored by most tourists, and the private, hidden life of those ancient industrial families —the mediaeval guilds in Berne *still* giving dowries, in the twentieth century, to the daughters of those whose membership of the guild goes back for centuries.

And I was glad to be writing about Switzerland—of all the foreign countries I have known and loved, the one I knew first, and best, and have loved most. It would have been fun for me, personally, to write about my climbing years there in the first decade of this century; but all that would have been out of date—who today climbs with guides?—and could not have been a truthful account without dropping such prodigious names that my family might have been embarrassed. Better just to let Julia look at the Jungfrau from a distance, and pick flowers on Alpine meadows.

About the Author

The wife of a British diplomat, Ann Bridge has travelled around the world and has lived in China, Switzerland, Portugal, Italy, Hungary, France, and Germany. Drawing upon her unique international background and upon her formidable amount of knowledge about a vast variety of things, from botany to mountain climbing, she writes with the spell-binding detail and precision of a widely travelled, sensitive, and observant author. Her dramatic stories of the diplomatic world and of international intrigue and her brilliant discussions of everything from menus to rare wild-flowers have made such books as *The Lighthearted Quest, The Portuguese Escape, The Numbered Account,* and *The Episode at Toledo* great favorites among her enthusiastic public here and abroad.